ELECTROCONVULSIVE THERAPY

ELECTROCONVULSIVE THERAPY

Richard Abrams, M.D.

UNIVERSITY OF HEALTH SCIENCES
THE CHICAGO MEDICAL SCHOOL

Oxford   *New York*
OXFORD UNIVERSITY PRESS
1988

Oxford University Press

Oxford   New York   Toronto
Delhi   Bombay   Calcutta   Madras   Karachi
Petaling Jaya   Singapore   Hong Kong   Tokyo
Nairobi   Dar es Salaam   Cape Town
Melbourne   Auckland

and associated companies in
Berlin   Ibadan

Library of Congress Cataloging-in-Publication Data
Abrams, Richard, 1937–
Electroconvulsive therapy.
Includes bibliographies and index.
1. Electroconvulsive therapy.   I. Title.
[DNLM: 1. Electroconvulsive therapy.   WM 412 A161e]
RC485.A27   1988   616.89′122   88-1357
ISBN 0-19-504536-X

2 4 6 8 9 7 5 3

Printed in the United States of America
on acid-free paper

To my teachers

Lothar B. Kalinowsky, M.D.
Max Fink, M.D.

Foreword

Despite more than 50 years of controversy, electroconvulsive therapy (ECT) remains a principal treatment of the severely mentally ill. With the introduction of psychotropic drugs in the 1950s, ECT was temporarily abandoned. Disappointment with the efficacy of psychotropic drugs and the need to find treatments for therapy-resistant patients led to the reintroduction of ECT into practice and research. Public doubts as to the treatment's safety encouraged numerous examinations of the merits and pitfalls of the treatment. After many assessments, arguments, challenges, and experiments during the past two decades, we find the treatment to be increasingly accepted, and the simplicity of the early methods to be replaced by a highly technical and sophisticated treatment; one that requires considerable skill and training for its proper use.

For more than 20 years, Richard Abrams has been a student, researcher, teacher, clinician, and editor in the forefront of clinical and research assessments of the convulsive therapy process. In the present volume, he shares his extensive experience and provides an authoritative, useful, encyclopedic, and well-written book, which is a standard for clinical practice and a challenge for research.

Convulsive therapy was developed in 1934 by Ladislas Meduna who used camphor-in-oil and then Cardiazol to induce seizures. He developed the treatment based on the observation and belief that there was a biologic antagonism between the pathophysiology of dementia praecox (schizophrenia) and that of epilepsy. Within a few years, convulsive therapy was widely hailed as an effective treatment for the severe mentally ill. It was the genius of the Italian psychiatrists Ugo Cerletti and Lucio Bini to develop an electrical induction that elicited seizures more easily than did the chemical methods, establishing *electro*convulsive therapy as the induction of choice. The first human experiments with ECT were done in Rome in April 1938. The very ease of administration encouraged more extensive application, so that by the early 1940s, ECT was the most widely used treatment in psychiatry. This volume, an extensive review of our clinical and research experience with ECT, is a fitting contribution to the semicentennial celebration of its development.

Richard Abrams' ECT research and expertise is reflected in more than 40 citations. His studies of the effects of single and multiple seizures through unilateral nondominant, bifrontal, and bilateral electrode placements are central to our understanding of the role of electrode placement in clinical outcome, EEG, and cognitive performance. He has proposed a theory of the relation of EEG changes to clinical outcome. In recent studies, he examined the changes in prolactin secretion during the course of ECT and reported important relations among the strength of the stimulus, the amount of prolactin secreted, and clinical outcome. In these investigations he has been associated with Michael Taylor, Jan Volavka, Rhea Dornbush, Conrad Swartz, and myself. He is a student and long-time friend of Lothar Kalinowsky. In 1982, with Walter Essman, he edited a multi-authored volume on electroconvulsive therapy. This extensive experience has served him well in making the present volume authoritative.

The more we have learned about ECT, the more complex the actual treatment has become. Indeed, proper administration today requires the combined skills of the psychiatrist, nurse, and anesthetist. As more high-risk patients are recommended for treatment, consultation with knowledgeable physicians, neurologists, and cardiologists become more frequent. As the age of patients is extended, we deal more frequently with geriatricians.

This book has much to offer. For the clinician, it provides a sophisticated guide to the selection of patients for treatment; a step-wise manual of treatment procedures; and an understanding of the proper role of the electrical stimulus and electrode placement in treatment practice. It is up-to-date in its clinical applications and case descriptions, and contains a comprehensive presentation on the treatment of high-risk patients. It includes a detailed explanation of informed consent, with helpful suggestions on how to deal with patients, their families, and others who may express concerns about the long-term effects of the treatments.

For the researcher, it provides timely information on the effects of electric currents and electrode placement on behavior, brain function, memory, cognition, and biochemistry. For students, it is an excellent guide to case selection, cerebral and systemic physiology, patient attitudes, and legal issues. It is a rewarding update of the 1978 American Association Task Force report, my 1979 volume *Convulsive Therapy: Theory and Practice*, and the 1982 texts of Kalinowsky, Hippius and Klein, and Abrams and Essman.

ECT is said to be controversial. The 1985 NIH Consensus Conference on Electroconvulsive Therapy, while agreeing that the treatment's efficacy and safety compares very favorably with alternate treatments for severely depressed, manic, and schizophrenic patients, labels the treatment as the "most controversial in psychiatry." What is controversial?

There is no controversy about the indications for ECT and its efficacy in alleviating severe mood disorders, nor about the safety of the procedure when properly done, nor about the characteristics of optimal practice. There is no controversy about consent, although there are times when our present antiauthoritarian attitudes prevent the administration of this effective treatment in patients for whom it may be life saving. There are those who argue that the treatments are brain-damaging and brain-disabling, but neither they nor our present research has been able to muster tangible evidence on long-term changes in brain functions when the treatments are properly done.

We do not understand its mode of action. But then, we are no worse off with regard to ECT than in our lack of understanding of the mode of action of psychoactive drugs, or psychotherapy, or behavior modification, or psychoanalysis. (I believe we actually know more about the effects of induced seizures in man than we do about the effects of psychoactive drugs, and a concerted effort at research into the mode of action of ECT would be particularly rewarding in our understanding of mood disorders, psychosis, brain function, and behavior.)

We are not satisfied that our students are taught well enough to deliver these treatments effectively and safely. Only a few psychiatric training centers provide experience for their students in this complex therapy; and fewer still provide the research support to develop alternative treatments or to improve our understanding.

But none of these issues—complexity, safety, indications, consent, mode of action, or training—are sufficient justification for cries of controversiality. For this label we must look not at the treatment, nor in its history, but in ourselves. Primitive fears of electricity and of insanity make trained psychiatrists quake at the thought of this treatment. The persistent lobbying of a small band of antipsychiatrists encourages the scapegoating of one treatment over others. Inexperience, lack of training and knowledge—perhaps even laziness—encourage psychiatrists untutored in the practice of ECT to shun it, and to decry its use by others. These anxieties and a desire for anonymity encourage otherwise intelligent men and women to join in shrill cries that the treatment is controversial, and to justify their distance from it.

The present volume describes our knowledge in sufficient detail and simplicity that an intelligent person can comprehend it. Should a relative or a friend have a severe mental illness, one for which a course of ECT is recommended, this book should reassure the reader that there is much known about ECT, and that the treatment is remarkably safe and effective. He should ask of his psychiatrist or physician, does he know the material in this book? If not, the knowledgeable layman should seek a therapist who has an understanding of the present state of our knowledge.

For the practitioner, student, administrator, and educator, this summary of our knowledge is an important milestone in the practice of modern clinical psychiatry, and a fitting celebration of the fiftieth anniversary of the introduction of electroconvulsive therapy.

Nissequogue, New York   Max Fink, M.D.
November 11, 1987

Preface

It is now six years since Walter Essman and I wrote, in the preface to our edited volume on electroconvulsive therapy (ECT): "As scientists, we believe that a presentation of experimental data and verifiable clinical experience is the strongest antidote to the misplaced emotionalism that has embroiled the treatment" (Abrams and Essman, 1982). During these six years interest in ECT has bourgeoned. In 1985 alone, the journal *Convulsive Therapy* was born, the National Institutes of Mental Health (NIMH) and the New York Academy of Sciences jointly sponsored a three-day international conference entitled *Electroconvulsive Therapy: Clinical and Basic Research Issues* (the proceedings were published the next year), and the NIMH sponsored a two-day *Consensus Development Conference on Electroconvulsive Therapy*, published later in the year as a special section of the *Journal of the American Medical Association*.

What is responsible for this *volte-face* in American psychiatry? Disenchantment with the antidepressants, perhaps. None has been found that is therapeutically superior to imipramine, now over 30 years old, and the more recently introduced compounds are often either less effective or more toxic than the older drugs, or both. The greying of America, perhaps. The aged are more prone to melancholia than younger cohorts, more often resistant to antidepressants, and with their multiform medical disabilities, much more sensitive to the side-effects of medications. The pressures of geometrically escalating costs of medical treatment, perhaps, leading inevitably to the kind of cost–benefit analysis that recently demonstrated that ECT dramatically reduces the length and cost of hospitalization for patients with major depression (Markowitz et al., 1987).

Whatever its cause, the phenomenon seems real and the need for an updated volume on ECT justified. I have tried not to duplicate Max Fink's masterful coverage of the topic from its inception through the mid-1970s (Fink, 1979); such an effort would be in vain, in any case, and the experience accumulated in the decade since his volume was written provides challenge enough. Of course, some overlap is inevitable; history does not change (except in the minds of historians), and certain basic clinical principles remain inviolate. I have emphasized the use of ECT in medically compromised and aged populations, stressing an understanding of the basic medical physiology of the treatment as central to its appropriate application in high-risk patients. The neuropsychological and neurochemical correlates of ECT have been subjected to intense scrutiny during the past decade, and I have attempted to cover these in suitable detail. Finally, an accumulation of incremental advances in instrumentation and technique have led to what is now a rather sophisticated treatment method, and I have endeavored to present this method in sufficient detail to permit the novice as well as the venerable but rusty practitioner to administer ECT with safety and finesse.

As before, my goals have been to present the "experimental data and verifiable clinical experience" that is required for the student and practitioner to develop and perfect their skill and understanding of this unique psychiatric therapy, and to erect a bulwark of fact between inexperienced and vulnerable patients and their families and the flood of emotional misinformation daily generated by its opponents.

Chicago, Illinois   R. A.
December 1, 1987

Acknowledgments

Most of the research presented here was the result of a collaboration with many colleagues, including Max Fink, M.D.; Michael Taylor, M.D.; Jan Volavka, M.D., Ph.D.; Conrad Swartz, M.D., Ph.D.; Rhea Dornbush, Ph.D.; Stanley Feldstein, Ph.D.; Walter Essman, M.D., Ph.D.; and Raymond Faber, M.D. I am further indebted to Dr. Max Fink for his careful review of earlier versions of the manuscript and to Dr. Conrad Swartz for his thoughtful comments on several of the chapters. Charles Ludmer, M.D., Ph.D., provided helpful discussion on the nature of the electrical stimulus. Mary Lou Liebert worked indefatigably through several revisions to prepare the final version of the manuscript.

Contents

ELECTROCONVULSIVE THERAPY

1

History of
Electroconvulsive Therapy

The traditional litany on the history of the medical uses of electricity, beginning with the Roman use of electric fish to treat headaches (Harms, 1956; Sandford, 1966; Brandon, 1981), is simply beside the point; electroconvulsive therapy evolved solely as a result of Ladislas von Meduna's original investigations on the effects of camphor-induced convulsions in schizophrenic patients, and it is the chronology of the medical (and, specifically, psychiatric) uses of *convulsions* that provides an appropriate historical perspective to his work.

This chapter draws extensively from the excellent historical reviews of the subject by Mowbray (1959), Sandford (1966), Fink (1979, 1984), Brandon (1981), Kalinowsky (1982, 1986), and Endler and Persad (in press), as well as from Cerletti's (1950) personal recollections and the recently published English translation of the autobiography of Meduna (1985).

According to Mowbray (1959), Paracelsus, the sixteenth century Swiss physician and alchemist, "gave camphor by mouth to produce convulsions and to cure lunacy." The first published citation, however, is generally attributed to Leopold von Auenbrugger, the originator of the percussion method of examining the heart and lungs, who, in 1764, treated "mania vivorum" with camphor every 2 hours to the point of convulsions (Mowbray, 1959; Sandford, 1966). The next publication (and the first in English) was by one Dr. Oliver, whose case report in 1785 in the *London Medical Journal* described the successful use of camphor in a patient who had been "seized with mania with few intervals of reason" (Kalinowsky, 1982). Fifteen minutes after a single dose of camphor the patient had a grand mal seizure and awakened in

3

a rational state. The case was later cited by Burrows in his 1828 textbook, *Commentaries on Insanity*:

> In a case of insanity, where two scruples of camphor were exhibited, it produced a fit and a perfect cure followed. When given to the same gentleman 2 years afterwards, upon a relapse, i.e., a recurrence, it had the same effect, even to an alarming degree; but the patient did not, as before, progressively recover from a single dose, for it was repeated afterwards in smaller doses of ten grains.

Next came Weickhardt, a councilor of the Russian Imperial College, who reported in a Viennese textbook in 1798 that he had obtained cures in 8 out of 10 cases of mania with camphor-induced seizures (Mowbray, 1959; Sandford, 1966; Meduna, 1985). The last citation given before the method fell into obscurity for almost a century is from an unpublished 1851 manuscript in Hungarian by a Dr. Szekeres, who described the technique for treating mania of a Dr. Pauliczky who recommended

> camphor, beginning with a dose of 10 grains and increasing the dosage by five grains daily up to 60 grains a day. After this the patient will have dizziness and epileptic attacks. When he awakes from these, his reasoning will return (Sandford, 1966).

In the recently published English translation of Meduna's autobiography (1985) it is revealed that none of this work was known to Meduna until a year after he had published his first report on induced seizure therapy in schizophrenia, at which time a Hungarian psychiatrist accused him of plagiarizing Weickhardt's eighteenth century ideas. Stung by the unfairness of the accusation (which was subsequently published in a Hungarian medical journal), Meduna says

> I began to read old manuscripts and found that the convulsive method had been used 20 years before Weickhardt by Auenbrugger . . . I found other reports: Simmon, whose nationality I could not ascertain, used camphor to produce epileptic attacks to cure insanity; as did Pauliczky, a Polish scientist of the eighteenth century, and a Dr. Laroze of Paris, probably at the beginning of the nineteenth century.

Meduna's decision to attempt the treatment of schizophrenic patients by inducing epileptic seizures stemmed directly from neuropathological studies (Meduna, 1932) in which he observed an "overwhelming and almost crushing growth of the glial cells" in the brains of epileptic patients, contrasted with an equally evident lack of a glial reaction in the brains of schizophrenic patients. He thought these observations to be evidence of a "biological antagonism" and decided to pursue this line of inquiry further. He was very encouraged in this by a friend and colleague, Dr. Julius Nyirö, who had observed that epileptic patients had a much better prognosis if they were also diagnosed as having schizophrenia, and actually had attempted (unsuccessfully) to treat epileptics with injections of blood from schizophrenic patients (Nyirö and Jablonszky, 1929). (Although not mentioned by Meduna in his autobiography or in Fink's [1984] historical review, Mowbray [1959] asserts that these authors also had reported using pentylenetetrazol to produce convulsions in their schizophrenic patients.)

After unsatisfactory animal trials of strychnine, thebaine, Coramine, caffeine, brucine, and absinthe (!), Meduna learned from the International League Against Epilepsy that one of its officers had written a monograph about producing artificial convulsions with camphor monobromide. Choosing the less toxic simple camphor, Meduna successfully produced experimental epilepsy in guinea pigs (Meduna, 1934). Two months later, on January 23, 1934, Meduna gave an injection of camphor in oil to a schizophrenic patient who had been in a catatonic stupor for 4 years, never moving, never eating, incontinent, and requiring tube-feeding.

> After 45 minutes of anxious and fearful waiting the patient suddenly had a classical epileptic attack that lasted 60 seconds. During this period of observation I was able to maintain my composure and to make the necessary examinations with apparent calm and detached manner. I examined his reflexes, the pupils of his eyes, and was able to dictate my observations to the doctors and nurses around me; but when the attack was over and the patient recovered his consciousness, my legs suddenly gave out. My body began to tremble, a profuse sweat drenched me, and, as I later heard, my face was ashen gray.

Thus, convulsive therapy was born. The patient went on to full recovery after a short series of seizures, as did the next five patients treated, and by the end of a year Meduna had collected and published his results in a sample of 26 schizophrenic patients: 10 who recovered, 3 who enjoyed good results, and 13 who did not change (Fink, 1984). Meduna soon replaced camphor with the chemically related pentylenetetrazol (Cardiazol, Metrazol), which he preferred because of its solubility and rapid onset of action.

Pentylenetetrazol convulsive therapy spread rapidly throughout Europe; however, the extremely unpleasant sensations induced in conscious patients during the preictal (or myoclonic) phase of the treatment soon led investigators in Rome to seek alternative methods of induction (Cerletti, 1956). Von Fritsch and Hitzig had already demonstrated that epileptic seizures could be produced in dogs by electrical stimulation of the exposed brain, and von Schilf had suggested the feasibility of producing convulsions in humans with extra-cerebral electrodes (Mowbray, 1959; Sandford, 1966).

In 1934, Chiauzzi, working in Cerletti's laboratory, had produced seizures in animals by passing a 50-Hz, 220-V stimulus for 0.25 seconds across electrodes placed in the mouth and rectum. In May 1937, Bini, another of Cerletti's assistants (and himself a fine clinician and author of a textbook on psychiatry), reported similar animal studies at an international meeting in Münsingen, Switzerland. About 50 percent of the dogs thus stimulated died, and, according to Kalinowsky (1986), it was Bini who first realized the danger of passing current through the heart with oral–rectal electrodes and who demonstrated the safety of applying both electrodes to the temples of the dogs he was studying. This was confirmed by Cerletti in a visit to the Rome slaughterhouse where, he had been told, pigs were killed by electricity. In actuality, the pigs were first convulsed by an electrical stimulus to the head and then dispatched while they were comatose. The fact that such transcerebral electrical stimulation did not actually kill the pigs provided encouragement for continued attempts by Cerletti and Bini to define the electrical stimulus parameters that might be safe and effective for human application (Cerletti, 1950).

This was soon accomplished, and the first patient to receive electroconvulsive therapy (ECT) was a 39-year-old unidentified man found wandering about the train station without a ticket. He was hallucinating and alternating between periods of mutism and incomprehensible, neologistic speech. After several weeks of observation, a diagnosis of schizophrenia was made, and the first treatment was given in mid-April, 1938. The first stimulus was unintentionally subconvulsive (70 V for 0.2 seconds): the patient exhibited a brief myoclonic reaction without loss of consciousness and began to sing loudly. He lapsed into silence while those in attendance discussed what to do next, and then solemnly intoned clearly and without jargon "Not another, it will kill me!" Despite this ominous warning, which understandably caused some apprehension among those present, the patient was restimulated at a higher dosage (110 V for 0.5 seconds) and a grand mal seizure ensued. After awakening,

> The patient sat up of his own accord, looked about him calmly with a vague smile, as though asking what was expected of him. I asked him: "What has been happening to you?" He answered, with no more gibberish: "I don't know; perhaps I have been asleep."

The patient's eventual full recovery with a course of 11 ECTs was dramatic, but not the important contribution made by the Italian investigators—the striking effectiveness of induced convulsions had already been shown many times since 1934—rather, it was the demonstration that such convulsions could safely, reliably, and inexpensively be induced by electrical means that constituted the technical advance for which Cerletti and Bini justly achieved fame, and that stimulated the rapid spread of this uniquely effective therapeutic modality.

As Fink (1979) pointed out, convulsive therapy burst upon the scene during an era of unprecedented therapeutic optimism in psychiatry, following hard upon the heels of Wagner-Jauregg's malarial fever therapy for general paresis of the insane (1917) and Klaesi's prolonged sleep therapy (1922), and virtually coeval with Sakel's insulin coma therapy (1933) and Moniz' psychosurgery (1935). One by one, the other treatments briefly flourished and then fell into desuetude, replaced by less complex and more definitive methods; only ECT flourished and remains widely used to this day, doubtless because of its demonstrable efficacy, safety, and relative ease of administration, all due, in large measure, to the advances in technique (e.g., succinylcholine muscle-relaxation, barbiturate anesthesia, oxygenation, unilateral electrode application, brief-pulse stimulation) that have been introduced regularly over the years.

Will ECT also be replaced by a less intrusive, perhaps pharmacological, therapy that alters brain function in the desired direction (e.g., via a hypothalamic releasing factor) but without the auxilliary convulsion and its attendant risks and drama? Probably, but I think not very soon. For one thing, the rate of accumulation of new techniques and discoveries in the application of neurotransmitter pharmacodynamics to the treatment of mentally ill patients (and depressives, in particular) has slowed considerably in the last decade, and despite manufacturers' claims, no significant progress in the pharmacological treatment of depression has occurred since the introduction of imipramine in 1958.

For another, incremental advances in the method of administering ECT have refined the treatment to the point that, with brief-pulse unilateral technique, most patients can enjoy the full therapeutic benefit of ECT without the usual cognitive side effects that were so prominent with the original method (Weiner et al., 1986).

It is more likely in the foreseeable future that the application of increasingly sophisticated research methodologies will both augment the understanding of the mechanisms inherent in the therapeutic action of ECT and promote continued refinement of its technique of administration, resulting in a highly efficacious treatment without serious side effects, thus obviating the need for its replacement by a more refined method for some time to come.

2
Efficacy of Electroconvulsive Therapy

Experimental Data

It is axiomatic that rigorous experimental methods are required to demonstrate the efficacy of a medical treatment. Whether the comparison is against placebo (sham treatment) or an alternative active therapy, a prospective design with random assignment of consecutive patients to treatment groups and blind assessment of outcome using objective measures are absolute requirements. Both the diagnostic criteria and the precise treatment parameters must be specified, and appropriate statistical analyses must be employed (or the data presented in sufficient detail for readers to perform their own calculations). Scrupulous adherence to these rules is especially crucial when studying an emotionally charged and physiologically active treatment such as ECT, given as it often is for illnesses (depression, mania) with a high spontaneous remission rate.

The first part of this chapter will assess the efficacy of ECT by reviewing the evidence from controlled trials in the three disorders for which such data are available: depression, schizophrenia, and mania. The results of uncontrolled or otherwise methodologically weak studies, anecdotal reports, and case history studies will be referred to in the second part.

Depressive Illness: Sham ECT Studies

The studies of genuine versus sham ECT published through 1966 and reviewed by Barton (1977), Fink (1979), and Taylor (1982) generally support the efficacy of ECT in severe depression, although each suffers from inadequate methodology of varying degree (Crow and Johnstone, 1986). The following review concentrates on the random assign-

9

ment studies published since then, each of which satisfies the methodological requirements outlined earlier.

Freeman, Basson, and Crighton (1978) treated 40 primary depressives with either two genuine (bilateral, partial sine-wave) or two simulated ECTs during their first week of treatment, after which, for ethical reasons, all patients received genuine bilateral ECT for the remainder of the course. Anesthesia was identical for both groups and included atropine, barbiturate, and muscle-relaxant. Mean scores on the Hamilton, the Wakefield, and the Visual Analogue depression scales after the first two treatments were significantly lower after genuine than simulated ECT, and patients in the simulated ECT group ultimately received significantly more treatments as prescribed by clinicians who were blind to group assignment. (The Beck self-rating depression scale did not reveal any significant between-group differences, perhaps because depressed patients, particularly those with retardation, have difficulty completing it.)

Lambourn and Gill (1978) assigned 32 patients with psychotic depression to receive either six brief-pulse, low-dose (10 joules, J), unilateral ECTs or an equal number of identical anesthesia inductions without the passage of electricity. Mean Hamilton rating scale scores obtained 24 hours after the sixth treatment did not differ significantly for the two groups.

In the Northwick Park ECT trial, Johnstone et al. (1980) gave 70 endogenous depressives a 4-week course of eight partial sine-wave bilateral ECTs or eight anesthesia inductions without electrical stimulation. Mean Hamilton depression scale scores after 4 weeks were significantly lower in the genuine ECT group by about 25 percent, a difference that was no longer present at 1- and 6-month followup intervals, during which additional treatment (including ECT) had been given ad libitum. The advantage of genuine over sham ECT in this study was most marked in the subgroup of delusional depressives (Clinical Research Centre, 1984).

West (1981) treated 22 primary depressives with courses of six genuine or sham ECTs, after which they completed the Beck self-rating scale for depression, were blindly rated on both doctors' and nurses' rating scales, and were then switched to the alternate treatment if indicated. There was a highly significant and clinically important improvement in the genuine compared with the sham ECT group, and 10 out of 11 sham ECT patients (but no genuine ECT patients) were switched to the alternate method, from which they derived the expected degree of improvement.

In the Leicestershire trial Brandon et al. (1984) studied 95 major depressives who were allocated to courses of up to eight genuine (bilateral, partial sine-wave) or sham ECT, administered twice-weekly. A significantly greater improvement in Hamilton depression scale scores was seen in the genuine (versus the sham) ECT group at 2 and 4 weeks, but not at 12 and 28 weeks. As in the Northwick Park trial, the largest between-group differences occurred in the subgroup of delusional depressives.

In the Nottingham ECT study Gregory et al. (1985) randomly assigned 60 depressives to partial sine-wave ECT with bilateral or unilateral placement, or to sham ECT. Both genuine methods were superior to sham ECT after two, four, and six treatments, as measured by the Hamilton and the Montgomery and Asberg depression scales, which were administered blindly.

Thus, five out of six methodologically impeccable studies of simulated versus real ECT in the treatment of depressive illness show both a statistically significant and clinically substantial advantage for the genuine article in reducing depression scale scores during and immediately following the treatment course. It is not surprising that evaluations done later in the maintenance phase of the treatment course or at follow-up generally fail to show such an advantage; during the intervening weeks patients typically received a variety of "doctor's choice" treatments, including both ECT and drugs, administered unsystematically.

The single study (Lambourn and Gill, 1978) that failed to show an advantage for real versus sham ECT also differs from all the others in having used brief-pulse, *low-dose* (10 J stimulus energy) unilateral ECT as the active treatment. A similar low-dosage technique using an even higher stimulus energy (mean = 18 J) was recently shown by Malitz et al. (1986) to be clinically ineffective for unilateral ECT and substantial evidence exists from a variety of sources for a reduced therapeutic effect of unilateral ECT regardless of stimulus type (see Chapter 8).

Depressive Illness: ECT Versus Antidepressant Drugs

The case for a therapeutic advantage of ECT over antidepressant drugs rests primarily on three studies: Greenblatt, Grosser, and Wechsler (1964), the Medical Research Council trial (1965), and the more recent report of Gangadhar et al. (1982). Although other studies have provided interesting and useful insights into special aspects of the relative efficacy of the two treatment methods, none has the scientific rigor necessary for an unequivocal demonstration of the superiority of ECT. Abrams (1982) lists the methodological flaws of the published comparisons of ECT and antidepressant drugs in the treatment of depressive illness. Almost 50 percent of the studies have to be excluded from consideration because of a retrospective design; nonblind evaluation and faulty data analyses account for most of the remainder. These are by no means trivial points. In a retrospective study, for example (they are all chart-reviews), patients have not been assigned randomly to treatments, there is no sure way to equate the groups for psychopathology or illness severity, the reasons why physicians or patients chose one or the other treatment constitute a major source of bias, there is no control over drug dosage or numbers of ECTs administered, and the assessment of outcome (even if done by "blinded" reviewers) is necessarily based on the nonsystematic observations recorded at the time by nonblind clinicians with their unknown biases.

Even studies that apparently follow a rigorous method may fade into insubstantiality upon closer scrutiny. A case in point is the previously mentioned study by Greenblatt, Grosser, and Wechsler (1964) that is widely cited as a demonstration of the therapeutic superiority of ECT over imipramine in the treatment of depressive illness. In this trial, 281 patients were randomly assigned to receive either ECT, a maximum obligatory dose of 200 mg/day of imipramine, phenelzine, isocarboxazid, or placebo, and evaluated blindly. The authors indeed found ECT to be superior to imipramine in the total sample studied, but diagnoses were heterogeneous and included psychoneurotic depression, schizophrenia, and a large number categorized only as "other," in addition to the diagnostically relevant categories of manic-depressive, depressed, and involutional psychotic reaction. Clearly, a combined analysis is noninformative with such diagnostic heterogeneity. Although a table provides separate percentages for each diagnostic subgroup of patients who were markedly improved with each treatment, the actual numbers of patients receiving each method are not given, nor are chi-square values or significance levels provided. The authors, however, affirm that their analyses show ECT to be significantly more effective than imipramine for the treatment of involutional psychotic reaction (85 percent versus 42 percent markedly improved) but not the depressed phase of manic-depressive illness (78 percent versus 59 percent markedly improved); these groups were not combined for analysis.

In the multihospital Medical Research Council trial (1965), 269 patients with endogenous depression were randomly assigned to four different treatment groups, two of which were four to eight ECTs (65 patients) and 100–200 mg/day (mean = 193 mg/day) of imipramine (63 patients). Fifty-eight patients in each group completed the first 4 weeks of treatment, at which time physicians' blind global assessments showed 71 percent of the ECT group to have no or slight symptoms, compared with 52 percent of the imipramine group ($\chi^2 = 8.75$, $p = 0.0005$).

Gangadhar, Kapur, and Kalyanasundaram (1982) studied 24 primary endogenous depressives who were randomly assigned to receive a course of genuine bilateral or sham ECT given over a 12-week trial in conjunction with either placebo capsules or 150 mg/day of imipramine. The first six treatments were given over 2 weeks, followed by one treatment per week for 2 additional weeks, and then one "maintenance" treatment at the sixth, eighth, and twelfth weeks of the trial (total = 11 treatments). Genuine ECT plus placebo capsules was significantly superior to sham ECT plus imipramine in lowering Hamilton depression scale scores after six treatments; no significant between-group differences on this scale were observed at subsequent assessment intervals. Assuming that imipramine does not antagonize the antidepressant effects of ECT (and Price et al. [1978] suggest that this may *not* be the case), this study also demonstrates the efficacy of genuine versus sham ECT. Although its sample size is small, this is the only study to employ the critical format of genuine ECT plus placebo versus sham ECT plus active drug in conjunction with all of the other methodological requirements.

All three studies, however, can be criticized for the low drug dosages employed. While there is little doubt that 100 to 200 mg/day of imipramine is an effective treatment for some patients, most psychopharmacologists today would peg the therapeutic range of this antidepressant at 200 to 300 mg/day, and would probably also require plasma-level monitoring. The two-phase study of Wilson et al. (1963) addresses the question of dosage, albeit in a rather small sample. In the initial phase, depressives were randomly assigned to four treatment groups, of which two (six patients each) were ECT plus placebo and sham ECT plus imipramine at a dose of 150–220 mg/day (mean = 180 mg/day). Assessment on the Hamilton Scale after 5 weeks showed a large and highly significant advantage for ECT. In the second phase of the study, 14 new patients were treated, 4 with ECT and 10 with imipramine alone, at a higher dosage: 215 to 270 mg/day. After 5 weeks on this regimen, the high-dose imipramine group showed significantly more improvement than the first- and second-phase ECT groups combined (although the authors erroneously identify the two methods as identical). The rating procedure, however, presents an important problem in this study—different numbers of raters were used at different assessment periods: one of the raters was never blind and one was not a psychiatrist. Moreover, the authors do not say which raters participated in the second-phase assessments, or how the Hamilton scores were derived when more than one rater was used.

Another aspect of the imipramine dose–response relationship was studied by Glassman et al. (1977) who treated 42 nondelusional psychotic depressives with a fixed milligram per kilogram dose of imipramine and examined the relation of plasma level to clinical outcome. The proportion of imipramine-responders increased directly with plasma levels: 29 percent for plasma levels of 150 ng/mL, 64 percent at 150 to 225 ng/mL, and 93 percent for levels of 225 ng/mL. The study is seriously marred, however, by the authors' failure to specify their criteria for defining treatment response.

Thus, although ECT is clearly more effective than moderate doses of imipramine in the treatment of several endogenous depression subtypes, it is less obvious that this difference would obtain under the optimal conditions of higher drug dosages and plasma level monitoring. To be sure, most practitioners neither administer high-dose antidepressant drug therapy nor routinely monitor plasma levels; in this sense ECT can justifiably be considered superior to antidepressant therapy as generally prescribed.

ECT Versus Drugs in Depressive Illness: Other Studies of Interest

The study of DeCarolis et al. (1964), as reviewed by Avery and Lubrano (1979), provides unique information on an important clinical question: What is the response to ECT in depressives who have failed high-dose antidepressant drug therapy? These authors initially treated a diagnostically heterogeneous sample of 437 depressives with 200 to 350 mg/day of imipramine. All patients who failed to improve after 30 days on this regimen were then given a course of 8 to 10 ECTs. Endogenous depressives constituted the largest diagnostic subgroup ($n = 282$), of which 172 (61 percent) responded to imipramine. Of the remaining 109 patients (one patient dropped out), 93 (85 percent) then responded to a course of ECT. In the subgroup of 181 delusional depressives, only 72 (40 percent) responded to imipramine, compared with 91 (83 percent) of the 109 imipramine nonresponders who went on to receive ECT. Although the assessment of the outcome was not blind in this study, this seems at least partially counterbalanced by the powerful bias against ECT response introduced by reserving this treatment for patients who had first failed high-dose antidepressant drug therapy.

A paper by Coryell (1978) considers a different question: what is the response of patients who had received ECT and antidepressants during different depressive episodes? In this study, hospital charts were reviewed and blindly rated for all patients who received ECT for depression in the preantidepressant era (1920–1959), and who later received tricyclic antidepressants from 1961 to 1975 for a different episode. Complete recovery occurred in 94 percent of the episodes treated with ECT, compared with 53 percent of those treated with antidepressants. Drug dosages were low by present standards, however, and no data is provided on the relative efficacy of the two methods within patients (e.g., how often the ECT response was superior to the tricyclic response).

Efficacy in Mania

Only one prospective controlled trial of ECT in mania has been completed at the time of this writing (Small et al., in press). After publishing an interim report on 21 patients [Small et al. (1986)], these authors went on to study a final sample of 34 newly admitted manic patients who were diagnosed as bipolar I according to the Research Diagnostic Criteria and who were randomly assigned to receive a course of brief-pulse ECT ($n = 17$) or lithium therapy ($n = 17$). The mean number of ECTs administered was 9.3, and lithium dosages were adjusted to yield serum lithium levels between 0.6 and 1.2 mmol/L. Concomitant neuroleptic drug therapy was permitted ad libitum. After completion of the ECT course, patients in this group were placed on maintenance lithium therapy.

Ratings by nonblind observers as well as blind evaluations of videotaped interviews were done at weekly intervals for the first 8 weeks, using a variety of rating instruments, including the Brief Psychiatric Rating Scale, Clinical Global Assessment scale, and Bech–Rafaelson Manic Rating Scale. At all rating intervals after the first week, and for each of the three previous measures, ECT induced greater improvement than lithium, a difference that generally reached statistical significance at weeks 6, 7, and 8. The blind and nonblind ratings were in general agreement throughout the study. The mean daily dose of neuroleptics received during the trial was similar for both groups. It is notable that a significant advantage for ECT emerged in this study despite the fact that the first group of ECT patients treated initially received unilateral electrode placement, failed to respond (or got worse), and then responded to bilateral placement, thereby confirming an earlier retrospective study that demonstrated a therapeutic advantage for the latter method in manic patients (Small et al., 1985; Milstein et al., 1987). Had all ECT patients received bilateral ECT from the outset, the observed advantage over lithium might well have been larger.

In a double-blind, random assignment, prospective study of ECT in mania now in progress (Mukerjhee et al., 1986), patients who have completed a pretreatment period of lithium or neuroleptic pharmacotherapy are randomly assigned to either an intensive high-dose pharmacotherapy with combined lithium and haloperidol or to 2 weeks of daily ECT (10 treatments) with right-unilateral, left-unilateral, or bilateral electrode placements. In the first 14 patients studied, five of 11 patients assigned to ECT achieved a full remission after 2 weeks of therapy, compared with none of three patients assigned to intensive drug treatment. In this sample, as in the study of Small et al. (in press), there was a tendency for bilateral ECT to be more effective than unilateral ECT: no patient failed to respond to bilateral ECT, although several either failed to respond to unilateral ECT or showed early relapse and had to be switched to bilateral ECT.

Efficacy in Schizophrenia

Evaluating the efficacy of ECT in schizophrenia is more difficult than in depression because of the greater variability in the diagnostic criteria for the former disorder. Most investigators who were quite specific in their description of the signs and symptoms of endogenous depression were unaccountably satisfied with simply proclaiming their schizophrenic patients as *chronic* or *acute*, with an occasional subtype thrown in. Moreover, no attempt was made until the 1980s to exclude schizophrenic patients who had prominent affective symptoms from ECT studies, raising the spectre of misdiagnosis as many patients with a mixture of affective and schizophrenic symptoms actually suffer from affective disorder (Abrams and Taylor, 1976, 1981; Pope & Lipinski, 1978; Pope et al., 1980).

Moreover, just as in the studies in depressive illness already reviewed, most of the older ECT studies in schizophrenia are methodologically defective. The few acceptable studies from this era will be briefly reviewed here, followed by a more detailed examination of the very few methodologically acceptable studies conducted in recent years.

Miller et al. (1953) assigned 30 chronic catatonic schizophrenics to genuine ECT or to pentothal anesthesia with or without the addition of nonconvulsive electrical stimulation. Partially blind assessment (two of the four interviewers were blind) after 3 to 4 weeks of treatment showed no differences among the three groups for reduction of psychotic symptoms or improvement in social performance. Brill et al. (1959) compared 20 genuine ECTs with an equal number of thiopental or nitrous oxide anesthesia inductions in 67 male chronic schizophrenics and found no significant difference among the methods as blindly assessed on three separate outcome measures 1 month after treatment. Heath et al. (1964) gave short courses of four or eight genuine or sham (thiopental anesthesia) ECTs to 45 chronic schizophrenics and found no significant changes or intergroup differences 1 month after treatment on a blindly administered nurses' behavior rating scale.

Langsley, Enterline, and Hickerson (1959) randomly assigned 106 acutely schizophrenic or manic patients to a course of 12 to 20 ECTs or 200 to 2000 mg/day chlorpromazine (CPZ) (mean = 800 mg/day). Blind evaluation at 8 and 12 weeks revealed no between-group differences on either a psychiatrist's or nurse's rating scale. King (1960) randomly assigned 84 newly admitted female schizophrenics to a course of 20 ECTs or 900 to 1200 mg/day CPZ for 1 month. Hospital discharge rates were the same for both groups, as were the subsequent relapse rates while on maintnance CPZ.

It is reasonable to conclude from these data that ECT is no better than sham ECT in the treatment of chronic schizophrenia, and no better than neuroleptics in the treatment of nonchronic schizophrenia.

Modern Studies Including a Sham ECT Group

Taylor and Fleminger (1980) studied 20 paranoid schizophrenic patients diagnosed according to the Present State Examination (PSE) and referred for ECT after having failed at least two weeks of low-dose neuroleptic therapy (e.g., 300 mg/day CPZ, 15 mg/day trifluoperazine). Chronically ill patients were excluded from this study, as were those who had a very short (6 months) psychiatric history. Patients were randomly assigned to a course of 8 to 12 genuine or sham ECTs (10 in each group), administered thrice-weekly, during which neuroleptic drugs were continued at the same low pre-ECT dosages in both groups. Blind ratings on the Comprehensive Psychiatric Rating Scale revealed lower scores for the genuine ECT group at 2 weeks ($p = 0.02$), 4 weeks ($p = 0.004$), and 8 weeks ($p = 0.07$), but not 1 month after the treatment course ended. Half of the patients in each group had pre-treatment Beck Depression Inventory scores of 20, indicative of clinical depression; although genuine ECT caused a greater reduction in these scores than sham ECT at 2, 4, and 8 weeks, the differences were not quite significant.

In a separately published part of the Leicester ECT trial described earlier (Brandon et al., 1984), Brandon et al. (1985) randomly assigned 17 patients who were diagnosed by the PSE-based Catego program as having schizophrenia to receive eight genuine ($n = 9$) or sham ($n = 8$) ECTs administered over a 4-week course. Those patients already on stable doses of neuroleptics were continued on them; there was no difference in mean dosage between the groups. Blind psychiatric evaluations on the Montgomery–Asberg Schizophrenia Scale at 2 and 4 weeks showed significantly greater improvement with genuine than sham ECT; this was no longer the case at the 12- and 28-week follow-up examinations. No effort was made in this trial to exclude patients with affective symptoms: mean Hamilton Depression scale scores were 26 and 37 for the genuine and sham ECT groups, respectively—well within the range of most studies of ECT in major depressive disorders.

The small sample sizes and failure to exclude patients with prominent affective symptoms limits the conclusions that can be drawn from these two studies: they both clearly demonstrate a therapeutic effect of ECT in nonchronic schizophrenic patients receiving neuroleptic drugs and diagnosed according to modern British criteria.

Bagadia et al. (1983) randomly assigned 38 predominantly non-chronic schizophrenic patients diagnosed according to the Research Diagnostic Criteria (RDC) to receive either six genuine bilateral ECTs plus placebo ($n = 20$) or six sham ECTs plus 600 mg/day CPZ ($n = 18$). Blind evaluation on the Brief Psychiatric and Clinical Global Impressions rating scales (BPRS, CGI) after 7 and 20 days of treatment revealed no significant between-group differences. This study is notable for its larger sample size and for excluding patients who had exhibited depressive or manic symptoms sufficient for a diagnosis of schizoaffective or affective illness. Although the number of ECT given was small by any standard, the study design demonstrates that a short course of ECT is no more or less effective a treatment for schizophrenia than an equally short course of moderate-dose neuroleptic treatment.

Studies Without a Sham ECT Control Group

Janakiramaiah et al. (1982) randomly assigned groups of 15 schizo-phrenic patients each to receive 6 weeks of treatment with one of four methods: ECT plus 500 mg/day CPZ, ECT plus 300 mg/day CPZ, 500 mg/day CPZ, or 300 mg/day CPZ. Diagnoses were made according to the RDC. Eight to 15 bilateral sine-wave ECTs were administered at a thrice-weekly rate. Blind ratings on the BPRS at weekly intervals were significantly different among the four methods by analysis of variance at the first through fifth weeks of treatment: the ECT plus 500 mg/day CPZ group was the most effective at the end of the first week, and the 300 mg/day CPZ group fared worse than any of the others at the two-to-five-week assessments. In the main effects analysis, ECT always resulted in lower BPRS scores than no ECT (regardless of CPZ dose), but these differences only reached significance at the end of the second and third weeks of treatment. The interactive effect of CPZ and ECT—that is, the efficacy of combined treatment versus either treat-ment given separately—was significant at the end of the third through fifth treatment weeks. (The study is marred by the fact that five patients in the ECT plus 300 mg/day CPZ group revealed to the "blind" examiner that they were receiving ECT.) In sum, this study shows that although at different times during the treatment course ECT was better than no ECT, and ECT plus CPZ was better than either treatment given alone, by the end of 6 weeks schizophrenic patients fared equally well with or without ECT. Essentially, ECT served to accelerate the treatment response to low-dose CPZ.

The literature is best summarized by the following statements:

1. ECT is no better than sham ECT in the treatment of chronic schizophrenia.
2. ECT is better than sham ECT in the treatment of nonchronic schizophrenic patients who have a lot of affective symptoms.

Efficacy in Other Disorders

No data exists from controlled trials to support the use of ECT in disorders other than those described earlier; such usage belongs to the art rather than the science of psychiatry. Of course, such art has an important place: ill patients must be treated, emergencies responded to, and families assured that no reasonable treatment alternatives have been overlooked. In truth, most suffering patients are primarily inter-

ested in seeking out a physician with great experience and reputed
success in the treatment of their illness, correctly believing that if he is
also honest, and learned, he will choose the most effective method to
cure them. Does it really matter to patient or doctor that data from
controlled trials does not exist to support the use of ECT in the
particular disorder under consideration? If a clinician has successfully
used ECT under similar clinical circumstances in the past, he has
ample justification for yet another therapeutic trial, especially when
other treatments have already failed.

Clinical Considerations

This section is a personal interpretation and elaboration of the anecdotal clinical lore that has evolved during a half-century of ECT
practice. Such uncontrolled observations are useful for the following
reasons.

1. *Controlled trials of ECT do not exist for all diagnoses.* Some
psychiatric syndromes for which ECT is often prescribed (e.g., mania)
have not yet been the subject of completed controlled trials, and others
(e.g. catatonic stupor, depressive pseudodementia) occur infrequently
enough to make it doubtful that they ever will be. Yet the universal
clinical experience has been that manics, catatonics, and depressive
pseudodements respond to ECT at least as well as to other treatments,
even in those patients who have failed to respond to intensive pharmacotherapy, and occasionally achieve dramatic remissions that surprise
even ardent foes of ECT.

2. *The results of controlled trials may be conflicting.* For example, how to view the carefully controlled and sharply contradictory
study of Wilson and Gottlieb (1967) that clearly demonstrates that
right-unilateral ECT causes more verbal impairment than bilateral
ECT, or Lambourn and Gill's (1978) methodologically impeccable
demonstration that sham ECT was just as effective in relieving depressions as the genuine article? After attempting vainly to incorporate
these and other similarly contradictory studies into a comprehensive
view of the ECT process, most writers have chosen simply to ignore
them, albeit without scientific grounds for doing so. The point is that
practicing clinicians, as well as their more rigorously scientific colleagues, pick and choose daily from among the available data those
results that best support their personal biases and experience and
reject those that do not.

3. *Controlled trials do not have a monopoly on truth.* This sentiment may seem strange in view of the opening sentence of the preceding section, but only because truth is here being considered at a different level of discourse. Double-blind, random assignment methodology was not required to demonstrate the efficacy of penicillin in meningococcal meningitis, and will not be needed to prove the efficacy of the first drug that cures a few patients with acquired immune deficiency syndrome. When a drowned boy is restored to life through phased warming and the intravenous administration of complexly balanced electrolyte solutions no one suggests the need for a placebo-controlled study to confirm the results. Likewise, the dramatic response of a mute, stuporous, rigid, incontinent, and drooling catatonic patient to one or two induced seizures also partakes of the truth, a truth that has generally been more difficult to accept with regard to ECT than most other treatments.

4. *Data from controlled trials may be incomplete.* Some psychiatric disorders (e.g., melancholia), although subjected to controlled study for their responsiveness to ECT, have protean manifestations that have not always been examined with enough thoroughness to draw definitive conclusions. The presence of depressive delusions, for example, long considered by clinicians to define an extremely ECT-sensitive subpopulation (e.g., Crow and Johnstone, 1986), has never been used to stratify a sample of melancholics in a prospective, random-assignment study of the efficacy of ECT.

Finally, although much of this volume is devoted to a critical review of the supporting research data for each topic covered, it is nevertheless intended as a clinical guide to ECT, and clinicians can never allow themselves to be bound solely by the narrow confines of data from controlled trials. This is simply because many, if not most, psychiatric patients present with syndromes that do not fit the nicely defined categories of research studies that have the luxury of specifying inclusion and exclusion criteria and minimal scores on standardized rating scales; for these patients there simply is no existing research data to guide the clinician's choice of treatment, yet treat he must. As is true for anyone who publishes frequently on the topic of ECT, I receive several calls a month from clinicians asking for advice on the management of a particularly difficult patient. The question is never "what objective data from controlled trials is there to support the use of ECT in my patient," but always "in your clinical experience, how should my patient be treated?" The present section addresses the latter class of questions, relying not only on an extensive clinical literature but on the cumulative wisdom of teachers and colleagues, all filtered through the residue of personal clinical experience.

Considerations in the Choice and Timing of ECT

It is no secret that patients with affective disorder, unipolar or bipolar types, are prime candidates for ECT; however, despite the chastening lessons of the cross-national study (Kendell et al., 1971) and several articles documenting the pitfalls of misdiagnosing affective disorder as schizophrenia (Lipkin et al., 1970; Carlson and Goodwin, 1973; Taylor and Abrams, 1974; Abrams and Taylor, 1974, 1976, 1981; Pope and Lipinsky, 1978; Pope et al., 1980), many affectively disordered patients who might otherwise have fully recovered or substantially benefited from ECT (or lithium, for that matter) still receive neuroleptic drugs instead in the mistaken belief that their psychotic symptoms indicate a diagnosis of schizophrenia. DSM-III has not been much help in this regard as it traps the clinician into diagnosing schizophrenia whenever psychotic symptoms evolve first in a patient's progression toward a full-blown manic or depressive syndrome. Thus, a patient who first develops a delusion of guilt for some imagined past transgression, followed shortly by anorexia, weight-loss, early waking, retardation, hopelessness, and suicidal ruminations, must receive the incongruous DSM-III diagnosis of schizophrenia. An analogous scenario for misdiagnosing manic patients is readily appreciated.

DSM-III notwithstanding, *melancholia* often presents with a stereotypical syndrome that is easy to recognize: agitation or retardation, weight loss, early waking, self-reproach, anhedonia, impaired concentration, low self-esteem, and ruminations of guilt, worthlessness, hopelessness, or suicide present an unmistakable clinical picture that augurs well for a full remission with ECT. The presence of such psychotic features as delusions (e.g., of guilt, sin, poverty) or hallucinations (e.g., a rotting odor, a voice counselling suicide), far from suggesting a diagnosis of schizophrenia, is more favorable still in predicting recovery (e.g., Kantor and Glassman, 1977; Dunn and Quinlan, 1978; Brandon et al., 1985; Lykouras et al., 1986). If a delusional mood is present or the patient appears dazed, perplexed, or clouded, the effects of ECT can be dramatic, with the patient awakening from the first or second treatment as if from a dream, thoroughly astounded to learn of his whereabouts and recent strange behaviors.

Although 6 to 8 ECTs constitute the modal treatment course in melancholia (Fink, 1979), an occasional patient may require considerably more. I remember well one woman in her early 70s whose severe unipolar depression did not respond at all to the first 10 ECTs. Treatment was continued despite these disappointing results because of her classical presentation and a history of an excellent response of similar symptoms to ECT 30 years earlier. Improvement became evident by the twelfth ECT and was complete after the fifteenth, illustrating the general rule that so long as the clinical syndrome is prognostically favorable, ECT should be continued until the expected degree of improvement is obtained. Although there is probably a maximum number of ECTs that should not be exceeded in a single treatment course, I know of no way to determine it. (I have only seen one patient with classical melancholia who did not respond to ECT, a late-onset unipolar depressive whose presentation was so typical, and symptoms so severe, that he received 22 ECT without significant improvement before the treatment was finally declared a failure.)

Conversely, there is no reason to slavishly adhere to a fixed minimum number of treatments either. I can think of several instances, especially in older patients, where marked improvement occurred after the third or fourth ECT, only to fade and then disappear with additional treatments. Whether this course of events represents a dose-response curve analagous to that reported for the tricyclic antidepressant nortriptyline, or simply the deleterious effects of developing cognitive dysfunction, the advisable course of action when a patient has shown marked improvement early in the treatment course is to withhold further ECT pending the return of symptoms. The rationale for the common clinical practice of giving two additional ECTs to prevent relapse after full recovery has been achieved was not confirmed in a controlled follow-up study by Barton et al. (1973). Finally, some depressed patients who do not respond to the usual rate of administration of three times a week may nonetheless recover if double ECTs are given each session (Swartz and Mehta, 1986).

Of all the possible behavioral responses to ECT, the euphoric–hypomanic pattern (Fink and Kahn, 1961) is best. It always indicates that enough ECT has been given. Its occurrence after right-unilateral ECT as well as after bilateral ECT suggests that it represents not merely a nonspecific organic frontal lobe response, but rather a focused limbic effect of ECT (a *direct hit*), producing an affective overshoot with gradual return to euthymia several days after treatment has stopped.

Antidepressants should be discontinued during ECT. No additive or synergistic effect of combining ECT and antidepressants has been demonstrated (Abrams, 1975; Siris, Glassman and Stetner, 1982), and Price et al. (1978) actually found a statistically significant *reduction* in affective improvement in patients in their ECT sample who had received tricyclic antidepressants compared to those who had not. Lithium, as noted in Chapter 6, should not be coadministered with ECT as it may cause severe organic confusional states and prolong the apnea induced by succinylcholine.

Two clinical variants of melancholia are exquisitely responsive to ECT: catatonic stupor and depressive pseudodementia.

CATATONIC STUPOR

Known in the older literature as *melancholia attonita*, this syndrome of stupor, mutism, negativism, catalepsy, and incontinence of saliva, urine, and feces may linger for weeks or months until abruptly dissolved by a few (sometimes, just one) induced seizures. Again, a diagnosis of schizophrenia is not inherent to this syndrome, which is diagnostically nonspecific and occurs most frequently in patients who satisfy research criteria for affective disorders (Abrams and Taylor, 1976). Other individual catatonic features (e.g., echolalia, echopraxia, mannerisms, stereotypies) are not associated with a particularly good response to ECT, perhaps becauase they are more often seen in patients with chronic schizophrenia. A positive, albeit transient, response of catatonic stupor to intravenous sodium amobarbital (the *amytal interview*) often predicts a favorable outcome with ECT. Indeed, while awaiting completion of the pretreatment workup before starting ECT in a catatonic patient, 250 mg of sodium amytal given intramuscularly 30 minutes before meals will often enable him to eat and drink.

DEPRESSIVE PSEUDODEMENTIA

If this syndrome of disorientation and impaired memory accompanying depressive symptoms in an older person is misdiagnosed as senile dementia and the luckless patient placed in a nursing home, he may not have long to live. A few ECTs, however, can rapidly restore such an apparently deteriorated individual to rosy health, an occurrence rendered all the more remarkable by the family's frequent comment that "——— hasn't looked this well in years." There is little risk in inadvertently treating a patient whose depressive symptoms are only an early manifestation of Alzheimer's dementia. ECT has been used successfully under such circumstances without worsening the cognitive symptoms or accelerating the progression of the underlying disorder (see Chapter 5), so there is nothing to be lost by a therapeutic trial in questionable cases.

A melancholic patient should receive ECT in preference to any other treatment under circumstances of increased clinical urgency or intolerance to psychotropic drugs.

1. *The presence of delusions or hallucinations.* Psychotic depression is notoriously resistant to antidepressant drugs but very responsive to ECT (Hordern et al., 1963; Glassman et al., 1975; Davidson et al., 1978; Crow and Johnstone, 1986). Although tricyclic–neuroleptic combinations are reported to be more effective in delusional depression than tricyclics alone (Spiker et al., 1986), it seems unwarranted to expose a depressed patient to the risk of tardive dyskinesia when the safe and rapidly effective alternative of ECT is available.

2. *The presence of stupor.* Neither full-blown catatonic stupor nor the more severe degrees of psychomotor retardation respond well to antidepressant drugs, yet both are rapidly responsive to ECT. Moreover, there is often some urgency involved, as such patients do not eat well, or at all, and have often lost significant body mass by the time they are first seen.

3. *The presence of suicidal ruminations or behavior.* Completed suicide presents the single greatest risk in melancholia, yet rarely occurs once ECT has been initiated. No similar experience has been accumulated for antidepressant drugs, which are traditionally held to increase the risk of completed suicide early in the treatment course if psychomotor retardation is relieved before despondency.

4. *Coexisting severe medical disease.* The pronounced cardiovascular effects of some tricyclic antidepressants have been reported to increase the risk of sudden death in cardiac patients (Coull et al., 1970; Moir et al., 1972), making ECT often seem to be the more conservative treatment choice. Hepatic and renal disease also increase the risks of drug therapy, due to impaired metabolism and excretion, but not the risk with ECT.

5. *Depressive pseudodementia.* Antidepressants seem only to aggravate this syndrome, perhaps because of their anticholinergic effects.

6. *Old age.* Elderly melancholics also seem particularly intolerant of the anticholinergic effects of many tricyclics, which often cause severe constipation or even precipitate a pseudodementia syndrome

(anticholinergic delirium). If anything, the response to ECT improves with the age of the patient, and fewer treatments are generally required to achieve remission.

7. *Pregnancy.* All psychotropic drugs, including lithium, cross the placental barrier and exert unknown, but doubtless protean and unfavorable effects on the fetus both during and after development, continuing into the postnatal period if the mother nurses. ECT is not known to exert any such adverse fetal effects (Chapter 5) and should be used in preference to drugs in pregnant women and during the nursing period.

8. *Drug therapy failure.* Any patient who has failed a course of adequate antidepressant therapy should be offered ECT in preference to another trial with a different compound. In practice, this covers many depressives who are admitted to the hospital after failing to respond to outpatient pharmacotherapy. Of course, any patient with a history of prior unresponsiveness to antidepressants should receive ECT as the initial treatment.

Mania

Mania, the obverse of melancholia, responds so well to ECT that it is difficult to account for the absence until very recently of any prospective controlled trials of induced seizures in this disorder. Perhaps the rapidly spreading use (and remarkable efficacy) of lithium therapy at a time when the importance of controlled trials of ECT was also being recognized had an inhibiting effect; probably the general disinclination of manics to cooperate with any form of treatment, let alone random assignment to ECT or drugs, also played a role. In any case, the studies in progress of Small et al. (in press) and Mukerjhee et al. (1987), cited earlier, have broken the ice and more are sure to follow.

There are three retrospective studies that shed some light on the efficacy of ECT in mania. In a chart-review study, McCabe (1976) compared a sample of manic patients who received ECT in the pre-drug era (1945–1949) with an age- and sex-matched control sample of manics who were hospitalized at the Iowa Psychopathic Hospital before ECT had been introduced (1935–1941). All subjects were selected on the basis of the same research criteria, and the resultant groups were remarkably similar on most of 27 clinical psychopathological variables studied. On all outcome measures (duration of hospitalization, condition at discharge, percent discharged home, degree of social recovery) the ECT-treated group fared substantially and significantly better than the untreated control sample, with the most striking difference being that 96 percent of the ECT patients were discharged to their homes, compared with only 44 percent of the untreated patients. A second chart-review study from the same hospital (McCabe and Norris, 1977) examined the question from a different vantage point, comparing the outcome in the same two groups already described with that obtained in a third age- and sex-matched sample of manics who received CPZ therapy during the period from 1958 to 1964. Not surprisingly, ECT and CPZ were both superior to no treatment, and were about equal overall in their beneficial effects in mania; however, 10 patients who did not respond well to CPZ therapy went on to recover with ECT. In another retrospective chart-review study (Thomas and Reddy, 1982), ECT, CPZ, and lithium were reported equally effective; however, the three groups were not as well-matched as in the studies from Iowa, and the sample sizes (10 in each group) were much smaller.

Most manic patients come to ECT only after lithium or neuroleptics have failed and the patient, who has typically been in a state of relentless excitement for several days, is on the verge of exhaustion. Even under these unfavorable circumstances ECT works, and bilateral ECT is the preferred method (Abrams and Fink, 1984; Small et al., 1985; 1986). Other than psychomotor excitement, a particularly favorable feature that is usually present in patients with acute mania, no individual manic symptom or symptom-cluster is especially predictive of a good response to ECT. Conversely, the presence of psychotic symptoms, however outlandish or bizarre, in no way reduces the likelihood of recovery so long as the full manic syndrome is also present (Taylor and Abrams, 1975).

It has long been standard clinical practice to administer double bilateral ECTs on consecutive treatment days during the first session or two of a manic patient's treatment course, perhaps reflecting the clinical urgency often felt by the time such patients are finally referred for ECT. Recent evidence (Small et al., in press; Mukerjhee et al., 1987), however, suggests that manics are quite responsive to conventional single bilateral ECTs when administered at the usual rate.

Schizophrenia

There is little doubt that many patients diagnosed as having acute or schizoaffective schizophrenia respond remarkably well to ECT; there is also little doubt that most of these patients are misdiagnosed manics (Taylor and Abrams, 1974; Abrams and Taylor, 1974, 1976c, 1981). When the diagnosis of schizophrenia is made by first excluding patients with prominent affective syndromes (Taylor and Abrams, 1978), most of the ECT-responsive clinical variance is thereby also excluded. This should not be taken to mean that patients with an early, insidious onset of emotional blunting, avolition, first-rank symptoms, and formal thought-disorder should never be offered ECT. On the contrary, *every* such patient deserves one full trial of ECT (preferably earlier rather than later in their illness course) so that no treatment will be overlooked that has a chance, however slim, of halting the otherwise relentless progression of this devastating illness (Abrams, 1987). Two recent, uncontrolled studies (Friedel, 1986; Gujavarty, Greenberg and Fink, 1987) suggest that such a trial, in conjunction with neuroleptic drug therapy, may yield unexpectedly favorable results. Controlled studies, with and without coadministration of neuroleptics, should now be undertaken to demonstrate the efficacy of such treatment.

In those rare instances when the catatonic syndrome of negativistic stupor is a manifestation of schizophrenia, ECT works just as well to remove the stupor as in patients with affective disorder, but often reveals a core schizophrenic syndrome that is resistant to further ECT.

SYMPTOMATIC PSYCHOSES

Numerous individual case reports over the last half-century testify to the effectiveness of ECT in psychotic states secondary to a wide variety of toxic, metabolic, infectious, traumatic, neoplastic, epileptic, and endocrine disorders (Taylor, 1982). Particularly striking are the results that are often achieved with ECT in drug-induced states, especially amphetamine psychosis, and in the acute epileptiform psychoses. Where the underlying disorder has been chronically in place or remains uncorrected at the time of treatment a favorable response is less likely. In general, it is reasonable to reserve ECT for those symptomatic psychoses that have neither responded to medical treatment of the underlying condition nor to a week's trial of neuroleptic drugs.

NEUROSES AND PERSONALITY DISORDERS

Whatever the current terminology used to classify these disorders, they are rarely responsive to (and often aggravated by) ECT.

3

Prediction of Response to Electroconvulsive Therapy

Prediction in medicine is more aptly termed prognostication and usually constitutes an assessment of variables that determine the likelihood of developing a given illness (e.g., myocardial infarction risk factors), surviving one (e.g., the staging of cancers), or of enjoying a favorable outcome following an intervention.

Some earlier prognostic methods are now mainly of historical interest. These include physiological measures, such as the methacholine (Mecholyl) and sedation threshold tests (Funkenstein et al., 1952; Shagass and Jones, 1958), and personality variables as assessed by the Minnesota Multiphasic Personality Inventory (MMPI) (Feldman, 1951), Rorschach test (Kahn and Fink, 1960), and California F scale (Kahn et al., 1959). These have been reviewed in detail elsewhere (Fink, 1979; Hamilton, 1982) and are not included here as they provide no practical guide to the present-day administration of ECT. Somewhat more relevant to modern practice are the prognostic scales derived from the clinical and psychopathological features of the depressed state, although, as we shall see, they are also of limited utility.

Hobson (1953) was the first to construct such a predictive index, recording the presence or absence of 121 clinical and historical features in a sample of 127 patients ("almost all" of them depressed) prior to ECT. Two weeks after the treatment course patients were classed as having had a "good" or "poor" response, and each of the 121 features was examined for its correlation with this measure. Thirteen features correlated significantly with the outcome. Five were favorable (sudden onset, good insight, obsessional personality, self reproach, duration of illness less than 1 year) and 8 unfavorable (mild-to-moderate hypochondriasis, depersonalization, emotional lability, adult neurotic traits, hysterical attitude, above average intelligence, childhood neurotic traits). By adding 3 "very suggestive" features (a favorable one of pronounced retardation and 2 unfavorable ones of ill-adjusted or hysterical personality) to this list, a checklist of 16 features was provided and scored by assigning 1 point for the absence of a favorable feature or the presence of an unfavorable one. Scores ranged from 1 to 14, the lower the better. A mean score of 7.5 was found to provide the fewest misclassifications into the good and poor outcome groupings, yielding a "hit rate" of 79.7 percent.

Roberts (1959a) found that the Hobson index successfully predicted the outcome in 80 percent of depressives, and Mendels (1965a) in 78 percent, but Hamilton and White (1960) and Abrams et al. (1973) found it to be of no value. Mendels (1965b) also employed an item analysis (similar to Hobson's method) to construct his own index of all variables associated with a 50 percent or greater reduction in depression scale score 1 month after ECT. Four favorable items (family history of depression, early waking, delusions, retardation) and 4 unfavorable ones (neurotic traits, inadequate personality, precipitating event, emotional lability) correctly predicted the outcome in 90 percent of the cases; a subsequent study with an enlarged sample and slightly different index (Mendels, 1967) yielded a predictive accuracy of 86 percent. In this study, personality traits (e.g. histrionic) that were associated with reactive or neurotic depression were better predictors of outcome than the clinical variables (e.g., early waking) that were classically associated with a diagnosis of endogenous depression. Abrams et al. (1973) were unable to confirm the predictive value of Mendels' (1965b) index in a sample of 76 primary depressives studied before and after a course of 4 ECTs.

Multiple regression analysis is a more sophisticated procedure for weighting the prognostic value of variables. It was first used for this purpose by Hamilton and White (1960). These authors included 5 pretreatment variables in their regression analysis that were selected for their significant correlation with the Hamilton (1960) depression scale score after ECT: duration of illness, body index, postmethacholine fall of systolic blood pressure, and pretreatment Hamilton depression scale score. The multiple correlation achieved was a modest +0.62, somewhat lower, but in the same general range, as that reported by subsequent investigators using similar techniques. Nyström (1964) selected 24 variables that were correlated with the outcome and calculated individual prognostic values for each patient based on the partial regression coefficients of the items. Favorable features included early waking, retardation, and a profoundly depressed mood; unfavorable ones included seclusiveness, ideas of reference, depersonalization, obsessionality, and histrionic behavior. Outcome was correctly predicted in 76 percent of the cases. Carney, Roth, and Garside (1965) constructed their Newcastle Scale predictive index by applying multiple regression analysis to determine the weights for each of 35 clinical variables that best predicted the outcome 3 months after ECT. Five favorable features (weight loss, pyknic physique, early waking, somatic delusions, paranoid delusions) and 5 unfavorable ones (anxiety, worsening of mood in evening, self-pity, hypochondriasis, hysterical traits) were selected and yielded a score that had a multiple correlation with outcome of $+0.67$. Each item that correlated significantly with outcome also did so with a diagnosis of endogenous depression. The Newcastle scale was subsequently tested on a new sample of depressives by Carney and Sheffield (1972) and found to have a predictive accuracy of 76 percent.

The prognostic accuracy reported for these various indices is overestimated by the very nature of the statistical procedures employed (Abrams et al., 1973; Hamilton, 1982; Abrams, 1982). By selecting those items from a larger sample that are significantly correlated with the outcome and combining them in a coefficient of multiple correlation to "predict" outcome in the sample from which they were derived, the relationships involved are inherently inflated. This is because the item set was derived from (and therefore "tailored" to) the sample studied. When the same variables and weights are then used to predict outcome in other samples, the results always suffer substantially.

Moreover, workers from the University of Iowa have recently had less success in confirming the prognostic value of melancholic–endogenous features. Coryell and Zimmerman (1984) tested the predictive value of a DSM-III diagnosis of melancholia, along with a variety of other response predictors, in a sample of primary unipolar depressives receiving ECT. The presence or absence of melancholia was the only variable of 7 tested that bore an *inverse* relation to any of the 3 outcome measures employed (Hamilton scale score at discharge, global rating at discharge, and mean weekly follow-up symptom score): melancholics had higher follow-up symptom scores ($p < .05$) and poorer global ratings at discharge (N.S.). The presence of delusions was the most favorable predictor variable, followed by increasing age and female gender. The familial subtype of depressive spectrum disease was unfavorable, as was a longer duration of illness prior to admission. In a subsequent analysis of the same data set, Coryell, Pfohl, and Zimmerman (1985) also found secondary depressives to have a worse outcome than primary depressives. Depressed patients with a diagnosable personality disorder, however, do not fare any worse with ECT (Zimmerman et al., 1986). Another study from the same group failed to find any predictive value of a Newcastle scale diagnosis of endogenous versus reactive depression in predicting ECT response (Zimmerman et al., 1986).

One potential problem with the Iowa studies is the rather low efficacy of ECT that they found: about 60 to 65 percent improvement in Hamilton scale scores. This is probably a function of their choice of unilateral ECT as their results are similar to the 56 percent improvement with this method obtained by Abrams et al. (1983), but substantially less than the 81 percent these same authors achieved with bilateral ECT. By using a less effective method for ECT, the Iowa group may simply have demonstrated that unilateral ECT is equally *ineffective* in patients with endogenous and reactive depression. [True, Rich et al. (1984) also failed to find any predictive value of RDC and DSM-III subtypes of major depression (reactive, secondary, nonpsychotic) in 48 depressives receiving ECT, but as their sample consisted mostly of endogenous or melancholic depressives there was not much variance for their predictors to explain.]

Various and sundry clinical and demographic items have been reported to exhibit an association with ECT response. A favorable effect of increasing age on an outcome with ECT was found by several earlier investigators (Roberts, 1959b; Mendels, 1965; Carney et al., 1974), as was shorter duration of illness (Hamilton and White, 1960; Hobson, 1953; Carney et al., 1974; Herrington et al., 1974). Although there are disparate results (Hamilton, 1982), two studies beside Coryell and Zimmerman (1984) also report better results in women than men (Herrington et al., 1974; Medical Research Council Trial, 1965). Other variables predicting a favorable response to ECT include cyclothymic personality (Abrams and Taylor, 1974; Ottosson, 1962), pyknic physique (Abrams and Taylor, 1974), and diminished salivary flow (Weckowicz et al., 1971). The report of a better ECT response in bipolar than unipolar depressives (Perris, 1966) was not confirmed by Abrams and Taylor (1974) or Heshe et al. (1978). Although there are contradictory data, the presence of precipitating social stressors does not appear to predict the response of depressed patients to ECT (Zimmerman et al., 1987).

There has been a special interest in the dexamethasone suppression test (DST) as a possible predictor of treatment response in depressed patients receiving biological treatments (Fink, 1986a). In an analysis of pooled data from a number of studies that assessed the value of the DST in predicting treatment response of major depressives to adequate doses of an antidepressant or to ECT, Arana et al. (1985) found that more than 70 percent of responders had a positive DST (nonsupression) compared with fewer than 50 percent of nonresponders, a modest but highly significant difference. ECT response was not examined separately in this analysis, and few investigators have conducted prospective studies specifically relating suppressor status to ECT response. The limited number of studies reported, however, find modest or no differences between suppressors and nonsuppressors in their response to ECT.

Coryell (1982) obtained DSTs within 1 week of admission in 42 DSM-III major depressives who subsequently received ECT on clinical grounds. Blindly assigned global ratings of improvement based on a review of nursing and progress notes for the final 3 days of hospitalization were greater for nonsuppressors than suppressors, a difference not found for Hamilton Depression Scale scores. At follow-up 6 months later (Coryell and Zimmerman, 1983) no between-group differences were found on any measures. In a subsequent and different sample of unipolar depressives receiving ECT these authors (Coryell and Zimmerman, 1984) again found a significant correlation (0.33) in the predicted direction between the suppressor status and the globally rated outcome, but not in the outcome as determined by Hamilton Scale scores. Ames et al. (1984) found no significant difference in ECT response between seven suppressors and six nonsuppressors, although the percentage reduction in Hamilton Scale score was 15 points greater in the latter group. Coppen et al. (1985) found a significant correlation between post-DST plasma cortisol concentration and percentage improvement in Hamilton Scale scores in 44 major depressives receiving antidepressants, but not in 42 who received ECT. Lipman et al. (1986a, b) found no differences in depression scale ratings at discharge or at a 6-month follow-up between 26 suppressors and 12 nonsuppressors who had received ECT. Fink et al. (1986) found no short- or long-term differences in ECT response between nonsuppressors and suppressors, and Devanand et al. (1986) found no evidence that the pretreatment DST was useful in predicting the immediate clinical outcome of ECT—in fact, these authors found that 35 percent of the patients who were initially DST suppressors were converted to nonsuppressors by a course of ECT. The recent study by Katona et al. (1987) also found the DST to be unsuccessful in predicting either immediate or 6-month outcome.

A related question, although not precisely relevant to prognostication, is whether conversion from nonsuppressor to suppressor status during a course of ECT identifies patients who benefit from treatment. Albala et al. (1981) obtained serial DSTs during a course of ECT in a sample of six unipolar depressives who had been nonsuppressors prior to treatment, and monitored improvement with weekly Hamilton depression scale scores. Five of the 6 patients became suppressors (between the fourth and sixth ECT) and showed significant clinical improvement; the sixth patient failed to convert and had a poor clinical response to ECT. These results were confirmed in a subsequent study from the same laboratory (Grunhans et al., 1987), but contradictory data exist. Papakostas et al. (1981) found that of 10 unipolar melancholic DST nonsuppressors who responded favorably to ECT, 8 also exhibited concomitant normalization of the DST; the fact that there were no ECT nonresponders made it impossible to demonstrate the necessary corollary relationship, that is, that ECT nonresponders were also DST nonconverters. Moreover, 3 of the investigations cited earlier (Coryell, 1982 and 1985; Lipman et al., 1986) actually found a trend for patients who converted to suppressor status to have a *worse* outcome.

The prolactin response to ECT may be a more promising predictor of outcome. Abrams and Swartz (1985) studied serial postictal prolactin levels after each of 4 ECTs in a sample of 16 male melancholics. The mean ECT-induced prolactin elevation for the 4 induced seizures correlated significantly with the blind rating of global improvement after the sixth ECT and with the total number of ECTs prescribed by the treating psychiatrist, who was unaware of the prolactin values. The signs of the correlation coefficients demonstrated that a larger prolactin release predicted a worse outcome. When the patients were divided into fast ($n = 12$) and slow ($n = 4$) responders to ECT on the basis of global outcome ratings and number of ECTs ultimately received, the peak prolactin response to the first ECT was more than three times greater in the slow than the fast responders, perhaps because of relatively unresponsive pituitary dopamine receptors in the former group at baseline. Virtually identical results have been obtained by these investigators in a replication in progress in a different sample of 15 melancholic patients studied with serial postictal prolactin levels after each of six ECTs and with Hamilton rating scales for depression after the third and sixth treatments (Abrams and Swartz, 1986).

Scott et al. (1986), however, found no correlation between the prolactin response to the first ECT and improvement in depression scale scores; instead, they reported that release of estrogen-stimulated neurophysin was significantly greater in the depressed patients who improved than those who did not. Unfortunately, their study was confounded by the use of a nitrous oxide anesthesia control group (nitrous oxide raises serum prolactin levels) and co-administration of neuroleptics in several of their experimental subjects (Swartz, 1986).

Decina et al. (1976) found no predictive value of the TRH stimulation test for the response of depressives to ECT, although a significant reduction (blunting) of the TSH response occurred during the week following a course of treatment.

For the clinician, however, many of these "predictors" lack utility. The observation that a given depressed patient is female, or older, or has a stocky build is unlikely to influence the decision to give ECT. The fact is that favorable and unfavorable features do not exist independently of ill patients but tend to group together naturally into depressive syndromes, unfortunately often with substantial overlap. Favorable features generally characterize patients with endogenous or melancholic syndromes, and these are the patients who recover rapidly with ECT. The unfavorable features characterize patients with long-standing anxiety, hypochondriacal, and somatization symptoms, often dating from childhood, and personality traits of hysteroid dysphoria, dependency, and inadequacy. Such patients typically respond briefly or not at all to ECT and may even be made worse by the treatment. In practice, it is not very difficult to identify patients who are likely to benefit from ECT. For example, it is rare for a retarded patient with guilty delusions and suicidal intent not to respond to ECT. The difficulty usually arises in patients who would not generally be thought of as prime candidates for ECT but whose atypical depressive features remain despite adequate treatment with antidepressant drugs. In such instances there is little help to be derived from the predictors, and the administration of a "trial" course of ECT results in improvement with a frequency that is sufficient to maintain the strategy in clinical practice.

4

Cerebral Physiology and Metabolism

The combined physiological effects of the electrical stimulus for ECT and the resultant generalized seizure discharge are immediate and powerful and may be detectable days or weeks after the treatment course terminates.

Cerebral Electrographic Events

If an electrical stimulus depolarizes sufficient neurons a generalized, paroxysmal, cerebral seizure ensues, the threshold for which is defined as the electrical dose (in millicoulombs) that produced it. Subconvulsive stimuli elicit only an electroencephalographic (EEG) "arousal" response, characterized in the cat by low-voltage fast activity (Miyasaka, 1959) that is indistinguishable in appearance from that seen in the earliest phases of ECT-induced seizures (Penfield and Jasper, 1954; Chatrian and Petersen, 1960; Staton et al., 1981) and which Weiner (1982) has dubbed the "epileptic recruiting" stage. With substantially suprathreshold stimuli this initial low-voltage 18 to 22 Hz activity is rapidly replaced by a crescendo of high-voltage 10 to 20 Hz hypersynchronous polyspikes occurring simultaneously throughout the brain and corresponding to the tonic phase of the motor seizure. This discharge gradually decreases in frequency as the seizure progresses, evolving into the characteristic polyspike and slow wave complexes of the clonic motor phase, slowing to 1 to 3 Hz just prior to seizure termination, which is often abrupt and followed by "electrical silence" (*postictal suppression*). Clinically, the *tonic* phase is manifested by flexion of the arms, hyperextension of the neck, and extension of the legs with plantarflexion of the feet, and the *clonic* phase by bilateral clonic jerks of the extremities, corresponding to each polyspike and slow wave complex: symmetrical at first and then increasingly asymmetrical and uncoordinated just prior to seizure termination.

When the electrical stimulus is applied at, or just above, threshold, the seizure activity can be seen to originate in the neocortex (Miyasaka, 1959), spreading to older cortical and then subcortical regions. Multichannel EEG recording during ECT (Staton et al., 1981) confirms the neocortical origin of the initial polyspike activity and suggests that cortical spread, rather than cortical driving from diencephalic activation, is the mechanism for seizure generalization during ECT. The depth-electrode studies of Chatrian and Petersen (1960) are not informative on this point as no cortical electrodes were included in their investigation.

Termination of the clonic phase in EEG flattening is a phenomenon of varying clarity. Although it occurs abruptly in about one-third of the cases, and more often after bilateral than unilateral ECT (Abrams et al., 1973; Daniel et al., 1985), many records show a less precise end-point, with polyspike and slow-wave activity apparently stopping for a second or two and then resuming (Daniel et al., 1985; Swartz and Abrams, 1986), or gradually and imperceptibly blending into a mixture of alpha and beta activity (Small et al., 1970; Abrams et al., 1973). When clearly observed, the phase of postictal flattening lasts up to about 90 seconds, when high-voltage, irregular delta waves of 1 to 3 Hz gradually appear, followed by increasingly rhythmical theta waves that progressively merge into the preseizure rhythms by about 20 to 30 minutes after seizure termination. [Interestingly, Daniel et al. (1985) reported that the presence of postictal EEG suppression was associated with amnesia for a story told to patients 50 minutes before receiving ECT. In their study, however, it is difficult to determine whether seizure generalization or treatment electrode placement was the critical intervening variable, as bilateral ECT was strongly associated with both postictal EEG suppression and amnesia.]

The abruptness with which a seizure ended was attributed by Blachly and Gowing (1966) to a hypothetical "fit switch" that they believed became less precise with increasing numbers of treatments. They reported this phenomenon in patients receiving multiple electrically induced seizures in a single treatment session (see Chapter 6) with concomitant EEG and electrocardiogram (EKG) monitoring.

They also claimed that successive seizures induced during a single treatment session tended to increase in duration, in contrast to the reverse trend observed for seizures administered at the usual rate (Holmberg, 1955; Sackeim et al., 1986a). Our own data (Abrams et al., 1973) are at variance with theirs. We recorded the EEG during 45 sessions of multiple unilateral or bilateral ECT in 18 depressed patients. Most of the 160 seizures we blindly rated terminated precisely and abruptly on both sides of the head, regardless of treatment electrode placement, a finding consistent with that of Bridenbaugh et al., (1972) and Kurland et al. (1976). Concerning the ordinal position of seizures in a treatment session relative to the clarity of their endpoints, we found a trend for the final seizure to terminate *more* precisely than the first. In fact, in only 19 percent of the sessions did the final seizure terminate less abruptly than the first.

We also examined the characteristics of the postseizure EEG by dividing the records into those that were flat and those that exhibited mixed rhythms in the alpha–beta range; virtually all of the latter records occurred after unilateral ECT. When postictal flattening occurred after unilateral ECT it was always over the treated hemisphere. We did confirm an increasing duration of seizures within a single session, a phenomenon also reported by Bidder and Strain (1970).

The tendency for unilaterally induced seizures to terminate in mixed alpha–beta activity was also observed by Small et al. (1970), and may reflect a seizure for unilateral ECT that is in some way incomplete. A similar pattern of the immediate postictal activity was also observed by Kirstein and Ottosson (1960) for lidocaine-modified seizures, which were shorter in duration and less therapeutically active than those produced by conventional ECT.

At the level of the scalp-recorded EEG, the seizure'appears to be an all-or-none phenomenon. The titration procedures developed by Malitz et al. (1986) show that it only takes a small increment in electrical dosage to convert an entirely subconvulsive stimulus into one that yields a generalized seizure of adequate duration; moreover, substantial increases in stimulus intensity above threshold do not lengthen the seizure further (Ottosson, 1960). In the brain, however, seizure threshold, frequency, amplitude, and duration vary according to the structures involved. Miyasaka's (1959) implanted electrode studies in the cat show externally and electrically induced seizure activity starting first in the neocortex, followed by the archicortex (hippocampus), and, much later, the paleocortex (amygdala). And, whereas the neocortical seizure activity is characterized by the typical

10- to 20-Hz high-voltage polyspikes that gradually slow in frequency to 1 to 2 Hz, the hippocampal seizure begins at 30 to 40 Hz and gradually slows to 20 to 30 Hz, exhibiting the largest amplitude increase over baseline of any structure measured. Chatrian and Petersen's (1960) depth electrode recordings in patients receiving inhalant- or chemically-induced seizures also clearly demonstrate the polyspike phase starting at variable post-induction intervals:

> A high-voltage, rhythmic discharge already may be well developed in one area of the brain, while in other areas a similar discharge is only at the outset or the recording is still apparently flat.

In humans, as in cats, the seizure activity often terminates separately in different parts of the brain.

Seizure duration is variable in relation to stimulus wave-form and treatment electrode placement. Using a sine-wave stimulus Abrams et al. (1973) found significantly shorter seizures with unilateral than with bilateral ECT, but the same method in a younger population (Abrams et al., 1983) revealed slightly *longer* seizures with unilateral ECT. And, when brief-pulse ECT was studied in a small sample at the same center, seizure length was equal for both methods (Swartz and Abrams, 1984). In a four-cell comparison of unilateral, bilateral sine-wave, and brief-pulse techniques, Weiner (1980) reported significantly longer seizures with bilateral than unilateral ECT overall, a difference much more clearly seen with sine-wave stimuli. Although Horne et al. (1985) reported no statistically significant difference between unilateral and bilateral brief-pulse ECT, their raw data reflect about 30 percent more total seizure activity with bilateral than unilateral placement. The most recent brief-pulse ECT studies (Malitz et al., 1986; Weiner et al., 1986) find no differences in seizure length for the two methods when administered with just-above- or moderately above-threshold stimulation. To summarize these disparate results, it seems that a tendency for seizures to last longer with bilateral than unilateral ECT is augmented by sine-wave stimulation administered at substantially suprathreshold levels.

Prolonged seizures and status epilepticus have only very rarely been reported with conventional bilateral ECT (Weiner et al., 1980; Weiner, 1981). The clinical significance of the recent report of numerous prolonged seizures with brief-pulse unilateral ECT (Greenberg, 1985) is difficult to interpret as EEG seizure monitoring only became routine at about the time this latter treatment technique was introduced into general use. Nonetheless, no prolonged seizures were observed during the EEG monitoring of many dozens of consecutive unilateral and bilateral ECTs administered with both brief-pulse and sine-wave stimuli (Abrams et al., 1973; Weiner, 1980a; Abrams et al., 1983; Swartz and Abrams, 1984). There is no question, however, that prolonged seizures are more frequent with multiple ECT: despite its extremely limited use, two instances of status epilepticus have been reported (Strain and Bidder, 1971; Bridenbaugh et al., 1972) as well as numerous occurrences of seizures lasting more than 10 minutes (Bridenbaugh et al., 1972; Maletzky, 1978). It may be that Blachly and Gowing's (1966) recommendation for hyperventilation during Multiple monitored ECT (MMECT) is responsible for this phenomenon, as hypocapnia induced by hyperventilation during ECT increases seizure duration (Bergsholm et al., 1984).

Seizure monitoring during ECT has also provided the interesting observation that paroxysmal EEG seizure activity continues for about 10 seconds after all visible motor activity ends (Weiner, 1980; Fink and Johnson, 1982; Abrams and Volavka, 1982; Miller et al., 1985)—hence, the advisability of routine EEG monitoring during ECT in addition to observing the motor seizure in the "cuffed limb."

Intraseizure EEG patterns are usually symmetrical in both hemispheres with conventional bilateral ECT, but not for unilateral ECT. Small et al. (1970) reported asymmetrical paroxysmal EEG activity during the late clonic phase, with greater amplitude and persistence in the nonstimulated hemisphere. D'Elia and Perris (1970) also observed a variable amplitude of EEG seizure activity with unilateral ECT: their findings towards the end of the seizure were similar to those of Small et al. (1970), but were reversed at the beginning of the seizure. Kriss et al. (1978) continuously recorded the EEG for 30 minutes during left- or right-sided unilateral ECT and subjected the data to frequency analysis. During the seizure, paroxysmal slow-wave activity had significantly greater power over the *stimulated* hemisphere, in contrast to the findings by Small et al. (1970). This asymmetry extended to the immediate postictal period, with the treated side producing significantly more delta and less alpha and beta activity than the contralateral side. Confirmation of this finding comes from a recent EEG study of unilateral ECT (Gerst et al., 1982) that finds that polyspike activity on visual analysis is more prominent and of higher voltage over the stimulated hemisphere, where digitally analyzed seizure activity also showed the greatest energy content.

Since seizures induce physiological effects related to the activation of different regions of the brain, the duration of these effects should correlate highly for well-generalized seizures. Swartz and Larson (1986) recently calculated the correlation coefficients among four different measures of seizure duration (motor activity, EEG spike activity, total paroxysmal EEG activity, and tachycardia duration) and found them to be significantly higher with bilateral than unilateral ECT, suggesting greater generalization throughout the brain with the former technique. Using the same method, Larson and Swartz (1986) also demonstrated greater intracerebral generalization with the first than with the second of two seizures given consecutively in a single treatment session. As less well-generalized seizures may be expected to spread more slowly and therefore last longer (indeed, the duration of total paroxysmal EEG activity was significantly longer for the second ECT), the authors' finding may help explain the increased occurrence of prolonged seizures with multiple-monitored ECT.

Following a single ECT very little EEG change persists after the seizure patterns have terminated and been gradually replaced by the pretreatment rhythms. As the numbers of treatments increase, however, the EEG slowing persists into the postconvulsive period, accumulating as a function of the total number of ECT and their rate of administration (Fink, 1979). This EEG activity increases in amplitude and duration, and decreases in frequency, with each additional treatment as long as the rate of administration remains above 1 per week. These changes are accompanied by a decreased mean alpha frequency, decreased beta activity, increased mean EEG amplitude, and increased paroxysmal activity (Fink, 1979). With the usual three treatments per week the EEG obtained 24 to 48 hours after 6 to 8 seizures given with sine-wave bilateral ECT is often dominated by delta activity with a marked reduction in the abundance of normal alpha–beta rhythms. This postconvulsive (or interseizure) EEG slowing is also related to the pretreatment EEG, age, and method of seizure induction. The pretreatment EEG is a significant predictor of postconvulsive patterns. In our own work (Volavka et al., 1972) we subjected the pre- and post-ECT EEGs to computer analysis and found that the pretreatment EEG accounted for 14 percent of the variance of the total post-ECT slowing and for 41 percent of the variance of the pooled average frequency. ECT-induced EEG slowing was directly proportional to the number of treatments given and consisted mainly of an increase in delta activity. We also reported a significant correlation between increasing age and decreasing average frequency. The failure of Strömgren and Juul-Jensen (1975) and Weiner (1983a) to find a significant correlation between the number of ECTs administered and the degree of EEG slowing may be a statistical artifact of the small range of treatments given (Weiner, 1983a).

With bilateral ECT the induced EEG slowing is either symmetrical or accentuated over the left hemisphere (Green, 1957; Abrams et al., 1970; Volavka et al., 1971; Marjerrisson et al., 1975; Strömgren and Juul-Jensen, 1975; Weiner et al., 1986; Abrams et al., 1987). Schultz et al. (1968) found a similar asymmetry in patients receiving pentylenetetrazol convulsive therapy. Unilateral ECT also induces asymmetrical postconvulsive EEG slowing (Martin et al., 1965; Zamora and Kaelbling, 1965; Sutherland et al., 1969; Abrams et al., 1970; Volavka et al., 1972; Abrams et al., 1987; Weiner et al., in press), which is accentuated over the stimulated (usually, right) hemisphere. This differential lateralization of EEG slowing with unilateral and bilateral ECT is age-related, with increasing age associated with a relative reduction of left versus right hemisphere frequencies (Volavka et al., 1972). The visual evoked potential is also asymmetrical after unilateral ECT (Kriss et al., 1980), with the major positive component (P140) being significantly smaller and later on the treated side.

Following the final treatment of a series of ECTs the cumulative EEG slowing typically diminishes gradually over time and eventually disappears (Weiner, 1980). The time required for this to occur varies directly with the total number of treatments received (Pacella et al., 1942; Mosovich and Katzenelbogen, 1948; Roth, 1951). Most studies show a return to baseline by 30 days post-ECT (Moriarity and Siemens, 1947; Bergman et al., 1952; Roth, 1951), although a few patients are described with persistent slowing up to 1 year later (Proctor and Goodwin, 1943; Taylor and Pacella, 1948; Klotz, 1955; Small, 1974). Similar findings have been reported with chemically induced seizures (Weiner, 1980).

Some early studies reported a direct relation of ECT-induced EEG slowing to the therapeutic response in depressed patients. Roth (1951) used quantitative measures to assess the EEG delta activity elicited by intravenous thiopental in endogenous depressives after a course of ECT. They found that the greater the amount of delta activity elicited, the less was the likelihood of a relapse 3 and 6 months later. (They found no relation between therapeutic outcome and thiopental-elicited delta activity 3 days after ECT.) Fink and Kahn (1957) also used objective methods to measure the ECT-induced delta activity in a large sample of patients and related this activity to clinical response as evaluated during at least 8 weeks of follow-up. They found the greatest amount of clinical improvement in patients with the most EEG slowing, and also reported that the early appearance of such slowing was related to assessments of global improvement. Other early workers reported either no relation between EEG slowing and improvement (Hughes et al., 1941; Taylor and Pacella, 1948; Bergman et al., 1952; Johnson et al., 1960; Ulett, 1962) or an inverse one (Honcke and Zahle, 1946; Mosovich and Katzenelbogen, 1948).

In a subsequent study from Fink's laboratory (Volavka et al., 1972) computer-derived frequency and power spectral analyses were used to measure EEG delta activity after ECT, and no relation was found between these measures and clinical improvement in depression as assessed by reduction in Hamilton Depression Scale scores. This study differed from the earlier ones both in its use of computer EEG analysis and a multiple regression data-analytic procedure that covaried the total number of treatments given out of the equation before calculating the correlation between EEG slowing and therapeutic response. This suggests that global EEG slowing and therapeutic response are both a function of the number of ECTs given, but are not themselves causally related. Indeed, recent EEG data from patients receiving brief-pulse unilateral ECT indicates that full recovery is possible in the absence of demonstrable slowing (Weiner et al., 1986).

The previous studies, however, were primarily concerned with measuring *global* EEG slowing, and our own recent study (Abrams et al., 1987) suggests that an existing relation between *lateralized* EEG slowing and improvement may be obscured with global analyses because it is opposite in direction for each hemisphere. In this study, we obtained Hamilton Rating Scales for depression and research EEGs for visual and computer analysis in a sample of 34 melancholics before and after 6 unilateral or bilateral ECTs. Depression scale ratings and EEG analyses were done blindly and independently. The two ECT methods were equally effective in patients who did not develop asymmetrical EEG slowing after ECT; however, a very substantial therapeutic advantage was observed for bilateral ECT in patients who developed asymmetrical EEG slowing: a right-sided asymmetry was associated with unilateral ECT and a lesser treatment response, and a left-sided asymmetry with bilateral ECT and a greater treatment response. Computer EEG analysis using a right:left ratio of the EEG slowing supported this relationship, which was not a function of age, handedness, pre-ECT EEG asymmetry, or drug administration.

In a study in progress using multichannel topographic EEG mapping, Weiner et al. (1986) confirmed this tendency for right-unilateral and bilateral ECT to induce EEG slowing of the opposite hemispheric lateralization, as well as the trend for ECT nonresponders to have greater right- minus left-hemisphere delta difference than ECT responders.

Cerebral Metabolism, Oxygenation, and Blood Flow

The induced cerebral electrical discharges during ECT and the subsequent changes in electrical rhythms are accompanied by changes in cerebral blood flow, oxygenation, and glucose utilization. Penfield et al. (1939) studied cerebral blood flow during induced seizures in animals and humans and reported that vasospasm played no role during a seizure, and that blood flow increased. They did not study oxygenation, however, and noted that it would have been quite possible for oxygen consumption to outstrip supply during a seizure, despite increased blood flow. Posner et al. (1969) studied patients undergoing ECT with general anesthesia, oxygenation, and muscle-relaxation, and measured oxygen, carbon dioxide, and lactate concentrations in blood samples drawn simultaneously from the femoral artery and jugular vein throughout the procedure. Probably because all patients were ventilated with oxygen the pO_2 always remained above 100 mm Hg. The most striking finding was the consistency of the cerebral venous oxygen tension, which remained steady at approximately 63 mm Hg throughout the seizure. At no time in any patient did pO_2 fall near the 20 mm Hg level that is usually taken to indicate cerebral hypoxia. Arterial pCO_2 did not change during the seizure, but cerebral venous pCO_2 increased significantly and returned to baseline during the postictal period. There were no significant changes in lactic or pyruvic acid during the procedure.

Brodersen et al. (1973) studied cerebral blood flow and metabolism in patients undergoing ECT with anesthesia, muscle-relaxation and oxygenation. They found that cerebral blood flow (CBF), oxygen consumption, and glucose uptake doubled during seizures, with modest increases in both cerebral venous pO_2 and pCO_2. In contrast to Posner et al. (1969) these authors found a very slight but significant arteriovenous lactate difference during the seizure amounting to 0.08 mmol/L 1 minute after ECT. These marked ECT-induced increases in

CBF and metabolic rate were also found in rats during chemically induced epileptic seizures (Meldrum and Nilsson, 1976). Bolwig et al. (1977) used a ^{133}Xe inhalation technique to demonstrate increased regional cerebral blood flow (rCBF) during ECT and postulated that a simultaneously observed increased permeability of the blood–brain barrier was secondary to the increased flow. The close coupling of regional blood flow and oxygen utilization in the brain (Raichle et al., 1976; Lebrun-Grandie et al., 1983) permits the interpretation of rCBF changes in terms of regional metabolic activity.

Using impedance plethysmography as a measure of CBF in patients receiving ECT under oxygenation, anesthesia, and muscle-relaxation, Doust and Raschka (1975) confirmed the marked increase in CBF during ECT. These changes in blood gases during ECT are associated with changes in brain electrical activity. Szirmai et al. (1975) measured femoral arterial and cerebral venous oxygen saturation, pO_2 and pCO_2 in patients receiving modified ECT and correlated changes in these gases with changes in the EEG, recorded simultaneously and divided into 6 phases: pretreatment, seizure, electrical silence, delta, theta–alpha, and alpha. Cerebral venous oxygen saturation did not change significantly during any of the EEG phases and remained more than 90 percent at all times. The venous pO_2 did fall significantly during the seizure, but rose about pre-ECT levels during the period of electrical silence, returning to baseline thereafter. The venous pCO_2 increased significantly during the seizure, remained elevated during the postictal slowing, and returned to baseline with the return of normal rhythms. These authors concluded, as did the others quoted previously, that there was no evidence of cerebral anoxia during modified ECT in humans. This was attributed in part to the small amount of oxygen used by the paralyzed muscles.

The markedly increased rCBF reported during the induced seizure contrasts sharply with consistent reports of postictal *suppression* of rCBF. Early studies using the nitrous oxide technique (Kety et al., 1948; Wilson et al., 1952) reported modest reductions in flow during the postictal phase. Silfverskiöld et al. (1986) used the ^{133}Xe technique to study rCBF before and after unilateral or bilateral ECT in depressed patients. They found rCBF to be significantly reduced for 1 to 2 hours after ECT with both treatment methods, much more so with bilateral than with unilateral ECT. Moreover, there was a significant lateralization of rCBF suppression to the stimulated (right) hemisphere with unilateral ECT. All rCBF differences were more pronounced earlier than later in the treatment course.

Similar findings were reported by Prohovnik et al. (1986), who examined depressed patients 25 minutes before and 50 minutes after inductions with low-dose unilateral or bilateral ECT. Bilateral ECT resulted in symmetrical frontal flow reductions of about 15 percent, and right unilateral ECT showed similar reductions over the stimulated hemisphere but only about 5 percent reductions over the nonstimulated hemisphere. These reductions in flow were greatly attenuated after the first ECT in a series, analogous to the attenuation over time of the increased flows observed during the seizure itself (Brodersen et al., 1973).

Positron emission tomography (PET) employing 2-deoxyglucose provides a measure of local glucose metabolism during seizures (Engle, 1984). Unfortunately, the present level of technology of this procedure only measures utilization over relatively prolonged periods of time (e.g., 30 minutes). This, therefore, does not permit the separation of ictal from postictal phases. Within this contraint, however, Engle et al. (1982) were initially able to demonstrate increased glucose utilization over baseline during ECT-induced seizures, and a sharp drop in utilization below baseline during the phase of postictal suppression. They were unable to confirm such a relationship in the next series of patients they studied (Ackermann et al., 1986), however, perhaps due to technical and methodological difficulties. Parallel autoradiographic studies conducted in rats by the same investigators clearly supported the initial findings: ictal metabolic rates increased 177 percent over baseline and postictal rates were suppressed 68 percent below baseline (Ackermann et al., 1986).

Cerebral permeability (the *blood–brain barrier*) is also affected by ECT. Some animal studies showing substantial penetration of large molecules into the brain with electrically induced seizures used methods that were entirely inconsistent with those employed for administering ECT, e.g., induction of 30 electroconvulsive seizures (ECS) in a single session (Lending et al., 1959; Petito et al., 1977). More relevant to humans is the study of Aird et al. (1956), who gave cats 12 ECS over 22 days with bifrontal placement, using a 400 mA stimulus applied for 0.2 seconds. Three days after the last ECS, treated animals showed significantly greater transfer of intravenously administered cocaine into brain than unshocked controls, demonstrating a substantial increase in cerebral permeability. More recently, Preskorn et al. (1981) used a double-isotope technique to measure both CBF and the transfer of water into the brain of rats 15 minutes after a single ECS or a course of 8 ECS given at the rate of 1 per day. Cerebral permeability to water in anesthetized and paralyzed animals increased linearly ($r = 0.98$) with CBF, a phenomenon that was *blunted* by ECS.

The only cerebral permeability studies in patients receiving ECT have been conducted by Bolwig and his associates (Bolwig, 1984). These investigators used a double-isotope technique to study both transcapillary escape and the capacity for capillary diffusion of small tracers (e.g. urea) into the brain during ECT. No increase in transcapillary escape occurred (e.g., as might be expected in a "breakdown" of the blood–brain barrier), but a net increase in passive diffusion of these small molecules across capillary endothelial cells was observed during a seizure, perhaps as a result of increased available capillary area due to stretching or recruitment of partially perfused capillaries. The fact that the same results were obtained during a period of increased CBF that was deliberately induced by hypercapnia 15 minutes postictally suggests that hyperperfusion is the mechanism through which seizures increase cerebral permeability.

Electrically induced seizures themselves exert a major effect on seizure threshold and duration. Early clinical observations of a progressive rise in seizure threshold across a course of treatments (Kalinowsky and Kennedy, 1943; Finner, 1954; Holmberg, 1954a; Brockman et al., 1956; Green, 1960) have been amply confirmed by the study of Sackeim et al. (1987c). These authors used a titration procedure of graduated electrical dosages to determine the seizure threshold before each seizure induction during a course of ECT and observed a progressive increase in seizure threshold averaging 65 percent from the beginning to the end of the course, an effect that was significantly more pronounced with bilateral than with unilateral electrode placement. A progressive reduction in seizure duration from treatment to treatment was also found, likewise confirming earlier clinical observations (Holmberg, 1954a; Small et al., 1981). These anticonvulsant effects of ECT have also been used clinically in the treatment of epileptic patients (Caplan, 1946; Kalinowsky, 1947; Sackeim et al., 1983).

The relevant animal data is primarily derived from studies of animals that have had epileptic foci induced ("kindled") by the repeated passage of small currents through electrodes implanted in their amygdylae. Although it has been suggested that ECT may itself kindle an epileptic focus (Pinel and Van Oot, 1975, 1977), several studies show that ECS exerts a pronounced *anticonvulsant* effect on amygdyla-kindled seizures. Babington and Wedeking (1975) showed that 1 electrically induced seizure administered from 15 minutes to 2 hours before an amygdyla-kindled seizure markedly reduced its duration, an effect confirmed by Handforth (1982) who found that the anti-convulsant effects of multiple ECS lasted for 1 to 2 days. Post et al. (1984) found no effect on amygdyla-kindled seizures 6 days after a single ECS, but demonstrated a marked protective effect lasting for up to 5 days after a 7-day course of once-daily ECSs. Moreover, these authors found that when ECSs were administered prior to stimulation given to induce kindling, this phenomenon was completely prevented. This action of ECS to inhibit the development and suppress the expression of kindling is similar to that of anticonvulsants, such as carbamazepine (Post, 1986), and raises the possibility that ECS in-duces the release of an endogenous anticonvulsant. An intriguing test of this hypothesis was conducted by Isaac and Swanger (1983), who induced a substantial and progressive increase in seizure threshold in cats by a course of daily ECS given over 22 days. Cerebrospinal fluid removed from these cats and injected intraventricularly into naive cats produced an elevated seizure threshold. Tortella and Long (1985) obtained similar results in rats that were subjected to a single ECS: CSF removed at varying postictal intervals (10 minutes providing the maximal effect) and introduced into the ventricles of donor rats signif-icantly raised the threshold to flurothyl-induced seizures. This effect was attenuated by naloxone, supporting the authors' hypothesis of endogenous opioid mediation of postseizure inhibition.

Although no prospective studies have been done to determine whether ECT induces kindling in humans, a survey of 1000 patients reported by Small et al., (1981) failed to reveal any clinical or EEG evidence of ECT-induced epileptogenic activity.

Do Persistent Brain Changes Occur?

In view of the large and diverse effects of ECT previously described on cerebral physiology and metabolism, is there convincing evidence that ECT is capable of permanently damaging the brain? Although there is very little data suggesting the possibility of such an occurrence, it remains a question of concern among many patients who receive ECT (see Chapter 11) as well as among a few outspoken medical opponents of this form of therapy (Friedberg, 1977; Breggin, 1980). For obvious reasons, the question must be considered in light of the present-day practice of ECT, using barbiturate anesthesia, muscle-relaxation, and oxygenation, and this constraint sharply truncates the available body of data that addresses the topic, much of it obtained before modern treatment techniques became standard. Might ECT given in the era before these advances were introduced have caused brain damage in certain patients under certain circumstances? Conceivably, as patients often became cyanotic during treatment, generally received substantially longer courses of treatment than are administered today, and even developed *tardive seizures* long after the treatment course was terminated (Fink, 1979), although this rarely happened. Even in the absence of oxygenation and muscular relaxation, however, it is notable that studies of artificially induced seizures in animals demonstrate that cerebral lesions do not occur unless seizures are prolonged for many multiples of the duration of those encountered during the administration of ECT (Weiner, 1981).

In his review of his own and other studies of the neuropathological consequences of induced seizures (primarily in baboons), Meldrum (1986) pointed out that selective brain damage involving neuronal loss and gliosis in the hippocampus (the brain region most susceptible to anoxia) requires sustained generalized seizures lasting more than 90 minutes, or more than 26 recurrent seizures in an 8-hour interval, or continuous limbic seizures lasting longer than 3 to 5 hours. These figures are for unmodified seizures; when curarization and oxygenation are employed during the procedure, continuous seizures for 3 to 7 hours are required to produce permanent damage. Although he raises the possibility that a prolonged period of limbic status epilepticus might conceivably be triggered in a susceptible patient, he also acknowledges that the potent anticonvulsant effects of ECT render such an occurrence extremely unlikely.

Virtually all of the animal literature reviewed by Weiner (1984) had to be discounted due to the excessive electrical dosages used or the fact that the seizures studied were unmodified by muscle-paralysis and oxygenation. Autopsy material from patients dying during or just after ECT is quite rare to begin with, considering the low mortality rates that will be described in Chapter 6, and almost impossible to interpret due to the lack of any information on the structure of these patients' brains before ECT, as well as the great likelihood of extensive coexisting agonal changes since most of the deaths were cardiovascular in origin.

The recent and widespread availability of brain imaging techniques raises the possibility of studying the effects of ECT on ventricular size and cortical geography; however, no systematic pre- to post-ECT studies have yet been reported. Several investigators have attempted to relate lateral ventricular size on computerized tomographic (CT) scans to a prior history of ECT in different patient samples, a procedure fraught with methodological problems (Schwartz, 1985), especially selection bias. It is difficult to see what useful information might be obtained from demonstrating an association (or lack of one) between lateral ventricular size and a history of ECT in a particular sample of patients, because preexisting cortical atrophy (or the lack of it) may well have influenced the initial decision to administer (or withhold) ECT. The problem is even further complicated when the patients studied (often schizophrenics) have also received a variety of other treatments (e.g., neuroleptic drugs), and have a greater-than-normal risk for cerebral atrophy for reasons presumably unrelated to the use of ECT.

Be that as it may, Owens et al. (1985) found no relationship between lateral ventricular size and a history of prior ECT in their schizophrenic sample, whereas Weinberger et al. (1979) found such a relation for cortical atrophy. More relevant, since depressives constituted the sample, is the study of Calloway et al. (1981) in 37 elderly patients who received CT scans and were then assessed for a history of having had ECT. Ventricular measures did not differentiate those who had received ECT ($n = 22$) from those who had not ($n = 15$), but a significant association between frontal atrophy and a history of ECT was demonstrated—it occurred in 68 percent of those who had ECT compared with 27 percent who had not. As the authors correctly point out, the possibility that patients with preexisting atrophy had symptoms that preferentially suggested the use of ECT to their physicians, makes the data difficult to interpret.

Although still lacking the sorely needed prospective design, the recent study of Kolbeinsson et al. (1986) employed the best methodology to date. These authors compared the CT scans of 22 patients with a history of ECT to those of two age- and sex-matched no-ECT control groups: one of comparably ill patients, and one of normal, healthy volunteers. Although both patient groups had significantly larger ventricular : brain ratios and cortical atrophy scores than normal controls, they did not differ significantly from each other.

Although little useful scientific information can be gleaned from the individual cases studied, it is nonetheless reassuring to note that a 63-year-old woman described by Kendell and Pratt (1983) received 325 ECTs over 4 years without any evidence of brain atrophy on CT scans obtained after a few treatments and at the end of the 4 years. In a similar vein, Menken et al. (1979) report that a 30-year-old woman, who received 10 ECTs *in a single 45-minute treatment session*, showed no brain changes as measured by CT scans obtained before the session and 3 hours afterward. Most striking in this regard is the patient reported by Lippmann et al. (1985), who received 1250 documented bilateral ECTs over a 26-year period in her life, with an additional 800 claimed but unsubstantiated by medical records. When she came to autopsy after her death at the age of 89 years, the neuropathological examination was normal.

Myelin basic protein is an antigen that constitutes 30 percent of the myelin sheath, and its immunoreactivity in serum and cerebrospinal fluid has been correlated with the degree of central nervous system (CNS) damage that occurs with stroke and cerebral trauma. Hoyle et al. (1984) found no difference in serially sampled serum myelin basic protein immunoreactivity between a sample of 13 patients undergoing ECT and a sample of 14 normal controls, nor was any pre- to post-ECT increase in mean reactivity observed in the patient sample. Likewise, ECT does not increase the brain-type serum CPK isoenzyme (BB) during 6 hours following treatment (Webb et al., 1984).

In sum, there seems little likelihood that ECT as administered today is capable of causing brain damage, although "absence of proof does not constitute proof of absence." Perhaps the main reason for pursuing the question further lies in the recent demonstration (see Chapter 10) that some patients may have persistent amnesia for selected autobiographical information as long as 6 months after a course of treatment. The fact that this amnesia does not occur with right-sided unilateral ECT suggests that it might have an anatomical (and, therefore, possibly structural) basis, although studies extending beyond 6 months are needed to confirm the "permanence" of the finding.

Even if permanent, however, such memory deficits by no means demonstrate permanent structural changes, at least not as commonly understood (e.g., gross alterations of defined anatomic structures, cell fall-out). More likely to occur, if at all, are changes in those microstructures (synaptic vesicles and terminals) that daily wax and wane as new material is learned or forgotten. Interference with protein synthesis can prevent consolidation of newly learned material, and neurotransmitter release at critical phases can enhance memory acquisition and storage. That ECT, with its multiform effects on neurohumors, neuropeptides, and neurohormones, might exert long-term influences on such processes is entirely within the realm of possibility, particularly when it is understood that memory consolidation is an evolving, rather than a discrete, phenomenon.

The question, then, is not to determine whether ECT does or does not cause "brain damage" in the sense of gross anatomic pathology—it almost certainly does not—but to define those short- and long-term (if any) effects that ECT exerts on the acquisition and retention of information, understanding that according to our present view, it is microstructural events that are involved.

5
Medical Considerations: The High-Risk Patient

Considerable evidence has been adduced in support of the safety of ECT. In particular, recent reviews of the mortality rate associated with ECT have generally agreed on a per-treatment rate in the neighborhood of three or four deaths per 100,000 treatments, or per 10,000 patients treated (Fink, 1979; Weiner, 1979, Babigian and Guttmacher, 1984; Crowe, 1984). A large-scale survey in the modern era of 55 psychiatric hospital departments in Denmark found one death in 22,210 treatments (3,438 series) for a per-treatment mortality rate of 0.0045 percent and a per-series mortality rate of 0.029 percent (Heshe and Roeder, 1976), the latter figure remarkably consistent with the per-patient mortality rates of 0.032 percent and 0.034 percent calculated by Fink (1979) by extrapolation from national and regional American surveys that were also conducted in 1976.

The most recent figure, reported by Kramer (1985) in his study of the use of ECT in California during the years from 1977 to 1983, is even lower: two deaths per 99,425 treatments (18,627 patients treated), yielding a per-treatment mortality rate of 0.002 percent and a per-patient mortality rate of 0.01 percent. As the author points out, a per-treatment ECT morality rate of 0.002 percent compares very favorably with the 0.01 percent mortality rate for childbirth in the United States. And, as Fink (1979) notes, the death rate from ECT is at the very bottom of the range of that reported for anesthesia induction alone (0.003 to 0.04 percent).

Most (about two-thirds) of the deaths reported during or immediately after ECT are cardiovascular in nature, and it is not overly optimistic to believe that an increased appreciation of the complex

cardiovascular effects of ECT (and their phamacological management) by its practitioners will help to further increase the safety of this
treatment.

Cardiovascular Effects of ECT

Heart Rate

By itself, the induction of anesthesia for ECT causes about a 25-
percent increase in baseline heart rate (Usubiaga et al., 1967; Rollason
et al., 1971; Kitamura and Page, 1984). When the electrical stimulus is
then administered, the immediate neural discharge it induces combines
with that of the seizure discharge, and a Valsalva effect secondary to
forced expiration against a closed glottis, to produce an immediate
and intense vagal parasympathetic outflow. In the absence of anticholinergic premedication (e.g., atropinization) a sharp but transient sinus
bradycardia occurs (Perrin, 1961), with periods of sinus asystole (cardiac standstill) occasionally recorded in excess of 7 seconds (Gravenstein et al., 1965). It is routine practice to attenuate or abolish this
vagal effect by anticholinergics administered parenterally about 1 hour
before ECT or intravenously immediately before giving the barbiturate. It is difficult to evaluate the contradictory study of Wyant and
MacDonald (1980) who found no effect of atropine on pulse rate or
cardiac irregularity in patients receiving ECT. Systematic EKG observations are not presented by these authors, and their statement that
"only a rare ventricular premature beat was noted" during 297 treatments does not jibe with the protean EKG abnormalities reported
during ECT by numerous other investigators (see especially Pitts,
1982), and seen every day in clinical practice. Miller et al. (1987)
confirmed the preventive action of atropine on vagal bradycardia in a
placebo-controlled, within-patient, design with Holter-monitoring of
the EKG, but, unlike several other investigators, did not observe any
effect of this medication on the frequency of ventricular arrhythmias.

A sympathoadrenal tachycardia then supervenes, initially effectu-
ated through direct adrenergic outflow via the paravertebral sympathetic ganglia and then rapidly amplified and sustained by the
epinephrine and norepinephrine released from the adrenal medulla
(Weil-Malherbe, 1955; Gravenstein et al., 1965; Anton et al., 1977).
This tachycardia is maximal during the clonic phase of the seizure
(e.g., about 150 to 160 beats/min.) and is virtually coterminous with

the EEG-monitored spike activity (Larson, Swartz, and Abrams, 1984). There is a progressive decline in the peak of this ECT-induced tachycardia with successive treatments in a course (Mann et al., in press), suggesting either a decline in the level of catecholamine release with repeated ECT, or a cumulative desensitization (down-regulation) of atrial beta$_1$ adrenergic receptors. Earlier reports (Griswold, 1958; Gravenstein et al., 1965) of a progressive decline in circulating noradrenaline levels with successive exposures to ECT support the former mechanism; the latter is suggested by the finding that ECT induces an increase in isoproterenol-generated cyclic AMP (Mann et al., in press).

Electrocardiographic (ECG) Effects

Abnormalities of cardiac rhythm and conduction are recorded much more frequently just after the induced seizure than during it, and are classified as either vagal or sympathetic. The vagal arrhythmias are of atrial, junctional, or nodal origin and include sinus bradycardia, sinus arrest, atrial premature contractions, paroxysmal atrial tachycardia (atrioventricular junctional tachycardia), atrial flutter, atrial fibrillation, atrioventricular block (first-, second-, and third-degree), and premature ventricular contractions during periods of sinus bradycardia. The sympathetic arrhythmias originate in the ventricles as premature contractions occurring during sinus tachycardia, bigeminy, trigeminy, ventricular tachycardia, and ventricular fibrillation (Perrin, 1961; Elliot et al., 1982; Pitts, 1982). ECG repolarization abnormalities reported during and immediately after ECT include increased T-wave amplitude, T-wave inversion, and S-T segment depression of nonischemic and ischemic types (Lewis et al., 1955; Green and Woods, 1955; Deliyiannis et al., 1962; Dec et al., 1985). The prevalence of ECT-induced ECG abnormalities is increased in patients with preexisting cardiac pathology and is significantly greater after thiopental than methohexital barbiturate narcosis (Pitts, 1982). The occurrence of these abnormalities is essentially limited to the ictal and immediate postictal periods; extensive examinations conducted 4–6 hours post-ECT do not reveal any persistent ECG changes, even in patients with preexisting cardiovascular disease (Dec et al., 1985). These authors have also stressed the neural origin of these phenomena, due to direct electrical stimulation of brainstem subcortical structures and thalamic and hypothalamic nuclei. Many of these phenomena (e.g., ectopy, repolarization abnormalities) are so regularly observed in young patients with no history or symptoms of cardiovascular disease that they must be considered normal physiological concomitants of ECT and not in any way contraindications to it (Deliyiannis et al., 1962).

Blood Pressure

Blood pressure parallels heart rate throughout the treatment, dropping sharply during the initial vagal bradycardia or asystole, and then rapidly increasing to peak systolic values that frequently exceed 200 mm Hg, especially when atropine premedication is given (Bodley and Fenwick, 1966). The initial rise in systolic pressure is proportionately greater than for the diastolic, is more pronounced in hypertensive than normotensive patients, and in males than females (Prudic et al., 1987). Although much more epinephrine than norepinephrine is released during ECT (Jones and Knight, 1981), only norepinephrine levels correlate significantly with the hypertensive response (Gravenstein et al., 1965).

An initial report that the hypertensive response to ECT was linearly related to its cognitive side effects (Hamilton et al., 1979) was not confirmed in subsequent studies (O'Donnell and Webb, 1986; Ottosson and Widepalm, 1987).

Rate Pressure Product

The rate pressure product (RPP = systolic arterial pressure $\times$ heart rate) is a rough correlate of myocardial oxygen consumption; it increases two- to fourfold (e.g., from 9000 to 30,000) at its maximum (Jones and Knight, 1981; Mulgaokar et al., 1985), in response to equally robust increases in plasma catecholamines, an effect that is substantially (50 percent) attenuated by beta adrenergic receptor blockade (Jones and Knight, 1981).

Cardiac Enzymes

During the hours after ECT, significant elevations occur in serum levels of creatine phosphokinase (CPK) and lacate dehydrogenase (LDH), but not in glutamic oxalaminase transaminase (Rich et al., 1975; Braasch and Demaso, 1980; Dec et al., 1985) Creatine phosphokinase is found in the skeletal muscle, myocardium, brain, and gastrointestinal tract; only the CPK muscle-brain (CPK-MB) isoenzyme is specifically elevated after myocardial damage (and the brain CPK isoenzyme does not cross the blood–brain barrier in the absence of brain damage). Lactate dehydrogenase is found in most human tissues, including skeletal muscle and myocardium; its LDH-1 and LDH-2 isoenzymes are considered fairly specific for myocardial damage. None of the myocardio-specific isoenzymes are significantly elevated when tested at multiple intervals up to 96 hours after ECT (Braasch and Demaso, 1980; Taylor et al., 1981; Dec et al., 1985).

Cardiovascular Risks with ECT and Their Management

The gravest cardiovascular complications of ECT include acute myocardial infarction, acute coronary insufficiency, ventricular fibrillation, myocardial rupture, cardiac arrest, cardiovascular collapse, stroke, and ruptured cerebral or aortic aneurysm. Although the occurrence is extremely rare—none were reported in the Danish study of 22,210 consecutive ECT treatments already described (Heshe and Roeder, 1976)—such complications constitute the primary mortality risk with ECT (e.g., Tewfik and Wells, 1957; Ungerleider, 1960; Perrin, 1961; Hussar and Pachter, 1968; McKenna et al., 1970; Hurwitz, 1974) and their medical prevention and management is of understandable concern. The detection and management of significant cardiovascular disease *prior* to administering ECT is overwhelmingly the most important factor in reducing consequent cardiovascular morbidity and mortality: one need only contemplate the difference in the risk of ECT to a patient in acute congestive heart failure before versus after he has been stabilized on digitalis and diuretics. The swelling number of older individuals with significant cardiovascular disease is amply represented among patients referred for ECT, and a great deal of experience has accumulated in recent years in the pharmacological management of such "high-risk" patients (Elliot et al., 1982; Weiner, 1983b; Alexopolous et al., 1984; Dec et al., 1985; Regestein and Reich, 1985). The management of ECT-induced alterations in cardiac rate, rhythm, and blood pressure has received the most attention as these phenomena have multiform potential adverse effects in the presence of preexisting cardiovascular disease.

Prevention of Vagal Cardiovascular Effects

Atropine remains the drug of choice for attenuating or blocking the direct vagal effects on the heart during and immediately after the passage of the electrical stimulus and in the immediate postictal period: sinus bradycardia and arrest (and the consequent sharp drop in blood pressure), the atrial and junctional arrhythmias, and ventricular premature contractions (VPCs) during sinus bradycardia. Glycopyrrolate is a recently introduced anticholinergic agent that does not cross the blood–brain barrier and is therefore unlikely to exacerbate post-ECT confusion as sometimes occurs with atropine, a known deliriant. A recent comparison of these two agents for ECT premedication (Kramer et al., 1986), however, revealed that although glycopyrrolate was associated with less post-ECT confusion than atropine, it was less effective in preventing bradycardia and ectopy, and produced nausea and vomiting in several patients. Although Cropper and Hughes (1964) recommend no less than a vagolytic dose of atropine (2.0 mg), a systematic study of the cardiac effects of four dosage levels of atropine (1.0 mg, 1.5 mg, 2.0 mg, and 2.5 mg) for ECT premedication revealed no advantage of exceeding a 1.0-mg dose, administered intramuscularly 45 to 60 minutes before treatment (Rich et al., 1969).

Prevention of the Sympathoadrenal Cardiovascular Effects of ECT

Prevention or attenuation of the acute *blood pressure* increases consequent to ECT may be desirable in patients with brain tumors, hypertension, recent myocardial infarction or stroke, and aortic or cerebral aneurysms. Each of the following methods has been advocated for this purpose:

1. The ganglionic blocking agent *trimethaphan* (Arfonad) lowers blood pressure both by blocking adrenergic ganglionic control of arterioles and by directly causing peripheral vasodilatation. Parasympathetic ganglionic blockade also occurs, producing an atropinelike effect on the heart. Tewfik and Wells (1957) were the first to use trimethaphan for alleviating the cardiovascular stress of ECT, choosing this agent because of its hypotensive action, its vagolytic action on the asystole and bradycardia occurring with delivery of the stimulus, its sympathetic blockade of epinephrine release, hypertension, tachycardia, and increased cardiac irritability, and its short (4 minutes) duration of action. In a within-subjects comparison of 1.2-mg atropine versus 20-mg trimethaphan (both given by intravenous bolus), these authors found substantial reductions in blood pressure with trimethaphan during the 4 minutes after the stimulus, an effect that was inversely related to resting blood pressure. Trimethaphan was just as effective as atropine in blocking the vagal effects of ECT. Egbert et al.

(1959) gave 10 mg of trimethaphan by rapid intravenous push to 20 healthy male patients 30 seconds before administering the electrical stimulus for ECT. This resulted in a mean reduction of peak systolic blood pressure of about 40 points (from 219 to 180 mm Hg), without causing hypotension during the postictal period. Anton et al. (1977) and Regestein and Reich (1985) have employed trimethaphan under similar circumstances but without specifying the dosages used. Today, a continuous intravenous drip of a 0.1-percent (1 mg/ml) solution of trimethaphan is the standard method of administration, at an initial rate of 3 to 4 mg/min, which is then adjusted under continuous blood pressure monitoring to maintain systolic pressure within a clinically acceptable range. Despite this technique, titration is difficult in some patients and overshoot is common. As an abrupt reduction of blood pressure (or reduction below the normal range) may be risky in the presence of coronary or cerebrovascular insufficiency, caution should be exercised when using trimethaphan in patients with such problems.

2. *Nitroprusside* (Nipride) is a powerful, directly acting vasodilator that relaxes both the arteriolar and venous smooth muscles. It has a rapid onset and offset, with a half-life of just a few minutes— titration of arterial pressure, therefore, is readily accomplished by altering the rate of infusion. It is administered as a freshly made solution of 50 mg of nitroprusside in 500 ml of 5-percent dextrose in water, using a microdrip infusion set and continuous blood pressure monitoring. Ciraulo et al. (1978) used this method to control the blood pressure in a 70-year-old man with long-standing hypertension and an old myocardial infarction, whose blood pressure had reached 240/160 mm Hg during a prior course of ECT, and 250/140 mm Hg during the first treatment of the present series. A nitroprusside drip was begun 15 minutes before ECT and continued until 5 to 15 minutes after treatment for the remaining 9 ECT, keeping the peak blood pressure elevation at 190/120 mm Hg throughout. An episode of transient hypotension during one treatment was controlled by discontinuing the nitroprusside drip; there were no other problems encountered. More recently, Regestein and Reich (1985) used nitroprusside in five hypertensive patients, ranging in age from 70 to 77 years, who were undergoing ECT. Compared with treatments during which nitroprusside was not used, these patients exhibited a mean reduction in baseline systolic pressure during ECT of 58 points (188 to 130 mm Hg), although peak pressures were not significantly lowered.

3. *Diazoxide* (Hyperstat I.V.) is a potent antihypertensive closely related chemically to the thiazide diuretics; when given intravenously

it produces a prompt and rapid lowering of blood pressure in hypertensive patients by directly dilating arterioles. Unlike thiazide diuretics, however, it causes marked *retention* of sodium and water. Kraus and Remick (1982) reported using diazoxide to manage severe immediate post-ECT hypertension in an 80-year-old man with moderate preexisting hypertension (160/100 mmg Hg). After each of his first treatments without any antihypertensive agents his blood pressure reached 240/170 mm Hg. Daily antihypertensive therapy with chlorthalidone and pindolol brought his resting blood pressure into the normal range, but had little effect on his hypertensive response to the next three ECTs. Before each subsequent treatment and immediately following succinylcholine administration, he was given 200 mg of diazoxide by rapid intravenous push, followed by 40 mg I.V. of furosemide (to overcome the salt and water retention). At this and all subsequent sessions his blood pressure peaked at 170/110 mm Hg. A possible side effect was the occurrence of significant post-ECT confusion, unusual in a patient receiving unilateral ECT. Diazoxide should be used with caution in patients prone to myocardial ischemia as it does not cause venous dilatation (and thereby reduce cardiac preload), but does increase myocardial oxygen consumption through reflex sympathetic nervous system activation.

4. *Hydralazine* (Apresoline) exerts its antihypertensive effects by direct relaxation of the vascular smooth muscle; the effect on arterioles is greater than that on veins. It is available in 20-mg ampules for intravenous administration by rapid bolus push. Blood pressure may begin to fall a few minutes after injection, with the maximal decrease occurring in 10 to 80 minutes. Like diazoxide, hydralazine causes cardiac stimulation through a reflex sympathetic response to the fall in blood pressure, an effect that can be prevented by beta-adrenergic or ganglionic blocking agents. The myocardial stimulation associated with hydralazine administration can produce anginal attacks and ECG changes characteristic of myocardial ischemia; therefore, the drug must be used carefully in patients with coronary artery disease. This is exemplified by a 77-year-old hyptertensive patient of Regestein and Reich (1985), with a resting blood pressure of 160/90 mm Hg and an old myocardial infarction, who developed chest pain and S-T segment depression in the recovery room after receiving his first ECT with hydralazine pretreatment, 15 mg I.V. Seven additional ECTs were given without complication after adding propranolol, 0.4 mg I.V., and trimethaphan, 5 mg I.V., to the regimen.

The patient of Husum et al. (1983), described below who had a clipped cerebral aneurysm, received a combination of hydralazine and propranolol to completely prevent any ECT-induced blood pressure elevation. Intermittent doses of hydralazine were given intravenously over a 25- to 30-minute period to a total of 18.75 mg, bringing the resting blood pressure down from 110/60 to 85/50 mm Hg. The ensuing compensatory heart rate increase from 85–95/min to 100–105/min was then blocked by intermittent intravenous propranolol to a total amount of 4 mg. Following the same regimen each time, a total of 10 ECTs was given without significant increase in blood pressure or heart rate.

5. The vasodilating effect of *nitroglycerine*, 1 tablet sublingual, has also been successfully used immediately prior to ECT to attenuate the hypertensive response (M. Fink, M.D., personal communication).

Prevention and management of the sympathoadrenal *cardiac arrhythmias* of ECT involves the use of lidocaine or beta-adrenergic blocking agents. The most frequent of these extravagal tachyarrhythmias are VPCs occurring later in the seizure or in the immediate postictal phase. Occasional VPCs are of no concern; it is the frequent or multifocal ones that present a risk due to the increased chance that one might coincide with the apex of the T wave of the ECG and precipitate ventricular tachycardia or fibrillation (Lown, 1979).

1. *Lidocaine* (xylocaine) is a local anesthetic agent that prolongs the refractory period of the cardiac conduction system and increases the myocardial threshold to abnormal stimulation; it has been used successfully for many years to control ECT-induced tachyarrhythmias (Usubiaga et al., 1967; McKenna et al., 1970; Hood and Mecca, 1983; London and Glass, 1985). It is available for intravenous administration in 100-mg ampules. In patients with preexisting multiple PVCs a constant intravenous infusion is administered at a rate of 1 to 5 mg/minute, permitting moment-to-moment titration of ventricular ectopic activity. For rapid control of multiple PVCs that develop for the first time during ECT, a rapid bolus push of 50 to 100 mg of lidocaine (1 to 2 mg/kg body weight) is safe and effective. A significant drawback of intravenous lidocaine, however, is that it shortens (Ottosson, 1960; Usubiaga et al., 1967) or even abolishes (Hood and Mecca, 1983; London and Glass, 1985) ECT-induced seizure activity when given at the preceding doses, thus partially (and sometimes entirely) blocking the therapeutic effect as well.

2. *Propranolol* (Inderal) is therefore of particular interest since it can block ventricular arrhythmias without affecting seizure duration; it also provides other beneficial cardiac effects. Propranolol is a nonselective beta-adrenergic blocking agent that is widely used in the treat-

ment of hypertension and the prevention of angina pectoris and certain cardiac arrhythmias. It reduces the sinus rate, decreases the spontaneous rate of depolarization of ectopic pacemakers, slows conduction in the atria and atrio-ventricular (A-V) node, and reduces myocardial oxygen consumption. Weiner et al. (1979) used oral propranolol, 160 mg/day, to slow the sinus tachycardia and associated ventricular arrhythmias (VPCs, bigeminy, trigeminy, and quadrigeminy) that occurred postictally in a 62-year-old man without a history of cardiovascular disease.

Propranolol is also available in 1-mg ampules for intravenous administration. Jones and Knight (1981) reported a 74-year-old woman with moderate hypertension whose blood pressure reached 250/140 mm Hg during ECT, with a peak RPP of 35,000. After 3 mg of propranolol given intravenously in 0.5-mg increments, peak blood pressure was reduced to 160/80 mm Hg with a maximum RPP of 16,000. However, the beneficial effects of propranolol on cardiac irritability, heart rate, blood pressure, and myocardial oxygen consumption during ECT can safely be enjoyed only after atropinization. Based on studies in dogs that received electrically induced seizures in the presence of high spinal anesthesia, Anton et al. (1977) predicted that ECT-induced "activation of the autonomic nervous system in the presence of a sympathetic block would lead to a vagally induced protracted asystole." The aptness of this warning is illustrated by the experience of Decina et al. (1984) and Wulfson et al. (1984) who separately reported their experiences with the same 68-year-old woman with preexisting hypertension and ischemic heart disease who was given 1 mg propranolol I.V. just prior to ECT in order to reduce the risk of ventricular ectopy. Atropine was omitted for fear of further increasing blood pressure. Over 5 seconds poststimulus there was a progressive slowing of sinus rhythm, ending in 15 seconds of asystole (cardiac arrest) from which the patient was successfully resuscitated without sequelae. The recently reported case of London and Glass (1985) affirms the necessity of atropinization before using propranolol during ECT. These authors treated a patient in whom 0.5 mg I.V. of propranolol alone was followed by significant sinus bradycardia, VPCs, and bigeminy, phenomena that were eliminated in subsequent treatments when atropine premedication was given.

An instance of acute organic mental syndrome with paranoid delusions has been reported after the use of the beta-blocker atenolol

(Kramer, 1986), an antihypertensive agent related to propranolol that is reputed to have the advantage of little central nervous system activity.

ECT and Cardiac Pacemakers

There are several reports of the successful use of ECT in patients with implanted cardiac pacemakers (Youmans et al., 1969; Gibson et al., 1973; Abiuso et al., 1978; Jauhar et al., 1979; Alexopolous and Frances, 1980; Alexopolous et al., 1984). Although the ECT stimulus itself is normally prevented from reaching the heart by the high resistance of the intervening body tissues, and pacemakers are constructed with protective electrical circuitry and shielding to withstand electrical stimuli within the range of those used for ECT, the low-resistance pathway to the myocardium created by an endocardial electrode may allow a large current to pass through the heart during ECT if the patient is in contact with ground. Thus, all monitoring equipment should be properly grounded, the stretcher on which the patient is lying should be completely insulated from ground (e.g., by rubber wheels), and the patient should not be held or touched during treatment by anyone who is in contact with ground. (Contact with an improperly grounded monitor is dangerous even if it is turned off at the time.) Pacemaker wires should be checked for breaks or faulty insulation as these also provide ready entry of currents into the heart. Demand pacemakers are *inhibited* by P or R waves and may occasionally respond to ECT-induced muscle potentials or contractions, resulting in severe bradycardia. Under such circumstances the pacemaker should be converted to fixed-mode operation during the seizure by placing a ring magnet over the pulse generator (Abiuso et al., 1978; Alexopolous and Frances, 1980). Synchronous pacemakers are *triggered* by P or R waves and might conceivably respond during ECT by inducing a tachycardia (Gibson et al., 1973). Should this unlikely and rather benign event occur, the pacemaker can also be converted to a fixed-mode of stimulation. External (temporary) cardiac pacemakers must, of course, be grounded; they are, therefore, substantially riskier than implanted ones as they provide a ready conduit through the heart for current flow from improperly grounded monitoring equipment, on or off, even if unattached to the patient and only touched by an assistant who is touching the patient at the same time.

Aortic Aneurysm

Of the many published reports of patients with aortic aneurysms who received ECT (Monke, 1952; Wolford, 1957; Weatherly and Villein, 1958; Moore, 1960; Chapman, 1961; Pomeranze et al., 1968; Abramczuk and Rose, 1979; Alexopolous et al., 1984), either for untreated aneurysms or after surgical grafting, no untoward effects occurred in any patient, despite the fact that no particular efforts were made to augment the usual degree of muscle-relaxation or to reduce the blood pressure response to treatment. In fact, one patient with multiple aortic homografts (Greenbank, 1958) safely received 10 ECTs without any muscle-relaxant at all. Although these cases suggest that the presence of aortic aneurysm is not an important risk for ECT, it seems prudent to recommend that succinylcholine dosages in such patients should be adequate to provide full relaxation of the abdominal musculature (e.g., 60 to 80 mg), especially in the presence of an untreated abdominal aneurysm.

Cardiac Surgery

There are six reported instances of patients who received ECT at varying intervals after cardiac valvular surgery, two of them after replacement of both aortic and mitral valves (Blachly and Semler, 1967; Weinstein and Fisher, 1967; Hardman and Morse, 1972; Viparelli et al., 1976). Again, no special precautions were taken and no untoward cardiovascular effects of ECT were observed, even in one patient who was treated only 27 days after surgery.

Myocardial Infarction

Ventricular arrhythmias and cardiac rupture constitute the primary fatal complications of ECT in the presence of recent myocardial infarction. Although the risk is likely greatest during the first 10 postinfarct days (Willerson, 1982), and probably least after 3 months have elapsed (Perrin, 1961), there is no hard data to support the safety (or lack of it) of administering ECT at any given postinfarction interval. Ungerleider (1960) reported the case of a 68-year-old woman who inadvertently received an ECT without any ill effect during an acute myocardial infarction that was documented electrocardiographically, and described another instance personally communicated to him of a patient successfully treated with ECT 3 days postinfarct. Despite these lucky outcomes, the risks of such treatment may be substantial and can be reduced by waiting as long as possible after infarction before giving ECT, and by the judicious use of antiarrhythmic and antihypertensive agents and the administration of 100-percent oxygen by positive pressure before, during, and after the seizure.

Central Nervous System Risks with ECT and Their Management

Brain Tumor

Considering the fixed cranium, noncompressibility of cerebrospinal fluid and blood, and the substantial increases in cerebral blood flow and blood–brain barrier permeability that occur during ECT, it is not surprising that major neurological problems can occur when this treatment is administered in the presence of a space-occupying lesion of the brain. However, as there are only 3 published instances of ECT being administered to a patient already known to have a brain tumor (Dressler and Folk, 1975; Hsiao and Evans, 1984; Alexopolous et al., 1984), most of the other case reports describing the consequences of such a procedure are subject to ascertainment bias, having come to the attention of physicians precisely because of neurological deterioration that occured in association with a course of ECT. Thus, Savitsky and Karliner's (1953) patient with occult glioblastoma who developed stupor, papilledema, and hemiparesis after ECT, Shapiro and Goldberg's (1957) 6 patients with previously undiagnosed brain tumors who deteriorated rapidly after ECT, Gassel's (1960) three patients with occult meningiomas who fared likewise, and Paulson's (1967) 3 cases of rapid neurological progression after ECT in the presence of undiagnosed brain metastases or cerebellar sarcoma are largely responsible for the widely quoted but probably overstated clinical dictum that "brain tumor is an absolute contraindication to ECT." Nevertheless, such case reports are indispensable as they provide the main source of information for assessing the risks and benefits of ECT in the presence of a brain tumor.

    Maltbie et al. (1980) conducted an extensive review of 28 cases reported in the literature, adding 7 from their own hospital files. Only 34 percent of the 35 cases exhibited improvement in their psychiatric symptoms with ECT, whereas 74 percent exhibited neurological deterioration, providing a risk about twice as large as the possible benefit. Only 21 percent improved psychiatrically *without* showing neurological morbidity. Four patients died within a week of ECT, and four more died within a month; all 8 had major neurological complications precipitated by ECT. Considering the rarity of ECT-induced mortality, even in the presence of severe cardiovascular disease, it is apparent that brain tumor constitutes a major risk for the administration of ECT. It seems unwarranted to conclude, however, as do Maltbie et al. (1980), that intracranial tumor is a contraindication to ECT. A quarter of their patients received the treatment without neurological sequel, a figure that is rendered conservative by the ascertainment bias already noted. Moreover, Dressler and Folk (1975) were able successfully to treat a patient with a metastatic carcinoma of the brain, and Hsiao and Evans (1984) and Alexopolous et al. (1984) treated patients with meningiomas, all without deterioration in neurological status.

A considerable portion of the risk in administering ECT in the presence of a brain tumor is attributable to the aggravation of increased intracranial pressure by the cerebral hemodynamic effects of ECT. Maltbie et al. (1980) do not present data addressing this point, but it is notable that Dressler and Folk's (1975) patient had a normal spinal fluid pressure and dynamics, and that the patients of Hsiao and Evans (1984) and Alexopolous et al. (1984a) had small, slow-growing (calcified) meningiomas that were unlikely to have caused increased intracranial pressure. An ECT-induced increase in peri-brain tumor edema may contribute significantly to increased intracranial pressure; steroids (especially dexamethasone), which effectively reduce such edema, should also reduce the risks of treatment (Carter, 1977). In this regard, it is noteworthy that Dressler and Folk's (1975) patient was receiving 6.0 mg/day of dexamethasone at the time ECT was given.

In considering whether to give ECT to a patient with a brain tumor, the risks are likely to be least in the presence of small, slow-growing (or calcified) lesions and in the absence of increased intracranial pressure. The administration of dexamethasone in doses sufficient to reduce peri-brain tumor edema seems prudent, although no prospective trials exist to demonstrate the effectiveness of this procedure. Oral dexamethasone started several days before ECT should suffice for patients without increased intracranial pressure, but where pressure is elevated, parenteral administration 4 to 8 hours before the first treatment may be advisable, followed by an oral maintenance dose until the course is completed.

Subdural Hematoma

Cerebral compression by subdural hematoma should increase the risk with ECT in the same fashion as a brain tumor. Paulson (1967) reported a 47-year-old agitated depressed woman who became unresponsive immediately after her first ECT and remained comatose for 2 days. A large subdural hematoma was demonstrated on angiography and evacuated, at which point the patient immediately became responsive and alert.

Craniotomy

The patient of Hsiao and Evans (1984) described earlier subsequently underwent elective craniotomy for removal of her meningioma, leaving a left parietal calvarial defect. Four months postcraniotomy a second course of ECT was given for a recurrence of her psychotic depression, using bifrontotemporal treatment electrodes placed well away from the cranial defect; no complications resulted from a course of nine treatments. Levy and Levy (1987) reported the case of a 72-year-old man with a plastic plate covering a skull defect over the entire right cerebral hemisphere resulting from an earlier removal of a meningioma and more recent surgery for a cerebral abscess. A course of nine left unilateral ECTs induced a full remission of his depression without any neurological sequelae. As Gordon (1982) has pointed out, it is important to place the ECT treatment electrodes well away (and equidistant) from a cranial defect in order to avoid local intracerebral concentration of the stimulus current through the defect.

Ries and Bokan (1979) described a 39-year-old woman who received a course of 12 right unilateral ECTs for a depressive psychosis 30 days after undergoing a transsphenoidal–transnasal removal of a basophil adenoma of the pituitary. She enjoyed a full psychiatric recovery without neurological complications or sequelae.

Cerebral Vascular Malformation

Husum et al. (1983) successfully administered a course of 10 ECTs to a severely melancholic 42-year-old woman who 6 months earlier had undergone a craniotomy for surgical clipping of a bleeding sacculate aneurysm of the upper internal carotid artery and muscular wrapping of another located on the right medial cerebral artery. Although the patient was normotensive, these authors elected to block the sympathoadrenal response to ECT with a combination of hydralazine, to relax arteriolar smooth muscle, and propranolol, to prevent hydralazine-induced reflex sympathetic activation and ameliorate the effects of ECT-induced catecholamine release. Under this regimen, no significant blood pressure response to ECT was observed, with the maximum increase being 10 mm Hg. Many patients with occult berry aneurysms must have received ECT without any ill effect as they occur in 1 to 2 percent of the population but have never been implicated in an ECT-related death. Untreated aneurysms that have previously bled presumably constitute a significant risk with ECT because of their inherent tendency to rebleed; however, there are no reported instances of ECT having been administered under such circumstances.

Greenberg et al. (1986) reported a 24-year-old man with a left parietal cerebral venous angioma who received a course of 12 ECTs without incident. Although a nitroprusside drip infusion was at the ready it was never used (venous angiomas are low-pressure malformations and the maximum ECT-induced systolic blood pressure levels recorded in this patient rarely exceeded 200 mm Hg). Of special interest is the fact that magnetic resonance imaging (MRI) performed 18 days after the last ECT revealed no change when compared with the pre-ECT record.

Stroke

Shapiro and Goldberg (1957) described 6 patients who were given ECT for severe depressive states occurring 4 weeks to 2 years after a cerebrovascular accident (CVA). Four of these patients, including 2 who were treated 4 and 9 weeks post-stroke, enjoyed remission of their depression without neurological complications. Two patients died during treatment: a 55-year-old woman with severe diabetes whose right-sided CVA preceded ECT by 6 weeks failed to recover consciousness after her sixth ECT, and a 48-year-old man with hypertensive cardiovascular disease whose right-sided CVA preceded ECT by 2 years suffered cardiorespiratory standstill during his first ECT.

Murray et al. (1986) recently reported more favorable results in 14 patients, aged from 46 to 86 years, who received ECT for poststroke depression, a sample selected from the records of 193 patients with stroke and depression who were treated at Massachusetts General Hospital from 1969 to 1981. All strokes had been completed and none were evolving at the time ECT was given. Twelve of the 14 patients improved markedly with ECT and none developed new neurological findings or exhibited worsening of old ones, despite the fact that 4 patients were included whose stroke preceded ECT by less than 1 month. Of great clinical importance is the observation that of 6 patients who exhibited cognitive impairment prior to ECT, 5 experienced improvement in this impairment (and in depression) as a result of ECT. Kwentus et al. (1984) reported the case of a depressed, catatonic 52-year-old woman with a history of a left-hemisphere CVA 2 years before who was successfully treated with a course of 9 right-unilateral ECTs without neurological complication. In fact, a coexisting neuroleptic-induced tardive dystonia also remitted with ECT and remained so at examination 7 months later. The shortest interval between stroke and ECT was reported by Alexopolous et al. (1984) who briefly mentioned the uneventful treatment of a patient *4 days* after a cerebral infarction documented by CT scanning.

The only instance of a specific neurological complication secondary to ECT in a patient with a history of stroke was reported by Strain and Bidder (1971), who gave 4 closely spaced seizures during a single treatment session (MMECT) to a 62-year-old woman who, unbeknownst to the authors, had a CVA 7 years earlier. Status epilepticus lasting 28 minutes occurred after the fourth seizure, from which the patient awakened with a left hemiparesis that gradually remitted over the following week. The fact that this patient had received 2 prior courses of 6 to 8 conventional ECTs without neurological sequelae since her CVA illustrates the special risk presented by MMECT in patients with a history of stroke.

Although it usually takes about 3 months for radio-imaging evidence of cerebral damage to resolve (Jeffries et al., 1980), the data of Murray et al. (1986) suggest that ECT given even as soon as 1 month after a CVA does not present a major risk to the patient.

Cerebral Trauma

Years ago, Savitsky and Karliner (1953) reported using ECT (sometimes combined with insulin coma therapy) in 3 patients with recent head injuries, each of whom responded without neurological sequelae (2 were instances of moderate concussion, and the third was a case of skull fracture followed by 5 days of coma). More recently Ruedrich et al. (1983) successfully gave ECT to a 21-year-old woman with a depressive psychosis 3 weeks after she had shot herself in the right parietal lobe in a suicide attempt, requiring debridement of her right motor and sensory cortex and resulting in a left hemiparesis. A total of 17 treatments were given with bitemporal treatment electrode placement in order to avoid the parietal skull defect, and concomitant anticonvulsant therapy to prevent prolonged seizures or status epilecticus. Not only was there no evidence of ECT-induced aggravation of her hemiparesis, but it steadily improved following the course of ECT until she had regained nearly full use of her left arm and leg.

Lupus Cerebritis

Guze (1967) described the successful use of ECT in 3 patients with affective episodes secondary to lupus cerebritis, but did not mention whether any adverse effects occurred as a result. Since then, 4 additional patients have been described (Allen and Pitts, 1978; Douglas and Schwartz, 1982; Mac and Pardo, 1983), each of whose lupus-induced organic affective syndromes responded fully to ECT without exacerbating the underlying disorder.

Dementia

Because of the transient, but occasionally pronounced, cognitive side-effect of bilateral ECT, psychiatrists have been understandably cautious in administering any form of ECT to patients with preexisting cognitive impairment. In a study of acute organic mental syndrome after bilateral ECT, Summers et al. (1979) reported that the only 2 instances of markedly prolonged confusional states (lasting 45 and 65 days post-ECT) occurred in the only 2 patients with preexisting mild chronic dementia. Tsuang et al. (1979) reported the development of profound disorientation and urinary and fecal incontinence after 6 ECTs (electrode placement unstated) in a 70-year-old woman with normal pressure hydrocephalus (NPH) and a right ventriculojugular shunt. (She had been stuporous, disoriented, and occasionally incontinent of urine just prior to starting ECT, but had become fully oriented and continent by the fourth treatment.) Her cognitive functioning gradually improved over 3 weeks post-ECT, and she was fully oriented at discharge.

Subsequent reports have been more sanguine. Demuth and Rand (1980) gave 8 unilateral ECTs to a depressed 80-year-old man with documented severe primary degenerative dementia who achieved a full remission without any increase in confusion. Snow and Wells (1981) gave 9 unilateral ECTs to a depressed 62-year-old woman with probable Alzheimer's disease who also improved significantly without evidence of any worsening of her organic state—in fact, her incontinence cleared during the course of treatment. McAllister and Price (1982) described 2 depressed patients with dementia (1 with NPH, 1 with Creuzfeldt-Jakob disease) who improved substantially with ECT without any exacerbation of their cognitive deficits. Unilateral ECT was used for 1 patient, but the other's treatment was not described. Perry (1983) reported the case of a demented man in his 50s whose muteness and catatonia responded dramatically to ECT without any worsening of his dementia. And Dubovsky et al. (1985) successfully treated a 53-year-old depressed man with dementia and increased intracranial pressure with a course of 9 ECTs (4 unilateral and 5 bilateral) with marked improvement in his memory as well as his depression. Not every depressive improves with ECT, of course, and Young et al. (1985) reported the case of a depressed 73-year-old woman with Parkinsonism and dementia who exhibited no relief from depression, but also no persistent worsening of her dementia after 7 unilateral ECTS (there *was*, however, long-term improvement in some of her Parkinsonian symptoms).

When prescribing ECT for patients with dementia, a brief-pulse stimulus should be delivered through right-unilateral treatment electrodes. Only if improvement fails to occur after 4 ECTs should the switch be made to bilateral electrodes. Twice-weekly treatments are also less likely to induce cognitive dysfunction than those given 3 times a week, yet they are ultimately no less effective (they just take longer). The improvement in the dementia syndrome noted after ECT in several cases reported earlier does not suggest any ameliorative effect of the treatment on the primary syndrome. Rather, the cognitive deficits of melancholia (depressive *pseudodementia*) that have been superimposed on the existing features of dementia remit with successful ECT just as they do in nondemented patients (McAllister and Price, 1982).

Mental Retardation

In his review and case studies of affective disorders among mentally retarded patients Reid (1972) noted in passing that "tricyclic antidepressants and ECT appeared to be effective in most of the cases where they were prescribed." There are two case reports that specifically address this use of ECT. Bates and Smeltzer (1982) report the case of a

25-year-old severely mentally retarded man (full scale IQ range of 21–25) whose persistent self-injurious head-banging behavior resulted in a wide-based staggering gait, loss of manual fine motor control, a Babinski sign, and other symptoms of upper motor neuron damage. Insomnia, agitation, and weight-loss were prominent. A course of 12 bilateral ECTs induced a dramatic improvement in all areas of behavior, without any adverse consequences. Guze et al. (1987) reported a 21-year-old bipolar man with spastic diplegia and mild mental retardation (WAIS-R verbal IQ of 65) whose depressive symptoms were rapidly and fully relieved by a course of 8 unilateral ECTs. Although published clinical experience is scant, there is little reason to believe either that ECT is less effective in depression associated with mental retardation, or that it adversely affects this condition.

Epilepsy

The anticonvulsant effects of ECT described elsewhere in this volume were well-known to older clinicians who used them to good effect in the treatment of epileptic patients with and without psychiatric symptoms (Kalinowsky and Kennedy, 1943; Caplan 1946; Kalinowsky et al., 1982, p. 267). More recently, Sackeim et al. (1983) reported using the seizure threshold-raising effect of ECT to successfully treat a 19-year-old patient with lifelong, intractable, idiopathic secondary generalized seizures. Although there are sporadic instances reported of status epilepticus or other paroxysmal EEG abnormalities developing during or immediately after ECT (Roith, 1959; Strain and Bidder, 1971; Bridenbaugh et al., 1972; Ray, 1975; Small et al., 1980; Weiner et al., 1980a, 1980b; Weiner, 1981; Prakash and Leavell, 1984; Peters et al., 1984; Kaufman et al., 1986), almost all can be attributed to some unusual aspect of the patient or the treatment: mental deficiency secondary to brain damage at birth (Roith, 1959), a preexisting paroxysmal EEG abnormality (Weiner et al., 1980a; Kaufman et al., 1986), the administration of multiple ECT in a single session (Bidder and Strain, 1971; Bridenbaugh et al., 1972), or the coadministration of lithium (Ray, 1975; Small et al., 1980; Weiner et al., 1980b), theophylline (Peters, 1984), or trazodone (Kaufman et al., 1986). The only instance of ECT inducing status epilepticus in a patient known to have epilepsy occurred after the administration of multiple ECTs in a single treatment session (Maletzky, 1981).

Thus, ECT is more likely to ameliorate than aggravate an epileptic disorder, at least temporarily, and can be especially useful in patients with the psychiatric manifestations of complex partial seiz-ures (usually temporal lobe epilepsy). Epileptic patients already receiv-ing anticonvulsants should continue to do so during the course of ECT as their abrupt discontinuation increases the risk of status epilepticus (Hauser, 1983). Considering the potent anticonvulsant properties of ECT there seems little rationale for initiating anticonvulsants prior to ECT in epileptic patients not already receiving them. In any case, although higher-than-usual electrical dosages may be required, seiz-ures of adequate length and therapeutic potency can be obtained despite concomitant therapy with anticonvulsants (Weiner, 1981; Sackeim et al., 1986; Kaufman et al., 1986), although some manipula-tion of their dosage may be required. In this regard, Kaufman et al. (1986) found it easier to obtain seizures in the presence of blood levels of carbamazepine than of diphenylhydantoin.

Hydrocephalus

In addition to the cases of NPH described earlier (Tsuang et al., 1979; McAllister and Price, 1982), Karliner (1978) and Mansheim (1983) have reported the successful administration of ECT to a hydrocephalic patient without untoward event. Mansheim's (1983) patient is particu-larly interesting as ECT not only relieved his depression but markedly improved some long-standing functional deficits despite the presence of meningomyelocele, a ventriculagastric shunt and epilepsy.

It is unclear whether shunting reduces the likelihood of severe cognitive side effects of ECT in patients with NPH. Improvement in depression but with marked post-ECT confusion and memory-loss occurred in a patient with NPH reported by Price and Tucker (1977) who received ECT prior to shunting, but Tsuang et al. (1979) and Levy and Levy (1987) had patients who received ECT after shunting that also developed severe disorientation (as well as incontinence in the former instance), both transient. Another NPH patient treated with a shunt in place (McAllister and Price, 1982) recovered fully from depression without any unusual cognitive side effects.

Tardive Dyskinesia:

Considering the evidence from numerous animal studies that repeated electroconvulsive shock (ECS) increases postsynaptic dopamine recep-tor responsivity (see Chapter 10), it might be expected that ECT would aggravate tardive dyskinesia (TD) in humans. The opposite is most often the case. Asnis and Leopold (1978) found that the frequency of oral movements in 3 of 4 women with neuroleptic-induced oral–facial dyskinesia fell below baseline during ECT and remained so after the course in 2 of the women; the other two showed increased abnormal movements after ECT. Price and Levin (1978) described a 49-year-old woman whose pronounced buccal–lingual dyskinesia improved suddenly and dramatically after her third ECT and remained so thereafter. Chacko and Root (1983) reported 2 women, aged 62 and 63 years, whose prominent orofacial and buccolingual dyskinesias also improved markedly after their third and fourth ECTs. One patient had no return of TD over the following 2 years; the other showed only an occasional dyskinetic tongue movement 1 year later. Tardive dystonia is a less well-known entity than TD and is diagnosed in the presence of a chronic dystonia in a patient exposed to neuroleptic drugs and without any other known cause or family history of dystonia. Kwentus et al. (1984) described a 52-year-old woman whose severely dystonic gait and posture completely remitted by her fourth ECT and remained so at a 7-month follow-up examination. Holcomb et al. (1983) report the only contrary case: a 72-year-old woman with Parkinson's disease and buccolingual dyskinesia whose formal ratings of TD worsened substantially during and after a course of ECT despite remission of her depressive state and improvement in her parkinsonian symptoms.

Lerer (1984) has suggested a possible mechanism for ECT-induced improvement in TD. He and his associates (Lerer et al., 1982) found that concurrent administration of ECS significantly attenuated both the behavioral and the biochemical dopamine receptor supersensitivity induced in rats by chronic haloperidol feeding. In their hands, ECS alone had no effect on dopamine receptor sensitivity, as measured by striatal ^{3}H spiperone binding. These findings were interpreted to suggest that ECS may stabilize dopamine receptor sensitivity in the face of exogenously induced changes in receptor function, thereby attenuating the molecular basis of TD.

Parkinson's Disease

The high incidence of depressive illness in patients with Parkinson's disease (PD) has been well-documented (Asnis, 1977), so it should come as no surprise that many such parkinsonian patients have received ECT, and that most thereby achieve relief from their depression. The surprise is that in many instances ECT also substantially relieved the parkinsonian symptoms, occasionally for prolonged intervals, and may do so even in the absence of depression. Savitsky and Karliner (1953) observed a decrease in tremor without any change in rigidity in some of their PD patients who received ECT for depression. Lebensohn and Jenkins (1975), however, were the first to report a striking and sustained improvement in parkinsonian motor signs in two patients with severe PD, and concluded that "ECT may be the treatment of choice for certain patients with Parkinson's disease, whether or not it is complicated by intractable depression." Virtually all subsequent case reports of patients with PD who received ECT describe a similar favorable effect on the parkinsonian motor symptoms (Dysken et al., 1976; Asnis, 1977; Yudofsky, 1979; Balldin et al., 1980, 1981; Holcomb et al., 1983; Levy et al., 1983; Young et al., 1985; Jaeckle and Dilsaver, 1986), whether idiopathic or drug-induced (Ananth et al., 1979). Improvement in depression is not a prerequisite for amelioration of the motor symptoms (Young et al., 1985), nor must significant depressive symptoms be present for the latter benefit to occur (Balldin et al., 1981). The only negative findings were reported by Ward et al. (1980), who were unable to confirm the improvement in the "on-off" syndrome reported by Balldin et al. (1980, 1981) in nondepressed parkinsonian patients, and by Brown et al. (1973), who found poorer than usual responses and more frequent relapses after ECT in seven parkinsonian patients who were severely depressed. As Brown (1975) points out, however, the study was a retrospective chart review and all of the patients had moderate to severe dementia.

Although increased postsynaptic dopamine receptor sensitivity is a handy explanation for the reported beneficial effects of ECT on the motor manifestations of PD (see Chapter 5), such a phenomenon has yet to be demonstrated in humans. Moreover, as noted earlier, such a mechanism ought to make TD worse, and the opposite usually occurs with ECT.

Neuromuscular Disorders

Affective symptoms (depression or euphoria) occur frequently in patients with *multiple sclerosis* and are occasionally severe enough to require ECT. Savitsky and Karliner (1951) successfully treated two such patients diagnosed as having manic depressive psychosis without any significant worsening in neurological status (indeed, one bedridden and incontinent woman regained bladder control and the ability to walk with a cane after treatment). In later papers, Savitsky and

Karliner (1953) and Karliner (1978) reported several additional cases, although it is unclear whether any were reported twice. Most patients showed improvement in psychiatric status with no change or modest improvement in neurological symptoms, although Savitsky and Karliner (1953) cite an additional case from the German literature of a catatonic woman with multiple sclerosis who improved after a single unmodified ECT but developed paraparesis with bilateral pyramidal tract signs and right upper extremity weakness and hyperreflexia that took 3 months to resolve. In general, however, a pattern of psychiatric improvement with at least no neurological worsening has been consistently observed by subsequent clinicians treating patients with multiple sclerosis (Gallinek and Kalinowsky, 1958; Hollender and Steckler, 1972; Kwentus et al., 1986; Coffey et al., 1987), with the exception being a 38-year-old manic-depressive man with multiple sclerosis in remission who developed a gait disturbance and dyscalculia requiring cessation of treatment after 8 ECTs, with only minor improvements in mental state (Regestein and Reich, 1985). A patient was examined with brain MRI by Coffey et al. (1987) before and after the course of ECT with no change observed in the preexisting white matter lesions as visualized on spin-echo images.

ECT has also been used successfully to treat psychiatric patients suffering from *cerebral palsy* (Lowinger and Huston, 1953; Guze et al., 1987), *myasthenia gravis* (Martin and Flegenheimer, 1971), and *muscular dystrophy* (Zeidenberg et al., 1976), all without any complications.

The *neuroleptic malignant syndrome* (NMS) is characterized by the development of fever, rigidity, and stupor in a patient receiving neuroleptic drugs. The rationale for treating NMS with ECT is obscure, but may derive from the resemblance of NMS to "febrile" or "lethal" catatonia, a rare and reportedly highly ECT-responsive syndrome (Lotstra et al., 1983). Although there are numerous instances of the successful use of ECT to alleviate NMS (Powers et al., 1976; Jessee and Anderson, 1983; Greenberg and Gujavarty, 1985; Liskow, 1985; Lazarus, 1986; Abbott and Loizou, 1986; Addonizio and Susman, 1986; Mann et al., 1986), two reports indicate an increased cardiac risk with such a procedure. Regestein et al. (1971) reported a 22-year-old man diagnosed as having catatonic stupor, who clearly met criteria for haloperidol-induced NMS (Abbott and Loizou, 1986), complicated by thrombophlebitis, atrial tachycardia, pneumonitis, and massive pulmonary embolism that required inferior vena cava clipping. Immediately after his sixth ECT he developed ventricular fibrillation and lapsed into a coma with decerebrate posturing in which he remained at the time the report was written 7 months later. This malignant outcome was doubtless aggravated (if not caused) by 5 days of parenteral administration of chlorpromazine just prior to the course of ECT in an unsuccessful attempt to treat the "catatonia." Hughes (1986) reported a 33-year-old woman with NMS who developed cardiac arrest during a session of multiple bilateral ECT, from which she was successfully resuscitated. Interestingly, neither of these 2 patients experienced significant relief of their NMS from ECT.

Anesthesia Considerations

Although many patients with multiple sclerosis have received ECT with succinylcholine muscle-relaxation without ill effect, Marco and Randels (1979) have warned that the potassium-releasing and muscle-depolarizing action of succinycholine might adversely affect patients with neuromuscular disorders. For this reason, Hicks (1987) used atracurium, the curariform nondepolarizing muscle-blocker, as a muscle-relaxant instead of succinylcholine when giving ECT to a patient with multiple sclerosis. Because of the resemblance of NMS to malignant hyperthermia, a syndrome induced by general anesthesia and succinylcholine, concern has also been raised that using this muscle-relaxant when giving ECT to patients with NMS might aggravate their condition (Liskow, 1985). This author also chose atracurium instead of succinylcholine in treating a patient with NMS. Addonizio and Susman (1986) feel such concern is unjustified, however, as they found that all 13 instances of succinylcholine administration during ECT in patients with NMS were without untoward effect.

Other Risk Factors with ECT

Pregnancy

Several early reviews of the effects of ECT during pregnancy (Boyd et al., 1948; Charatan and Oldham, 1954; Laird, 1955; Forssman, 1955; Smith, 1956; Sobel, 1960) failed to demonstrate any increased risk or complications of labor and delivery, fetal damage, or growth and development that could be attributed to the treatment. More recently, investigators using Doppler ultrasonography, external uterine tocodynamometry, ultrasonography, and continuous fetal heart electric monitoring have found no significant alterations of fetal heart rate, fetal movement, or uterine tone during ECT (Wise et al., 1984; Repke and Berger, 1984); both infants that were so studied were normal at delivery and at follow-up examination. In light of these facts, there seems little justification to routinely monitor mother and fetus during ECT (Remick and Maurice 1978; Wise et al., 1984; Repke and Berger, 1984); rather, these procedures should be reserved for patients with high-risk pregnancies. The call for performing ECT in pregnant women only under endotracheal intubation (Wise et al., 1984) seems particularly unwarranted, as this procedure requires substantially higher dosages of barbiturate and muscle-relaxant drugs and stimulates tracheal–laryngeal reflexes that increase pressor responses and the incidence of cardiac arrhythmias (Pitts, 1982).

Osteoporosis

With unmodified ECT, the presence of osteoporosis approximately doubles the risk of vertebral compression fracture (Lingley and Robbins, 1947; Dewald et al., 1954). The modern use of muscle-relaxant drugs however, has eliminated the risk of any type of fracture during ECT, along with the influence of osteoporosis on that risk.

Old Age

Increased age does not of itself increase the risk of ECT, and, as described in Chapter 2, some of the most rewarding results with convulsive therapy are obtained in elderly, debilitated patients whose primary affective disorder masquerades as senile dementia.

6

Technique of
Electroconvulsive Therapy

ECT is not a trifling or inconsequential procedure to be delegated to a junior resident or casually administered, unassisted, in the office. It is unique among psychiatric treatments: a significant medical intervention requiring general anesthesia and entailing risks, however small, of morbidity and mortality. The psychiatrist administering ECT adopts a role most like that of his medical and surgical colleagues; to perform it well requires an intimate knowledge of the physiology and biochemistry of induced seizures, an understanding of the pharmacology of anesthetic agents, familiarity with the physical properties of the electrical stimulus used, and the confidence and skill to lead a treatment team in the event of a medical emergency.

This chapter will first provide a detailed commentary on each aspect of the administration of ECT, from the training of personnel to the prevention of relapse after successful treatment. This will be followed by a stepwise presentation of a typical treatment.

Training

No requirements exist for the training of psychiatrists in giving ECT (Fink, 1986b); indeed, neither the Liaison Committee on Graduate Medical Education nor the American Board of Psychiatry and Neurology provide any guidelines in this regard. It is clear, however, that training in ECT has been sadly neglected by many institutions here and abroad—the surveys of Pippard and Ellam (1981) in Great Britain and Latey and Fahy (1985) in Ireland amply demonstrated how little attention has been paid to this subject in the British Isles; the Consensus Development Conference Statement (National Institutes of Health, 1985) from the United States likewise calls for the increased training of medical students and residents in the use of ECT.

A reasonable training program for psychiatric residents should provide didactic course-work on ECT early in the first year of training (usually the *inpatient* year), including at least 3 hours of lecture and discussion on history, clinical indications, treatment response, side-effects, precautions and contraindications, medical physiology, cognitive effects, EEG effects, the physical properties of the electrical stimulus, and the comparative and combined effects of psychotropic drugs. For practical experience the psychiatric resident should personally administer at least 30 to 40 treatments under the direct supervision of a faculty member; this will usually require a 1- or 2-month rotation on an ECT service. The resident's responsibilities should include both the performance of ECT consultations and assistance with the administration of ECT. After an initial week of observing all aspects of the treatment procedure with full discussion by his supervisor, the resident in training should be responsible for treating patients under direct supervision. He should learn to start the I.V., prepare and administer the anesthetic agents, apply the treatment electrodes for unilateral and bilateral ECT, deliver the electrical stimulus, and monitor the induced seizure. He should observe patients in the recovery room awaken from their treatments, and learn to manage emergence delirium. He must become thoroughly familiar with the requirements for informed consent for ECT, and participate in obtaining such consent from new patients.

For residents enrolled in programs at facilities where ECT is underutilized, it is possible that educational videotapes can augment their training (Fink, 1986b). Such tapes are available (Frankel, 1986; Ries, 1987) and should be used in conjunction with assigned readings and attendance at the training courses conducted for credit during the year at various medical centers and at the American Psychiatric Association's annual meeting.

The ECT Unit

The ECT unit is an integral functioning part of the psychiatric inpatient service and ought to be located closely to it, not set apart in a surgical suite or other remote area of the hospital.

Physical Requirements

Electroconvulsive therapy should be given in pleasant, well-lit surroundings, air-conditioned in summer and heated in winter, with ample room for staff and equipment, and with waiting and recovery areas designed to maximize privacy and minimize the apprehension engendered in patients by seeing or hearing others receiving or recovering from treatment. These points may seem self-evident, but the Pippard and Ellam report (1981) revealed them, sadly, not to be so.

The *treatment room* should be large enough to comfortably accommodate a patient on a stretcher, all of the equipment in the following list, and from 4 to 8 people, depending on whether any observers are present. (The ECT unit appropriately serves as a training site for nursing and medical students and should have adequate space for this important function.) This will require from 225 to 400 square feet of space with at least 4 grounded hospital grade outlets. A telephone will be needed for calling the patients' units and in the event that emergency assistance is required. The room should have 2 doors: one for patient entry, the other leading to a recovery area. Recommended equipment is as follows:

Six rolling stretchers, operating room type, with wheel locks and I.V. pole holders.
ECT instrument and cart.
EEG monitor (if not incorporated into ECT instrument).
Defibrillator and cart.
EKG machine and cart (if not integral to defibrillator).
Oxygen tank with valve, flow meter, and positive pressure bag.
Tracheal suction pump and cart.
Refrigerator with lock.
Wheeled I.V. pole and stand.
Lockable cabinet for medication and supplies.
Medication cart.
Emergency medication tray (not lockable) containing
    atropine (20-ml vial, 0.4 mg/ml)
    diazepam (2-ml ampules, 5 mg/ml)
    diphenhydramine (30-ml vial, 50 mg/ml)
    epinephrine (1-ml ampules, 1 mg/ml)
    levarterenol (4-ml ampules, 1 mg/ml)
    lidocaine (50-ml vial, 20 mg/ml)

methylprednisolone (125-mg vial, 62.5 mg/ml)
propranolol (1-ml ampules, 1 mg/ml)
Laryngoscope with 3 sizes of blades and assorted cuffed endotracheal
    tubes.
Rubber mouthguards (autoclavable).

The *recovery area* should be large enough to hold at least 3
stretchers, separated from each other by curtains or screens, and have
its own tracheal suction apparatus, portable positive pressure ventilation device (e.g., Ambu™ bag), and I.V. pole.

Staffing Requirements

To maximize safety and efficiency ECT should be given by a team
consisting of a psychiatrist, a registered nurse, an anesthetist or anesthesiologist, and a licensed practical nurse or nursing assistant. A
resident will be assigned to assist, as well as any additional nursing
staff who accompany their patients to the ECT unit and remain to
observe them in the recovery room until they are ready to return to
their wards.

The *psychiatrist* directs the treatment; his overall medical responsibility for the procedure is analagous to the surgeon's role in the
operating suite. He must ascertain how clinically appropriate ECT is
for each patient referred, weigh the treatment risks against the potential benefits, monitor the patient's treatment response, and decide
(with the primary physician) when maximum benefit has been obtained. He selects the anesthetic agents and their dosage, determines
the treatment electrode placement, sets and subsequently adjusts the
treatment stimulus parameters, administers the electrical stimulus, and
observes the patient throughout the treatment course for the occurrence of side effects.

The *ECT charge nurse* has a large administrative responsibility in
coordinating the unit, as well as substantial traditional nursing functions. These responsibilities include the verification that patients have
been appropriately prepared for ECT and that all necessary paper-
work and laboratory examinations are complete, including consent
forms. Medical supplies for the unit must be ordered and maintained,
records must be kept of the controlled substances used, and intravenous solutions and injectable medications must be prepared freshly

each treatment day. Patient flow from the waiting area to the treatment room to the recovery room must be facilitated, vital signs must be recorded before, during, and after treatment, and nursing personnel must be supervised in the treatment and recovery rooms.

The *anesthetist* or *anesthesiologist* [the former are generally less inclined to unnecessarily complicate a basically simple procedure (Pitts, 1982)] induces the anesthesia with the assistance of the psychiatric resident, maintains the airway, ventilates the patient, determines when it is safe to move the patient to the recovery area, and initiates any required resuscitative or corrective procedures (e.g., as intubation, treatment of cardiac arrhythmias).

The *nursing assistant* ensures that patients have voided their bladders and are properly attired, that they do not smoke before or chew gum during treatment, and that dentures, jewelry, and eyeglasses have been removed to a safe place. Other duties include wheeling patients to and from the treatment room, applying the EKG monitoring electrodes, and maintaining the unit in clean and orderly condition (by check-list) for the next treatment day.

The Pre-ECT Workup

As for any procedure conducted under general anesthesia, a medical history and physical (including neurological) examination are prerequisite. No laboratory tests are specific to ECT; the purpose of requesting routine examinations of the blood and urine (CBC, SMA-6, SMA-12, urinalysis), a chest x-ray, and an EKG is simply to screen for medical conditions that may complicate the procedure so that they may be remedied or controlled beforehand. Some examinations that traditionally have been obtained prior to ECT, or suggested by some authorities, are not recommended here for the reasons given in the discussion.

X-Rays of the Spine

Prior to the introduction of succinylcholine muscle-relaxation for ECT (vide infra), when up to 40 percent of the patients receiving this treatment experienced compression fractures of the dorsal spine (De-Wald et al., 1954), it was de rigueur to obtain spinal films before treatment for medical–legal purposes. Although the need for x-rays was abolished in the mid-1950s, some facilities continue to require them, which does not add at all to the patient's security, but adds very considerably to his bill.

Skull X-Rays

Skull films are occasionally requested to "rule out brain tumor" before giving ECT. Such films, however, are quite insensitive to intracerebral pathology of whatever etiology, and along with spine films needlessly increase the cost of treatment and add to the patient's lifetime radiation exposure. Brain tumors large enough to cause psychiatric symptoms are likely to manifest themselves during a careful behavioral neurological examination—any clinical suspicion of such a neoplasm should then be investigated with one of the newer imaging techniques (CT scan, MRI).

EEG

Conversely, the high sensitivity and low specificity of the EEG render it a poor screening tool prior to ECT. One-quarter to one-third of melancholics exhibit EEG abnormalities (Abrams et al., 1970; Abrams and Taylor, 1979) that are usually in the form of nonspecific slowing, which is not infrequently asymmetrical. Such slowing does not predict a poor outcome with ECT (Abrams et al., 1970) and may even disappear after the acute EEG effects of ECT have passed.

Pseudocholinesterase Testing

Pseudocholinesterase is the enzyme responsible for degrading succinylcholine, the muscle-relaxant used in ECT. Absence of this enzyme is transmitted as a rare genetic abnormality affecting less than 1 in 3000 (Lehmann and Liddell, 1969) and is responsible, along with liver disease, polyphosphate insecticide poisoning, anemia, malnutrition, or the administration of anticholinesterases, for the complication of prolonged apnea after ECT (Mathew and Constan, 1964; Packman et al., 1978). A rapid screening test for pseudocholinesterase deficiency is available (Swift and LaDu, 1966), but when a sensitive test is used to screen for a rare disorder, virtually all positive responses are false and therefore unhelpful (Galen and Gambino, 1975). Concomitant therapy with lithium, certain antibiotics, aminoglycosides, magnesium salts, procainamide and quinidine (Hill, Wong, and Hodges, 1976; Packman et al., 1978) may also prolong post-ECT apnea by enhancing the neuromuscular blockade induced by succinylcholine.

Medical Consultation

The mean age of patients receiving ECT has increased in recent years, probably as a combined result of increased longevity, the greater risk for depressive illness in later life, and insurance coverage under Medicare. More high-risk patients are thus receiving ECT, and medical consultation in their management will often by sought. The consultation process should not be viewed simply as "clearance for ECT"; no such clearance is really possible. Rather, what the referring psychiatrist needs is the consultant's opinion on the nature and severity of the medical disorder in question, its amenability to medical management, and the degree of risk imposed by a grand mal seizure induced under controlled conditions of anesthesia, muscle-relaxation, and oxygenation. In order for the consultant to provide a valid opinion on these matters he must have an understanding of the medical physiology of ECT, the risks of alternate therapies (e.g., tricyclic antidepressants), and the deleterious effects of the untreated psychiatric illness itself. As such considerations are not routinely taught in most medical residencies, psychiatrists should seek out consultants with some experience in ECT or provide the requisite information themselves through personal discussions and citations from the literature. (Some internists, not fully aware of the very brief duration of ECT anesthesia or the precise physiological effects of a medically controlled seizure, overestimate the stress of the procedure and reject some patients as inappropriate risks for whom ECT is actually a more conservative treatment than pharmacotherapy.)

Consent for ECT

Except for rare instances of judicially ordered treatment or treatment given in a genuine emergency to "preserve life or limb," patients may not receive involuntary ECT any more than they may receive involuntary surgery. The topic is treated in greater detail in Chap. 11, but the essential elements of informed consent include:

1. A full explanation of the procedure in layman's terms.
2. A presentation of the risks and potential benefits of the treatment offered, as well as those of alternative available therapies.
3. A statement that the patient may withdraw his consent at any time and for any reason.

An educational videotape is useful both to orient patients and their families to the procedures for ECT and to unambiguously document the information that has been presented to the patient when obtaining informed consent (Barbour and Blumenkrantz, 1978). Such videotape aids have become commercially available recently (Baxter and Liston, 1986; Ries, 1987).

Seizure Monitoring

Prior to the introduction of succinylcholine muscle relaxation for ECT there was seldom any doubt as to whether or not a patient had a seizure. With succinylcholine-induced attenuation of the motor convulsion, however, it may be difficult, if not impossible, to verify the occurrence and duration of the induced seizure through observation of muscle activity alone. The importance of such verification derives from studies suggesting that it is the induced cerebral seizure, more than any other aspect of the treatment, that is responsible for the fully developed therapeutic effect of ECT (Ottosson, 1960). Although direct electrical stimulation of the brain may itself play a therapeutic role during ECT (Abrams and Taylor, 1976; Robin and deTissera, 1982; Robin et al., 1985; Malitz et al., 1986), no one doubts that the cerebral seizure is central to the therapeutic process, hence the necessity for ensuring that a seizure of sufficient duration has occurred (an arbitrary minimum of 25 seconds is now generally agreed upon). Seizure monitoring is particularly important during unilateral ECT, which requires a substantially greater electrical stimulus than does bilateral ECT and yields an inadequate therapeutic response at just-above-threshold stimulation (Sackeim et al., 1986). Moreover, a recent study employing EEG monitoring (Pettinati and Nilsen, 1985) reported significantly more missed seizures with unilateral than with bilateral ECT (63 percent versus 29 percent). As such missed seizures are not always detected clinically, the authors suggest that without EEG monitoring, patients receiving unilateral ECT may inadvertently receive an inadequate treatment course.

Several methods are available for seizure monitoring. Of these the simplest was devised by Addersley and Hamilton (1953), and requires that a blood pressure cuff be applied to one limb and inflated to 10 mm Hg above systolic pressure prior to the administration of succinylcholine in order to occlude this drug from the muscles distal to the cuff. Seizure duration measured in this fashion correlates highly with that obtained by EEG (Fink and Johnson, 1982). The duration of the muscular convulsion in the cuffed limb correlates highly with the simultaneously recorded EEG (Fink and Johnson, 1982; Larson, Swartz, and Abrams, 1984). The heart rate may also be used to measure seizure length (Larson, Swartz, and Abrams, 1984) as the point of greatest decrease in the rate of the ECT-induced tachycardia is highly correlated with both EEG and motor measures of the induced seizure. Moreover, the heart rate is a sensitive enough measure of intracerebral seizure generalization to differentiate right-unilateral from bilateral ECT (Lane et al., 1987). Only the EEG, however, directly represents the brain's electrical activity and remains the standard against which other techniques must be measured. There are two methods incorporated in ECT instruments for amplifying and presenting EEG activity during ECT. The earlier method uses a chart-drive and penwriter to record the EEG signal on paper—the resulting record is then read by the clinician as it is generated in order to determine the seizure end-point. A recently introduced EEG monitor for ECT provides an auditory representation of the EEG signal in the form of a tone that fluctuates with the frequency of the seizure activity and becomes constant when the seizure ends. This method is as reliable as the paper EEG and correlates highly with it (Swartz and Abrams, 1986; Weiner et al., 1987), and it has the advantage of not needing paper or any EEG expertise and does not require the treating physician to divert his eyes from the patient during treatment.

The particular characteristics of seizures monitored with motor, visual, and auditory techniques are as follows. The motor seizure is observed in the limb distal to the blood-pressure cuff and consists of an initial sudden contraction of the muscles during the passage of the electrical stimulus and an equally abrupt relaxation as the stimulus terminates. The *tonic phase* is then ushered in by a gradually increasing, sustained, tetanic contraction of the muscles (arms flexed, legs extended), lasting from 10 to 15 seconds and characterized by rigidity and a fine tremor. This is gradually replaced by the increasingly rhythmical jerking movements of the *clonic phase*, starting at a frequency of 10 to 12 per second and gradually slowing over the next 20 to 45 seconds to 3 to 4 per second at seizure termination. This always occurs abruptly in the muscles, about 10 seconds before cerebral seizure activity ceases (Abrams, Volavka, and Fink, 1973). It is useful to monitor the motor seizure as well as the standard two-lead bifrontal EEG as the latter can not distinguish partial or focal from generalized seizures (Welch, 1982). Conversely, as the cerebral seizure activity occasionally continues for several or more *minutes* after the motor component ends (Weiner, 1980; Abrams and Volavka, 1982; Greenberg, 1985), and may require termination by intravenous diazepam, EEG monitoring of the induced seizure is also mandatory.

The EEG characteristics of induced seizures are described in greater detail in Chapter 4. The principles of EEG monitoring are identical regardless of whether a visual or an auditory EEG representation is provided by the particular ECT device used. The passage of the stimulus automatically excludes the EEG amplifiers from the circuit in order not to overload them. The tonic phase is then manifested by high-frequency, high-amplitude activity that is gradually replaced by increasingly rhythmic burst activity that corresponds to each myoclonic contraction and progressively slows in frequency until seizure termination, typically in electrical "silence."

EKG Monitoring

Although ECT is one of the safest procedures that is carried out under general anesthesia, whatever risk the treatment does entail falls primarily on the cardiovascular system and specifically on the heart (see Chapter 5). This risk primarily takes the form of cardiac arrhythmias engendered by the abrupt and massive autonomic stimulation resulting from both the electrical current and the induced seizure. Although such arrhythmias almost never need treatment, an awareness of their presence increases the likelihood of an efficient medical response in the rare instance when corrective measures are indicated. For this reason, and because of the increased numbers of "high risk" patients receiving ECT, EKG monitoring of the procedure is now standard. Any oscilloscope monitor or electrocardiograph is suitable for this purpose as all that is generally required is a determination of the rhythm and a display of the QRS complex. Should any evidence of myocardial damage appear, however, it would also be useful to have full limb and chest lead capability.

Benign neglect is a successful strategy for handling the vast majority of transient ECT-induced cardiac arrhythmias. Although propranolol, for example, has been recommended in the prevention or management of post-ECT sympathetic arrhythmias (McKenna et al., 1970; Weiner et al., 1979; Jones and Knight, 1981), its use for this purpose has also been implicated in cardiac arrest (Decina et al., 1984). Electroconvulsive therapy is a very safe procedure. It was given for tens of thousands of consecutive treatments without cardiac arrest long before EKG monitoring or beta-adrenergic blockade were ever dreamed of (Kolb and Vogel, 1942; Impastato and Almansi, 1942; Barker and Baker, 1959), and is remarkably benign even in the presence of cardiac disease (Pitts, 1982). It would be ironic if the introduction of sophisticated cardioactive agents into the procedure only increased the risk.

Protection of Teeth and Tongue

The direct electrical stimulation of the temporalis muscles during ECT causes the teeth to clamp shut powerfully, stressing them and risking a severe tongue bite. For this reason, a rubber mouthguard is always inserted between the teeth just prior to delivering the electrical stimulus, cushioning the force of contraction and preventing the tongue from protruding between the teeth. The mouthguard should be designed to direct much of the force of the bite to the molars and away from the more fragile incisors (Durrant, 1966). It should have a rim in the front to separate the teeth from the lips, as well as a channel to permit the flow of oxygen and the insertion of a suction catheter tip if needed. The rubber portion that fits between the teeth should be thick enough to substantially open the jaws, thus more efficiently diverting the biting strain rearwards. Under no circumstances should a Guedel-type plastic airway be in place in a patient with teeth when the stimulus is administered as this exposes the incisors to the full force of the bite on an unyielding surface, possibly fracturing them (Pollard and O'Leary, 1981; Faber, 1983). Of course, edentulous patients require no mouthguard.

Treatment Electrode Placement

The skin, with its oily secretions, presents the main impedance to the flow of current during ECT (Weaver et al., 1976), and special care should be taken to cleanse it thoroughly with an organic solvent before applying the electrode jelly. Alcohol is generally sufficient for this purpose, but some patients with particularly oily or sebaceous skin may require the use of ethyl acetate to bring their skin impedance down to an acceptable level. (Ethyl acetate is available at any local drugstore as nail-polish remover and is safer than acetone with its risk of hepatotoxicity.)

The relative indications for the use of bilateral or unilateral electrode placements are considered separately in Chapter 8. For bilateral ECT there is one standard placement: bifrontotemporal. One electrode is positioned on each side of the head approximately 1 in. above the midpoint of an imaginary line connecting the external auditory meatus and the outer canthus of the eye.

Unilateral ECT is preferentially administered to the hemisphere that is nondominant for language, based on the recommendation of Lancaster, Steinert, and Frost (1958), who believed that the reduced cognitive side-effects of this treatment method derived from avoiding the direct electrical stimulation of the speech and verbal memory centers of the dominant temporal lobe. Although it is now clear that these reduced cognitive effects (especially on short-term retentive memory) derive mainly from the fact that only one temporal lobe (rather than both) is stimulated, regardless of the side, nondominant placements remain standard. Moreover, although some workers have suggested adverse effects on depression from the administration of left-unilateral ECT (Deglin, 1973; Sackeim et al., 1986), a majority have not (Kronfol et al., 1978; Leechuy and Abrams, 1987), and there is substantial contrary data (Kronfol et al., 1978; Abrams, 1986) and even the suggestion that such treatment may be the *most* effective method in melancholia (Abrams, Taylor, and Volavka, 1987). Indeed, in a random-assignment, double-blind comparison of the therapeutic effects of bilateral, right-unilateral, and left-unilateral ECT now in progress, data from the first 29 patients demonstrates both left-unilateral and bilateral ECT to be equally effective in reducing depression scale scores, substantially more so than right-unilateral ECT (Abrams, unpublished data).

A variety of electrode placements have been employed for unilateral ECT, but a consensus has developed in recent years that the most efficient one is that recommended by d'Elia and Raotma (1975). In this method, the lower electrode is placed exactly as for bilateral ECT, and the upper electrode is placed on the same side of the head adjacent to the vertex of the skull. A frontoparietal placement (Muller, 1971) is often used by clinicians because of the ease with which both electrodes can be applied with a single head-band (the d'Elia placement requires a separate, hand-held electrode for the upper position). This method raises the seizure threshold, however, as the thick frontal bones substantially impede the passage of the stimulating current, leading to more missed seizures (d'Elia and Widepalm, 1974; Erman, Welch, and Mandel, 1979; Alexopolous et al., 1984b). The unilateral electrode handle should conceal the exposed electrode edge to protect the operator from any shock hazard.

Impedance Testing

The resistance to the passage of the stimulating current during ECT is called the dynamic impedance and is a function of the summed electrical properties of the skin, hair, scalp, subcutaneous tissues, periosteum, bone, dura and pia mater, brain, blood vessels, blood, and cerebrospinal fluid (Weaver et al., 1976). It would be useful to know the dynamic impedance prior to ECT as it would aid the physician in determining the appropriate treatment stimulus setting; however, this is not possible as the dynamic impedance can only be measured while the stimulus current is flowing, at which point the information is no longer useful. Modern ECT instruments use minute currents that are indetectable to the patient to test the static impedance prior to treatment. This procedure provides information about the quality of the electrode-to-skin coupling that is especially critical when administering unilateral ECT because this method is much more likely than bilateral ECT to be vitiated by reduced stimulus levels (Malitz et al., 1986). The static impedance cannot be used to estimate the dynamic impedance. It is not possible to provide a specific figure for the static impedance that is in the desirable range as different ECT devices use different test stimuli and are therefore not directly comparable. If the static impedance tests above the range recommended by the manufacturer, however, it should be reduced by 1) increasing the pressure on the treatment electrodes, 2) repositioning the treatment electrodes away from any hair, and 3) gently abrading the skin under the electrodes with a fine emery board to remove the top layer of dead cells and sebum. The specific risk incurred in treating a patient with a high static impedance is that of skin burns; if the impedance cannot be brought into the desired range by the preceding methods, then the decision must be made whether the risk (which is actually rather modest) outweighs the potential benefits of treatment. It usually will not.

If the impedance is too low (e.g., < 100 Ω) this means that a wet scalp or an electrode gel "bridge" has short-circuited the stimulus, usually between 2 unilateral ECT electrodes that have been placed too closely together. Treatment should not be given until this condition is remedied because no current will enter the brain under these circumstances.

Stimulus Selection

A detailed description of the nature of the electrical stimulus is provided in Chapter 7 of this volume. Suffice it to say here that the brief pulse square wave stimulus is the only appropriate one for modern ECT as the older sine-wave stimulus is excessively toxic, providing substantial subthreshold energy that contributes significantly to confusion and memory loss, but not to the therapeutic effect. All presently manufactured brief pulse ECT devices deliver stimuli that have essentially identical pulse configurations and energy levels, but differ mainly in the availability of additional features, such as skin impedance testing and EEG monitoring capability, as well as in reliability and ease of use (Nilsen et al., 1986).

The seizure threshold is multidetermined. It increases with age (Kalinowsky, 1947; Shankel et al., 1960; Weiner, 1980; Sackeim et al., 1987) and with the number of ECTs administered in a given treatment course (Kalinowsky and Kennedy, 1943; Essig, 1969; Sackeim et al., 1987). The threshold is higher in men than women and for unilateral than for bilateral ECT (Sackeim et al., 1987), it is increased by long-acting benzodiazepines administered for nighttime sedation (Strömgren et al., 1980), and it is decreased by pentylenetetrazol (no longer commercially available), theophylline, and caffeine (Shapira et al., 1985; Hinkle et al., 1987; Shapira et al., 1987). For many years the advice was to administer ECT at a level just above the seizure threshold in order to avoid the cognitive dysfunction induced by excessive electrical stimulation (Ottosson, 1960). A recent study by Sackeim et al. (1986), however, found that although just-above-threshold stimulation was effective for bilateral ECT it failed to produce a significant therapeutic effect for unilateral ECT. Thus, it is advisable to use a stimulus for unilateral ECT that is very substantially suprathreshold.

In any case, there simply is no way available at this time to determine the seizure threshold before treatment. The initial setting should be based on the device manufacturer's recommendation as a starting point, augmenting this value according to the presence of factors known to increase the threshold: unilateral electrode application, male gender, increased age, treatment later in course, received long half-life benzodiazepine the previous day. Seizure duration is correlated with seizure threshold and decreases with age and the number of treatments in the course (Holmberg, 1954b; Abrams et al., 1973; Sackeim et al., 1987). Oxygenation prolongs seizures modestly (Holmberg, 1953a,b; Bergsholm et al., 1984).

Oxygenation

Prior to the introduction of succinylcholine muscle-relaxation for ECT it apparently never occurred to those administering ECT that their patients might benefit from oxygenation during the treatment, despite the fact that hemoglobin oxygen saturations routinely fell to levels of around 40 gm % (in the old terminology), patients became profoundly cyanotic, and frequently lost sphincter control before the seizure terminated. Whether this cerebral hypoxemia contributed to the occasional occurrence of late (tardive) seizures through a kindling effect as a complication of ECT is not known; however, no more than one or two of such tardive seizures have been reported since oxygenation was introduced along with barbiturate anesthesia and succinylcholine as *modified ECT* in the 1950s. This is ironic because, in fact, succinylcholine-induced muscle paralysis obviates the need for oxygenation during the seizure as muscular activity is responsible for most of the oxygen consumed during a grand mal seizure (Posner et al., 1969). Nonetheless, it is standard recommended procedure to initiate oxygenation by forced ventilation as soon as the patient is unresponsive from the barbiturate, and to continue it throughout the treatment procedure until the return of spontaneous respirations. In patients with chronic obstructive pulmonary disease 100-percent oxygen should be replaced by room air or an oxygen–carbon dioxide mixture in order not to abolish the hypoxic drive to respiration.

Administration of Anesthetic Agents

Premedication with a parenteral anticholinergic agent 30 to 45 minutes before ECT prevents the excessive tracheobronchial secretions and slowing of the heart, which result from the powerful vagal outflow that occurs immediately after the treatment stimulus is passed. Atropine, 0.4 to 1.0 mg I.M., has traditionally been used for this purpose, but is sometimes replaced by intravenous glycopyrrolate, 0.2 to 0.4 mg, a compound that does not enter the CNS.

The anesthetic and muscle-relaxant are administered intravenously immediately prior to seizure induction. The ultrashort acting barbiturate methohexital is now the anesthetic agent of choice for ECT. It induces substantially fewer cardiac arrhythmias than the older thiopental (Pitts et al., 1965) and has the added advantages of a shorter sleep time and less postanesthesia confusion (Egbert and Wolfe, 1960; Osborne et al., 1963; Woodruff et al., 1968). The recommended initial dose of methohexital is 0.75 mg/kg of body weight (Pitts, 1982), given intravenously by rapid *bolus push*. The dosage for subsequent treatments should be adjusted according to the patient's response to the first injection.

Succinylcholine is the muscle-relaxant of choice for ECT and is given at a dosage of 0.6 mg/kg of body weight (Pitts, 1982), also by rapid bolus push.

The Seizure

Although recent evidence has been adduced for a direct therapeutic role of the electrical stimulus (Robin and deTissera, 1982; Abrams, 1986; Malitz et al., 1986), the seizure is generally considered to be the primary therapeutic agent of ECT (see the discussion in Chapter 7 of this volume). For this reason it is necessary to ensure that a fully developed bilateral grand mal seizure is obtained during each treatment session, as determined by the seizure monitoring techniques described earlier. As of this time, no objective guidelines have been established for a minimum seizure duration, but a consensus has developed in recent years that if a 25-second seizure is not induced the patient should be restimulated at a higher electrical dosage. Shorter seizures or those with indeterminate electrical activity are considered abortive or incompletely generalized and of reduced therapeutic benefit. The claim (Maletzky, 1978) that a specific minimum total seizure time is required for an effective treatment course is not supported by any objective data. Since most depressives require 6 to 8 treatments, and the average seizure lasts about 50 seconds (Abrams et al., 1973), most patients who recover will have experienced a total of from 300 to 400 seconds of seizure activity. This commonplace observation is, of course, *post hoc*, and cannot be elevated to a general statement of principle.

Postictal Care

With termination of the seizure the therapeutic portion of the treatment also ends—the goal of the postictal phase is primarily that of maintaining an adequate airway until the return of spontaneous respirations and, eventually, alertness. The anesthetist continues forced ventilation until the patient is breathing on his own, at which time he is transferred to a recovery area under the observation of trained staff until awakening. Occasionally, tracheobroncheal suction will be required in this phase, especially if the patient is a heavy cigarette smoker or has recently had an upper respiratory infection. About 10 percent of the patients will become increasingly restless and agitated during a 15- to 30-minute period of emergence from the anesthesia, moaning loudly, flopping about, and even trying to climb off the stretcher. This *emergence delirium* responds only minimally to calm reassurance, but is rapidly terminated by intravenous methohexital or diazepam. Since it usually occurs after each treatment in a given patient, it is best prevented in subsequent treatments by an intravenous injection of diazepam, 5 to 15 mg, given just when the seizure ends. If this does not prove adequate, a *methohexital drip* can be established using the butterfly assembly still in place while the patient is still in the treatment room. A solution of methohexital containing 2 mg/ml is dripped slowly into the patient's vein at a rate just sufficient to inhibit the delirium. This can be done easily in the recovery room, but it requires the direct supervision of a physician or registered nurse.

Frequency and Number of Treatments

In the United States ECT is invariably given 3 times per week, whereas in the United Kingdom semi-weekly treatment is the rule. This difference probably reflects national character more than any theoretical bias: Americans are impatient for results. The more leisurely pace of treatment enjoyed by the British, however, permits more time for the full effect of each treatment to develop, resulting in a generally shorter course of treatments and less cumulative memory-loss (at least where bilateral ECT is concerned). The advent of Diagnosis Related Groups to determine third-party reimbursements in the United States makes it quite unlikely that Americans shall ever adopt a more temperate rate of treatment. This is a shame because there is some recent evidence suggesting that the beneficial effects of a single ECT may not fully develop for a week or more.

Treatment may be given even more rapidly with unilateral ECT. Abrams (1967) demonstrated that unilateral ECT could be given 5 days/week without incurring significant dysmnesia, a finding later confirmed by Strömgren (1975). That such a schedule has not been universally adopted for this form of treatment is probably testimony to the general disinclination of psychiatrists to start their day at 8 AM any more frequently than is required by custom. Support for this hypothesis derives from the increasing tendency of some psychiatrists to surrender their role in the administration of ECT to the anesthesiologist, establishing their role in the procedure only at billing time.

It is not unusual for psychiatrists to administer two treatments per session (Swartz and Mehta, 1986), usually for conditions that constitute a serious threat to the patient's physical integrity. Delirious mania, melancholia with intense suicidal symptoms, and catatonic stupor may justify administering double bilateral ECTs in a single session, spaced 1 to 2 minutes apart to allow for the refractory period following a seizure. Double unilateral ECTs, on the other hand, are frequently given in an attempt to increase their therapeutic yield of this method, which many psychiatrists believe to be inferior to bilateral ECT (Abrams, 1986).

Required Number of ECTs

The total number of treatments administered to a patient in a single treatment course will be a function of the diagnosis, rapidity of response, prior ECT response (if applicable), severity of illness, and the quality of the response to treatments already received. Clinicians are readily able to weight these variables in practice and treat them accordingly as long as their patients improve with treatment. It is more difficult to specify the maximum number of treatments that should be given to a patient who is *not* showing the expected treatment response. Certainly 6 to 8 treatments achieve the desired result in the majority of melancholics receiving bilateral ECT, and it is by no means unusual to give as many as 12 to a patient who has all the clinical features generally associated with a good response but has not yet achieved one, or who exhibits incremental improvement with each additional treatment. It is only a rare melancholic who requires or substantially benefits from more than 12 ECTs in a single course; when this number has been given and the question arises whether or not to continue, it is generally prudent to withhold further treatment from several days to a week, observe the patient, and perhaps obtain another opinion before proceeding with additional treatments.

Manics may require more treatments than melancholics, with 8 to 12 ECTs sufficing in most cases, and only a rare patient requiring more than 16.

Catatonics may show an initial dramatic response to the first 2 or 3 ECTs, only to relapse if treatment is terminated at this point. It is advisable, therefore, to continue to 6 to 8 treatments in catatonia [which is not infrequently a manifestation of melancholic stupor (Abrams and Taylor, 1976)].

The common clinical wisdom of giving 2 additional ECTs after maximal improvement has been achieved was not borne out by the controlled study of Barton et al. (1973). These authors found no difference in improvement at 2, 6, and 12 weeks between those patients who stopped receiving ECT at the point of full improvement and those who received 2 additional treatments.

MULTIPLE MONITORED ECT (MMECT)

In 1966, Blachly and Gowing introduced the novel procedure of administering multiple ECTs in a single treatment session, while monitoring the patient's EKG and EEG. Their aim was to accelerate the treatment course and to reduce the required number of anesthesia inductions for a course of treatments. They treated 46 patients with 3 to 8 bilateral ECTs each session and claimed that the memory-loss produced by a single session was no greater than that observed after single treatments. They further claimed a specific relation between the EEG pattern of the seizure end point and the point of maximum improvement from treatment. Because these authors measured neither the memory-loss nor the therapeutic effect of their method, however, their claims can not be evaluated. Sadly, 20 years after this paper appeared, the therapeutic and cognitive effects of MMECT have yet to be studied in a controlled, prospective design.

White, Shea, and Jonas (1968) gave an average of 3.3 sessions of MMECT-5 (the standard notation for MMECT with 5 seizures per session) to 27 patients in an open clinical trial; bilateral treatment electrode placement was in every patient but one. They presented no data to support their claim that MMECT shortened the average hospital stay, reduced memory-loss, or increased safety in comparison with conventional ECT. Bidder and Strain (1970) gave 2 sessions of bilateral MMECT-4 to 14 patients and reported an excellent clinical response in only one. Four patients who were tested before and after their treatment course exhibited only minimal impairment on a verbal paired-associates learning task, but the authors noted the occurrence of frequent periods of prolonged postictal confusion, drowsiness, and disorientation, and described one patient who became severely confused after each treatment session. One year later (Strain and Bidder, 1971) these authors reported the occurrence of status epilepticus of approximately 53 minutes duration during the first session of MMECT-4 in a 62-year-old woman who had received prior conventional ECT without untoward event. A left hemisparesis ensued that cleared substantially over 24 hours, but neurological examination 3 weeks later revealed a residual mild left supranuclear weakness and the patient continued to feel that her vision and left arm were "not quite right" when she was discharged 4 weeks after the episode. Abrams and Fink (1972) treated 38 patients with an average of 2.5 sessions each of MMECT-4 or MMECT-6 in an open clinical trial that employed bilateral, right-unilateral, or anterior bifrontal (Abrams and Taylor, 1973) placements. Only one patient showed a dramatic response to a single session of MMECT; the remainder showed varying responses that were mostly similar to those obtained with conventional ECT. Postictal sleep was frequently prolonged after MMECT, and one 35-year-old woman was rousable only to deep painful stimulation for 10 hours after her first treatment. Post-ECT confusion and memory loss were often very prominent and 2 patients developed prolonged organic confusional states that cleared slowly but completely over 1 to 2 weeks posttreatment. Bridenbaugh, Drake, and O'Regan (1972) treated 17 schizophrenic patients in an open clinical trial of an average of 4.5 sessions of MMECT-5. They reported 16 seizures that lasted more than 15 minutes, one episode of aspiration penumonitis, and 5 occurrences of supraventricular tachycardia. A paper by Yesavage and Berens (1980), which purports to compare MMECT and conventional ECT by a retrospective chart review, is rendered uninterpretable by the fact that most patients studied received both forms of treatment. A recent paper by Maletzky et al. (1986) from a private-practice setting claims to demonstrate that right-unilateral MMECT and conventional ECT are equally effective, and that MMECT is associated with fewer adverse effects and a shorter hospital stay; however, the study is methodologically unsound (non-random assignment to treatment methods, nonblind assessment of adverse effects) and, therefore, unconvincing.

Record Keeping

Two permanent records should be kept of each treatment: one in the patient's chart and the other in the ECT unit. The latter should be maintained in a permanent ledger that sequentially records the essential data for each patient each treatment day, including the date, name, age, sex, hospital number, ward, ordinal treatment number, methohexital dose, succinylcholine dose, treatment electrode placement, stimulus setting(s), seizure type and duration, and pertinent comments concerning future adjustments in drug dosages or stimulus setting(s) or individual peculiarities such as "slow circulation time" or "develops emergence delirium." The same information should be entered in the patient's chart, which can most conveniently be done with a rubber stamp that has information headings followed by blanks to be filled in by the attending physician or his delegate.

Maintenance (Continuation) Therapy

Medication

As few illnesses are permanently relieved by a brief exposure to a therapeutic agent, most medical treatments consist of an acute phase followed by a maintenance phase. No one prescribing tricyclic antidepressants for melancholia, for example, would consider terminating therapy immediately after the patient had improved or recovered—the usual course of treatment continues for 6 months—yet this is precisely how patients are frequently treated with ECT. Relapse rates under these circumstances are quite high, ranging from 30 to 60 percent over 6 months. Fortunately, maintenance drug therapy with lithium or tricyclic antidepressants after a successful course of ECT reduces these rates by at least two-thirds (Seager and Bird, 1962; Wilson et al., 1963; Hordern et al., 1965; Imlah et al., 1965; Kay et al., 1970; Mindham, Howland, and Shepherd, 1973; Perry and Tsuang, 1979; Coppen et al., 1981). Examples of effective maintenance regimens for unipolar or bipolar patients are amitrityline, 150 to 200 mg at bedtime for 4 to 6 months post-ECT, or lithium in doses that provide blood levels in the neighborhood of 1.0 mEq/ L for the same period of time (or longer if the prior illness course warrants conventional lithium prophylaxis). Of course, failure with either compound is cause for a trial with the other.

Maintenance ECT

The widespread prescription and general efficacy of lithium prophylaxis for both bipolar and unipolar illness has doubtless reduced the popularity of maintenance ECT, as has the lack of any controlled trials demonstrating its efficacy. Nevertheless, the accumulated experience of a number of practitioners (Moore, 1943; Geoghegan and Stevenson, 1949; Stevenson and Geoghegan, 1951; Bourne, 1954, 1956; Wolff, 1957; Hastings, 1961; Holt, 1965; Decina et al., 1987a), suggests that maintenance ECT may be useful for the 10 to 15 percent of patients with affective disorder who will relapse during the 6 months post-ECT despite adequate maintenance drug therapy.

Maintenance ECT is an outpatient procedure for patients who have already exhibited satisfactory improvement with a conventional course of ECT and who have previously failed on maintenance drug therapy. The goal of continued treatment is to maintain the patient in remission by administering additional ECTs at a frequency sufficient to prevent relapse without incurring cumulative memory loss. The ideal vehicle for this purpose is right-unilateral ECT, which should be given an initial trial in the maintenance phase regardless of which method originally induced remission. The advantage of right-unilateral ECT is that it can be given virtually as often as desired without producing clinically significant dysmnesia (Abrams, 1967; Strömgren, 1975).

A typical schedule for maintenance ECT provides a treatment 1 week after the initial course is successfully completed, a second in 2 weeks, a third in 3 weeks, and the fourth and subsequent treatments at monthly intervals for up to 6 months. Some patients may not remain well on monthly interval maintenance ECT and will require treatments at 3-week intervals or, rarely, biweekly. This latter spacing should only be given for 2 to 3 consecutive treatments before again attempting to decrease the seizure frequency. Maintenance ECT should not be indefinitely prolonged. Such interminable treatment is unwarranted and if performed with bilateral placements may produce severe, continuous, cognitive deficits (Regestein et al., 1975).

Maintenance ECT patients are included in the treatment schedule together with inpatients. They should receive written instructions not to have breakfast, and although they may come to hospital alone, they must leave with a responsible person. Many patients on maintenance ECT find that they are able to go to work later that morning, especially if they have received unilateral ECT or monthly interval bilateral ECT. Regardless of who accompanies them from the hospital, each patient should be cleared for release that morning by a physician or nurse. The usual records are maintained in the ECT unit and the patient's outpatient chart. Laboratory tests other than those already obtained for the original treatment course are unnecessary.

Ambulatory ECT

This phrase refers to outpatient administration of the entire course of ECT—the patient is never hospitalized. Quite frequently performed in the United Kingdom, ambulatory ECT is little-used in the United States. This may soon change as free-standing outpatient treatment facilities (e.g., *Surgicenters*) flourish in response to universal cost-containment pressures on medical practice. ECT is ideally suited to the outpatient setting. It is brief, safe, and well-tolerated—far more so than a variety of endoscopic, plastic, and dental surgical procedures now routinely performed for outpatients. Ambulatory ECT is unsuitable primarily for those patients whose illness severity and consequent risk mandates inpatient observation and care (e.g., suicidal, agitated, or delusional melancholics; catatonics; acute manics).

Treatment Complications and Their Management

Elevated Seizure Threshold

Seizures may be increasingly difficult or impossible to obtain even at a maximum electrical dosage in older men during the latter part of their treatment course, especially if they are receiving benzodiazepines or if unilateral ECT is used. Intravenous pentylenetetrazol (Metrazol), 500 mg by rapid *bolus push*, 30 seconds before passing the electrical stimulus is an effective remedy, but this medication was no longer available at the time of this writing. Parenteral caffeine, in a dose of 250 to 1000 mg, is reportedly effective for this purpose (Shapira et al., 1987; Hinkle et al., 1987). The related compound theophylline also lowers the seizure threshold; status epilepticus was reported in an asthmatic patient who got ECT while taking 900 mg/day of Theodur, a long-acting preparation of this drug (Peters et al., 1984). The safe dosage of this preparation for lowering the ECT seizure threshold remains to be determined. If threshold-lowering medications are contemplated, it is prudent to have a syringe ready containing 15 mg of diazepam for intravenous administration in the event of an unduly prolonged seizure (e.g., one greater than 3 minutes).

There is evidence that methohexital itself shortens seizure duration from what would be obtained with unmodified ECT (Witztum et al., 1970). Jones and Callender (1981) have suggested that this may lead to inadequate treatment. Lunn et al. (1981) reported that methohexital shortened seizure length in rats as compared to those obtained in unanesthetized controls, ketamine increased seizure length, and a fentanyl–droperidol combination had no effect. Although these authors obtained longer seizures in an ECT patient with ketamine than he had previously exhibited with methohexital, they point out that the hallucinogenic properties of the former compound may seriously limit its use for ECT. Droperidol is also problematic as coma ensued when this drug was administered immediately following ECT (Koo and Chien, 1986).

Prolonged Seizures

Although no specific guidelines exist for determining when a given seizure has become excessively long, many practitioners would become concerned at a seizure that exceeded 3 minutes' duration, and most would elect to terminate one lasting longer than 5 minutes. Intravenous diazepam, 5–15 mg, is the drug of choice for terminating prolonged seizures.

Prolonged Apnea

There is no antidote for succinylcholine and no specific treatment to reverse prolonged apnea. Assisted respiration is simply continued for as long as it takes the patient's own pseudocholinesterase activity, however weak, to metabolize the succinylcholine (usually 30 to 60 minutes). Intubation is not required for this (Pitts, 1982) as long as good pulmonary exchange is achieved by face mask. If it seems that apnea will be prolonged for more than 1 hour, consideration should be given to the administration of a unit of typed and cross-matched fresh whole blood or plasma to supply an exogenous source of pseudocholinesterase (Matthew and Constan, 1964). Subsequent treatments can still be given with succinylcholine, but at a much lower dose: 5 mg is given and the degree of muscle-relaxation tested by repeatedly eliciting the patellar reflex—when it is abolished, ECT may safely be given (Impastato, 1966). If the patellar reflex persists 1 minute after the first 5-mg dose, a second 5-mg increment may be given, with continued reflex testing. By proceeding in this fashion, the safe dose of succinylcholine for that particular patient can be determined.

Emergence Delirium

About 5 to 10 percent of patients develop a short-lived delirium or acute confusional state as they emerge from the postictal state. Presumably the anesthesia, electrical stimulation, and seizure each contribute their part. Patients are restless, agitated, appear dazed, and mutter incoherently while fumbling with the bedclothes, rubbing their genitals in a stereotyped fashion, and incessantly and repeatedly attempting to climb out of bed. The physical restraint required to prevent this behavior only seems to make things worse. The delirium lasts from 15 to 30 minutes untreated and resembles nothing so much as a psychomotor seizure, which it may well be. It is readily terminated by intravenous methohexital or diazepam if a vein can be found and the patient held still long enough to inject it—both very unlikely propositions. Repeated episodes are likely to occur after each treatment in patients so disposed, making the best treatment prevention: 5 to 15 mg diazepam I.V. as soon as the induced seizure terminates. In the rare patient who fails to respond to such prophylaxis, the intravenous line can be left in place following the treatment and a 2-percent solution of methohexital infused at a rate sufficient to prevent the delirium from emerging. This procedure should be directly supervised by a physician or nurse-anesthetist.

Nausea or Vomiting

These are infrequent after ECT and can be prevented by dimenhydrinate, 50 mg I.M., given at the end of the seizure.

Headache

This occurs in about one-third of all patients after ECT and usually responds to aspirin or, if severe, ibuprofen.

Precautions and Contraindications

Drug Interactions

Reserpine is contraindicated in patients receiving ECT because several deaths and near-deaths due to cardiovascular collapse or respiratory depression have been reported with the combination (Foster and Gayle, 1955; Kalinowsky, 1956a; Bracha and Hess, 1956; Bross, 1957). Although the combination of chlorpromazine with ECT is believed to be safer (Berg, Gabriel and Impastato, 1959), a number of deaths and life-threatening incidents have also occurred with such coadministration (Weiss, 1955; Kalinowsky, 1956a, 1956b; Gaitz, Pokorny, and Mills, 1956; Grinspoon and Greenblatt, 1963), which must therefore be considered too dangerous to administer and in any case has no justification from controlled trials. If a neuroleptic must be combined with ECT (as in a manic patient who is early in the treatment course and has not yet responded adequately), haloperidol, fluphenazine, and thiothitene are good choices. As noted earlier, lithium should not be combined with ECT as it prolongs the neuromuscular blockade of succinylcholine (Hill, Wong, and Hodges, 1976) and has also been implicated in the causation of acute confusional states after ECT (Small et al., 1980; Weiner et al., 1980). The fact that Martin and Kramer (1982) treated a number of patients safely with this combination is irrelevant; there is no justification from controlled trials to support the use of the combination, however small the risk involved.

Tricyclic antidepressants may be safer than lithium or neuroleptic drugs in combination with ECT, although Freeman and Kendell (1980) noted that the only two deaths in a sample of 243 patients who received ECT occurred in patients with preexisting cardiac disease who were taking tricyclic antidepressants. Inasmuch as there is no controlled study demonstrating a synergistic effect of such combined therapy, and some evidence that it may actually antagonize the effects of ECT given alone (Price et al., 1978), there seems little reason to prescribe it.

Despite concerns frequently expressed over the safety of administering ECT to patients receiving MAOIs (Janowsky and Janowsky, 1985) the literature provides no specific evidence for an increased risk of such combined therapy (El-Ganzouri et al., 1985; Freese, 1987). Just as for tricyclics, however, no therapeutic advantage has been demonstrated for combining ECT and MAOIs.

A Stepwise Guide to the Technique of Administering ECT

The following is one specific sequence that I find useful in treating patients with ECT. It assumes that the patient has been properly prepared for treatment, as outlined earlier, and has received atropine or another appropriate anticholinergic premedication, that methohexital and succinylcholine syringes have been drawn up in advance in the appropriate dosages for each patient and labeled with the dose and the patient's name, and that the patient is lying on a stretcher in the treatment room, that vital signs have been recorded, and all necessary staff personnel are in attendance.

1. *Apply blood pressure cuff and record baseline blood pressure.* The same cuff will later be reinflated just prior to succinylcholine administration in order to block this drug from the muscles distal to the cuff and permit safe observation of the unmodified seizure. For this reason, if unilateral ECT is contemplated, the cuff should be applied initially to the arm ipsilateral to the placement of the unilateral treatment electrodes in order to document that a generalized, rather than a focal contralateral, seizure has occurred (Welch, 1982).

2. *Apply EKG electrodes.* The large self-stick EKG recording electrodes are applied precordially and to each shoulder (with a fourth applied anywhere for grounding) without any skin preparation. It saves time to apply them while the patient is waiting for treatment. The appropriate EKG leads are then connected and a baseline rhythm strip obtained.

3. *Apply EEG electrodes.* Disposable, pregelled, stick-on electrodes are now commercially available in a small size especially for EEG monitoring. They save time because they do not have to be smeared with electrode jelly first or cleaned up afterward, they will not pull loose during the seizure, and their adhesive surface allows them to be placed anywhere on the head rather than just under the perforated rubber headstrap, as does the older type that only permits recording from bifrontal forehead leads. This is a critical advantage for two reasons: 1) bifrontal placement is *least* effective for seizure monitoring because the EEG represents the *difference* in voltage between any two electrodes and there is very little difference between bifrontal leads, especially when the EEG signal is highly synchronous and symmetrical as during a seizure, and 2) bifrontal leads are incapable of differentiating focal contralateral seizures from generalized ones. Frontal-to-

mastoid electrodes on the same side of the head are preferred for EEG monitoring because they produce a large, easily read record and can be placed contralateral to the treatment electrodes during unilateral ECT to verify that a generalized seizure has occurred. (As for all monitoring of bioelectrical signals, a ground electrode is required and can conveniently be placed on the neck or shoulder.)

Patients should be instructed to shampoo their hair the night before and wash their faces with soap and water on treatment mornings. Careful rubbing of the skin over the recording sites with an alcohol-soaked swab followed by drying with a gauze pad is the only other preparation necessary to remove the oily residues and provide artifact-free recordings. The EEG leads are then connected; both available ECT instruments with EEG monitoring capability will automatically initiate monitoring when the stimulus is administered at the time of treatment.

4. *Start intravenous line.* An intravenous line is most conveniently started with a 19-gauge, thin-walled "butterfly" assembly attached to a saline-filled 20-ml syringe. When blood returns in the tubing it is flushed with a few milliliters of saline solution and clamped with a mosquito forceps until it is time to administer the anesthetic agents. (Alternatively, a continuous I.V. drip infusion may be started.)

5. *Apply treatment electrodes.* Two types of stainless steel disc electrodes (flat and slightly concave) are required to ensure a good fit under all anatomical configurations. Although esthetically less than pleasing, a properly applied perforated rubber headband ensures a firm electrode-to-skin coupling throughout the treatment procedure. The electrode sites should be carefully rubbed with alcohol and dried, and then rubbed again with a small amount of conductive electrode gel containing a mild abrasive (e.g., Omniprep™). The electrode treatment surfaces are then covered with a generous layer of conductive gel and applied firmly to the skin or scalp. Extra care must be taken to part the hair and expose the scalp when applying the upper unilateral ECT electrode in order to maximize contact. Clipping the hair to expose a circle of scalp is ideal for this purpose (Weiner et al., 1986), but is unlikely to be well-received by patients at non-Veteran's Administration facilities.

6. *Test impedance.*

7. *Administer methohexital.* While the patient counts aloud from 1 to 100, and after determining that the needle is still patent and in the vein, the saline syringe is replaced with one containing an initial dose of 0.75 mg/kg methohexital, which is then given by rapid bolus push

(Pitts, 1982). The methohexital dose may require adjustment for subsequent treatments depending on the patient's response to the initial injection.

8. *Inflate blood pressure cuff* to 10 mm Hg above the systolic pressure in order to occlude the succinylcholine to be administered next from reaching the distal muscles (Fink and Johnson, 1982).

9. *Administer succinylcholine.* As soon as the patient has stopped counting and is unresponsive to questions, the methohexital syringe is replaced by one containing an initial dose of 0.6 mg/kg succinylcholine, which is then also given by rapid bolus push. The empty syringe is then replaced with the saline syringe, and the tubing is flushed and clamped again for later availability in the event that additional intravenous therapy is required. The dose of succinylcholine may also require subsequent adjustment.

10. *Insert mouthguard and administer oxygen.* As soon as the succinylcholine has been given, the rubber mouthguard is inserted between the teeth and 100-percent oxygen is administered by positive pressure and continued throughout the treatment (including the seizure) until spontaneous respirations have returned.

11. *Observe muscular fasciculations* of the first (depolarization) phase of succinylcholine. These will appear first in the muscles of the head, neck, and upper chest, and spread to those of the trunk and limbs before reaching the small muscles of the feet and hands. When the fasciculations have died down in the small muscles of the feet (generally about 1 minute after the succinylcholine injection), the patient is ready to be treated. If the adequacy of muscle-relaxation is in doubt, abolition of the patellar reflex can provide complementary information. A more precise method for testing muscle-relaxation entails the use of a nerve–muscle stimulator set to provide intermittent pulses to a peripheral nerve (e.g., radial) at a rate of 1 or 2 per second. When the resultant muscle contraction response is abolished, muscle-relaxation is adequate.

12. *Administer the treatment stimulus.* When adequate muscle-relaxation has been achieved and the stimulus settings are adjusted according to the device manufacturer's recommendations, oxygenation is temporarily interrupted, the patient's head and neck are hyperextended with the jaw held tightly shut (a properly inserted mouthguard will automatically prevent the tongue from protruding between the teeth), and the stimulus is administered.

13. *Time the induced seizure.* The tonic and clonic muscular contractions observed in the cuffed limb provide a rough guide to the

occurrence and duration of the induced seizure. The EEG signal in its visual or auditory representations, however, remains the *sine qua non* of seizure monitoring because paroxysmal cerebral electrical activity can continue long after the motor convulsion has ceased. If an adequate seizure cannot be obtained, even after restimulation and at maximum device settings, no further stimuli should be given until the next treatment session, at which time consideration should be given to lowering the patient's seizure threshold with intravenous caffeine–sodium benzoate administered immediately following the methohexital injection, as described earlier in this chapter.

14. *Initiate routine postictal care.* After spontaneous respirations have returned and full ventilatory exchange has been established, the patient is wheeled on a stretcher to a recovery area to be observed by trained staff until alert, oriented, and able to walk without assistance. The main goal of postictal care is the maintenance of an airway. The patient should be turned on his side and carefully observed for any respiratory obstruction or distress. Stertorous breathing can be alleviated by hyperextending the neck with the jaw held tightly shut; excessive secretions may require suctioning, and the appropriate device should be maintained in readiness at all times in the recovery area. A manual assisted-respiration bag and mask (e.g., Ambu™) should also be available.

7

The Electroconvulsive Therapy Stimulus: Technical and Theoretical Considerations

Recognition of the importance of the physical charcteristics of the electrical stimulus for ECT historically has been biphasic: an initial peak from 1940 to 1955 was followed by a 20-year lull, with a second peak beginning around 1975 and increasing to the present. The lull coincided, of course, with the widespread reduction of ECT use following the introduction of the tricyclic and monoamine oxidase-inhibitor antidepressant drugs and ended with the realization among many clinicians that the widely heralded replacement of ECT with these agents and their derivatives had failed to materialize. Recent investigations into the nature of the electrical stimulus for ECT have built upon many of the principles elaborated during the early years, but with more precise quantification of their relation to cognitive and EEG effects.

A few basic electrical concepts are required to understand the properties of the ECT stimulus. Although all ECT devices utilize alternating current, some of the principles involved are more readily presented via the simpler situation that obtains for direct current. The primary variables of direct current electricity are voltage, current, and resistance, which are measured in units of volts, amperes, and ohms, respectively. *Voltage* is an electromotive force that drives the current of electrons through a conductor just as hydraulic pressure drives water through a pipe. The greater the resistance to the flow of current, the greater will be the voltage required to maintain the same current. Therefore, the flow of current through a conductor varies directly with the voltage and inversely with the resistance, a relationship known as *Ohm's Law* and expressed by the following equation:

$$\text{Current} = \text{voltage} / \text{resistance}$$

Energy

Energy is expressed as the product of voltage, current, and the duration of electron flow:

$$\text{Energy} = \text{voltage} \times \text{current} \times \text{time}$$

Since voltage = current × resistance (Ohm's law), the equation for determining the energy of a stimulus becomes:

$$\text{Energy} = \text{current}^2 \times \text{resistance} \times \text{time}$$

A stream of electrons flowing through a conductor dissipates energy (as heat) in proportion to the electromotive force (voltage drop) that drives it. If the current is kept constant, the higher the resistance, the more energy will be dissipated as the voltage rises in proportion to the resistance. Materials of low resistance (e.g., copper) conduct current with little dissipation of heat; those of high resistance (e.g., tungsten) dissipate more energy with the same passage of electrons—this is why tungsten and not copper is used for light bulb filaments.

Charge

Charge is the total quantity of electrons flowing through a conductor during a given period of time: it is the time integral of current. For a constant current, the charge is equal to the product of the current and its duration:

$$\text{Charge} = \text{current (in amperes)} \times \text{time (in seconds)}$$

The main difference in the principles governing the behavior of the alternating currents used to generate the ECT stimulus lies in the concept of *impedance*, which is analagous to direct current *resistance*. Impedance is a measure that includes resistance along with *capaci-*

tance (the property of being able to accumulate a charge) and *inductance* (the property of being able to induce an electromotive force, e.g., an electromagnetic field). Inductance does not occur during ECT because the brain contains no metal; as little is know about the capacitance of the brain during the passage of the ECT stimulus, it is generally assumed that the impedance during ECT is primarily attributable to resistance (e.g., Weaver et al., 1976; Sackeim et al., 1987a), making the necessary calculations easier (Ohm's law with regard to the electrical events during ECT can then be simply expressed as current = voltage/impedance); however, if the brain is capable of storing a significant charge during passage of the electrical stimulus [and this seems not at all unlikely, considering Maxwell's (1968) demonstration that the impedance during ECT varies with the voltage applied], the calculations provided later and by other authors on the relations among stimulus wave form, dosage, and seizure threshold may be inaccurate.

The amount of energy dissipated on and in the head during ECT largely depends on the impedance of extracerebral tissues and on the electrode-to-skin interface. The energy absorbed by the brain itself would be a useful measure of the stimulus because it is likely to be intimately related to any adverse cerebral effects consequent to ECT; unfortunately, no such separate measure is clinically obtainable.

The seizure with ECT is generated by the quantity (charge) of above-threshold electrons that flows through the brain, and it must be sufficient to depolarize cell membranes synchronously. The charge passing through the brain is related to the impedance of the head in a complex fashion. Most of the impedance is across the skull, estimated at 18,000 Ω/cm, compared with about 200 Ω/cm across the skin or brain (Weaver et al., 1976). Although the charge with a constant current device does not vary with the impedance, its distribution among the three compartments of scalp, skull, and brain will vary with the voltage. At low voltages there is insufficient force to drive enough current through the high-impedance skull to induce a seizure; most of it is shunted (short-circuited) between the electrodes via the scalp. As voltage increases, more and more current penetrates the skull to pass through the brain, increasing the likelihood of depolarizing enough neurons to induce a seizure.

This inverse relation for constant-current devices between seizure threshold (the charge required to induce a seizure) and patient impedance has been documented by Sackeim et al. (1987a). It results in the counterintuitive statement that the high-threshold patients in whom seizures are difficult to elicit are actually those with low impedances.

Stimulus Wave-Form

The electrical stimulus can be delivered in an infinite variety of forms, of which the two most common are the *sine wave* and *brief pulse*. Sine-wave currents are characterized by a continuously changing stream of electrons, flowing alternately in opposite directions, at a frequency of 50 to 60 wave-pairs (one negative, one positive) per second (Hertz, or Hz). This is the current wave-form that is universally supplied by wall outlets and was the first type to be used for ECT (Cerletti and Bini, 1938). The alternating rise and fall of the sine-wave current delivers substantial amounts of electrical stimulation below seizure threshold. Such below-threshold stimulation probably contributes little to seizure intensity or generalization, and, therefore, to the therapeutic effect, but may adversely affect memory functions (Ottosson, 1960).

The brief-pulse square-wave current was recognized early on to be a more efficient and physiological stimulus for inducing seizures (Merritt and Putnam, 1938). It rises and falls almost vertically, delivering all of its charge in about 1/1000 of a second and above the seizure threshold. The brief pulse is off (no charge flowing) during most of the time that the stimulus is administered. It induces seizures with substantially less charge and energy than do sine wave currents, achieving the same therapeutic effects with significantly less memory-loss and EEG abnormality (Weiner et al., 1986a, b). There may also be a cognitive advantage of the brief-pulse stimulus that is inherent to the wave-form itself and not to its reduced electrical charge, as Daniel et al. (1983) found a significant reduction in recent autobiographical amnesia with brief-pulse compared to sine-wave ECT that was *independent* of stimulus energy.

Sine-wave currents are now considered obsolete for ECT (Weaver and Williams, 1982), and the British government has ordered the replacement of all sine-wave devices in its National Health Service Hospitals with brief-pulse instruments (Health Notice, May 1982). The Ontario Psychiatric Association likewise recommends that all ECT instuments be of brief pulse rather than sine-wave type (Position Paper, 1985). For these reasons, and because of their increased neurotoxicity without increased therapeutic benefit (Weiner et al., 1986a, 1986b), sine-wave stimuli will not receive further consideration here.

Brief-pulse devices typically deliver a constant current, so the voltage varies with the impedance of the patient. As very high impedances would elicit very high voltages to drive the same current across the electrodes, markedly increasing the energy generated, all brief-pulse devices also limit the maximum possible voltage that can be applied. When this maximum is reached (e.g., 400 volts) the current will begin to decrease and, therefore, will no longer be "constant."

The brief-pulse square-wave stimulus can be described in terms of frequency, pulsewidth, and number of pulses. The standard stimulus is a train of *bidirectional* square waves, with each cycle consisting of one negative and one positive pulse. Thus, for this type of stimulus a frequency of 70 Hz delivers 140 pulses per second. For a typical pulsewidth of 1/1000 of a second (1 millisecond, msec), therefore, 1 second of stimulation will deliver 140 pulses of 1 msec each, or a total of 140 msec (0.14 seconds) of stimulation. The charge of this stimulus delivered by an instrument with a constant current of 0.9 amps is calculated as follows:

$$
\begin{aligned}
\text{charge} &= \text{current} \times \text{time} \\
&= 0.9 \text{ amps} \times 0.14 \text{ seconds} \\
&= 0.126 \text{ ampere-seconds} \\
&= 126 \text{ milliampere-seconds}
\end{aligned}
$$

(Ampere-seconds are known as *coulombs*, and milliampere-seconds as *millicoulombs*.)

The energy (in joules) of the same stimulus can only be calculated if the impedance is known or assumed, e.g., 200Ω. The equation is:

$$
\begin{aligned}
\text{Energy} &= (\text{current})^2 \times \text{impedance} \times \text{time} \\
&= 0.81 \text{ amp} \times 220 \ \Omega \times 0.14 \text{ sec} \\
&= 22.45 \text{ J}
\end{aligned}
$$

If the patient's impedance should double for the next treatment because the skin was not cleaned properly, the total stimulus energy would also double, suggesting to the unsophisticated operator that a greater stimulus had been delivered to the brain. Likewise, an ECT machine designed to deliver a stimulus determined by presetting the number of joules (a *constant energy* device) may produce numerous missed seizures if the skin is not well cleaned because stimulus duration will automatically fall as impedance rises (e.g., with oily skin), reducing the likelihood of obtaining a seizure.

Electrical Dosage and Seizure Threshold

Impedance to the electrical stimulus during ECT is primarily attributable to the patient, although corrosion may cause substantial impedances to develop for the stimulus leads delivering the current, their connectors, and the electrode discs themselves. During any given treatment, the high impedance of the skull relative to the skin and subcutaneous tissues causes 40 to 60 percent of the stimulus current to be shunted through the scalp (Weaver et al., 1976); the closer the treatment electrodes are placed to each other, the greater this shunt will be (e.g., as for unilateral ECT). The charge entering the brain is then distributed along the paths of least impedance, but as the various intracerebral components as a rule do not markedly differ in their ability to conduct electricity the overall effect is similar to that of a volume conductor (e.g., a bowl of Jell-O™). With bilateral ECT, current densities are greatest in the frontal poles, diminishing in more remote areas in proportion to the square root of the distance traversed; with unilteral ECT, current density is greatest in the pathway between the electrodes, across the surface of the brain (Weaver et al., 1976).

Measurement of patient impedance before administering the electrical stimulus for ECT provides important information on the quality of the skin-to-electrode contact: if the skin is oily, or if the electrodes are applied loosely or with inadequate conductive gel, a high impedance will be registered, informing the physician that his technique requires improvement. Such impedance testing is performed with a high frequency, very low milliamperage current that is undetectable by the patient. This procedure tests the *static* impedance, which is much higher than the *dynamic* impedance that would be recorded during the actual passage of the treatment stimulus. In one study of 756 brief-pulse square-wave ECTs received by 97 patients (American Psychiatric Association, 1982) dynamic impedances ranged from 120 to 520 Ω with a mean of 220 Ω and a 95-percent inclusive range of 155 to 340 Ω. Another study reported a range of 200 to 600 Ω with great intrasubject variability (Gordon, 1981). Since the dynamic impedance is so variable, can only be obtained after the fact, and is primarily a function of the voltage and frequency employed (Maxwell, 1968), it provides little clinically useful information.

In a careful comparison of dosage and seizure threshold with ECT, Sackeim et al. (1987b) measured the charge as well as the number of joules required to elicit a generalized seizure at just-above-threshold stimulus levels. A strong inverse relation was observed between the seizure threshold and the dynamic impedance: 48 percent of the variance in the seizure threshold could be accounted for in units of charge, compared to only 27 percent of the variance in units of joules. Moreover, units of joules were insensitive in detecting a rather strong gender difference in the seizure threshold that was demonstrated with the unit of charge (men had a higher threshold than women), and the authors concluded that for brief-pulse, constant-current stimulation, the unit of charge was superior to joules as a measure of ECT electrical dosage.

The likelihood of inducing a seizure varies directly with the charge passing through the brain and also, of course, with the energy. One study (American Psychiatric Association, 1982) of the brief-pulse square-wave stimulus during 2044 treatments showed that 70 J of energy were required to produce seizures with a virtually 100 percent probability. To maximize the likelihood of inducing a seizure in every patient, therefore, a brief-pulse ECT instrument must be capable of delivering at least 70 J of energy to a patient of 155 Ω dynamic impedance.

Ultrabrief Stimuli

The term *ultrabrief* describes pulsed stimuli of less than 0.5 msec duration. Cronholm and Ottosson (1963b) administered such stimuli with the Elther ES apparatus and obtained a smaller therapeutic effect in depression than with the higher energy Siemens Konvulsator III. As two quite different wave-forms were employed (the Siemens delivers a modified sine wave), it is unclear whether the wave-form or the energy differences account for the therapeutic discrepancy. Moreover, it was harder to get seizures with the Elther, suggesting that completeness of seizure generalization may have played a role. A similar criticism applies to a later study (Robin and De Tissera, 1982) that found a reduced therapeutic effect for ultrabrief pulsed spike stimulation (Ectonus "Duopulse") compared with pulsed square waves (Theratronic "Transpsycon"). Hyrman et al. (1985) was able to induce seizures in rabbits and a pig with 40–50 microsecond (0.04–0.05 msec) pulses, at frequencies of 100–300 Hz, generating only a fraction of the energy that would be expected from standard brief-pulse instruments. No human data are available for this technique as yet, but the much greater skull thickness and diameter in humans make it unlikely that seizures can reliably be induced with similar stimulus parameters.

8
Unilateral Electroconvulsive Therapy

Unilateral ECT represents the most important technical advance in the field of convulsive therapy since Cerletti and Bini (1938) introduced the electrical stimulus for seizure induction. More clinical research has been conducted since 1960 on the cognitive and therapeutic effects of this modality than on any other single topic in the ECT literature, yet controversy remains concerning the precise clinical role of this method in relation to the older bilateral ECT (Fink, 1979; Welch, 1982, Abrams and Fink, 1984; Abrams, 1986; Mathisen and Pettinati, 1987; Overall and Rhoades, 1986, 1987). This chapter will review the history and development of unilateral ECT, concentrating on studies of therapeutic efficacy in comparison with bilateral ECT; the cognitive studies will be considered in Chapter 10. Technical considerations that may lie at the root of the controversy will be discussed in detail, and specific clinical recommendations will be made for when to use unilateral, and when to use bilateral, ECT.

The early history of ECT research was largely characterized by attempts to reduce the side effects of seizures induced by the original sinusoidal currents as applied through bifrontotemporal electrodes. Only 3 years after the first English-language paper on ECT appeared (Kalinowsky, 1939), Friedman (1942) and Friedman and Wilcox (1942) published their results with unidirectional stimulating currents and left-sided unilateral electrode placement. These authors' primary interest was technical—to investigate the amount of electric current delivered—and they made no mention of therapeutic effects, memory-loss, or confusion. These studies were continued and expanded by Proctor and Goodwin (1943), Liberson (1944) (who introduced the brief-pulse square-wave stimulus, calling it *brief-stimulus therapy*, and was also the first to use right-side unilateral ECT placement), Liberson and Wilcox (1945), Moriarty and Siemens (1947), Medlicott (1948), and Liberson (1948). A variety of electrode placements were used (most of them right-unilateral), but not systematically, and these authors all reported reduced cognitive side effects with their new techniques.

Goldman (1949) was the first to specify that unilateral treatment electrodes should be placed over the right hemisphere in order to avoid the speech areas. In 112 patients he observed clinical improvement equal to that produced by bilateral ECT with a "marked diminution and, at times, absence of confusion associated with the electric shock therapy." His attribution of the beneficial effect to the brief-pulse square-wave stimulus he used was only partly correct—right-unilateral electrode placement probably played the more important role. Bayles et al. (1950) confirmed these results with brief-stimulus right-unilateral ECT and also reported reduced EEG effects compared with sine-wave ECT. Workers into the mid-1950s (Blaurock et al., 1950; Impastato et al., 1953; Liberson, 1953; Liberson et al., 1956) continued to report reduced memory-loss and confusion with unilateral placements, particularly right-sided ones, but they never attempted to separate the effects of stimulus type from electrode placement, or to characterize the specific benefits accruing from right-unilateral placement.

The Argentine psychiatrist Thenon (1956) was the first to demonstrate the specific link between right-unilateral electrode placement and reduced memory-loss and confusion; he also observed an accentuation of post-ECT slow wave EEG activity over the treated hemisphere. He called his method *monolateral electroshock*. Two years later, Lancaster, Steinert, and Frost (1958), apparently entirely unaware of Thenon's work, published the first English-language paper on this technique, giving it its present name of *unilateral ECT*. Their study was also notable for employing random assignment to treatment and blind assessment of depression and orientation using rating scales. In 21 patients receiving unilateral ECT, orientation and recall returned significantly faster than in 15 controls who received bilateral ECT. Moreover, they observed automatic behavior, dazed expression, and restlessness to be less prominent after unilateral ECT. They reported that four bilateral ECTs reduced depression scores by 71 percent, which compared with 54 percent for unilateral ECT (n.s.), noted "slightly better and more complete remission" with bilat-

eral ECT, and therefore recommended that bilateral ECT be preferentially given to involutional depressives, patients who were actively
suicidal, depressed patients who failed to show substantial improvement after six unilateral ECTs, and to catatonic schizophrenics who
were "dangerously impulsive" (these latter patients might well receive
a diagnosis of acute mania today). This report of Lancaster, Steinert,
and Frost (1958) already contained each of the elements of what later
was to become "the unilateral ECT controversy": 1) sharply reduced
memory-loss and confusion with unilateral ECT, 2) a formal equivalence for right-unilateral and bilateral ECT on objective outcome
measures, and 3) the authors' clinical impression that bilateral ECT
was nonetheless more therapeutically potent than right-unilateral
ECT.

By 1972 there were 15 published comparisons of unilateral and
bilateral ECT, of which only five unequivocally reported the two
methods to be equally therapeutic (Abrams, 1972). Most workers,
although finding the methods equally effective on the objective measures of rating scale scores or the total number of ECT prescribed by a
"blind" psychiatrist, nevertheless added their clinical impressions to
the effect that unilateral ECT was less rapidly effective, had to be given
more frequently or required more total treatments (Cannicott, 1962;
Halliday et al., 1968; Cronin et al., 1970; d'Elia, 1970), and that bilateral ECT was globally more effective or was to be preferred in patients
who were more severely ill, endogenously depressed, suicidal, catatonic, or dangerous (Lancaster, Steinert, and Frost, 1958; Levy, 1968;
Halliday et al., 1968; Small et al., 1970; Fleminger et al., 1970a;
Cronin et al., 1970).

By 1975 d'Elia and Raotma could find 24 published comparisons
of unilateral and bilateral ECT, which they tabulated for research
findings and clinical impressions. If one corrects their misidentifica-
tion of the Martin et al. (1965) study as showing unilateral ECT to be
"decidedly more effective" (these authors actually found the two methods to be equally potent), then 12 studies reported equal efficacy, 11
reported an advantage for bilateral ECT, and one an advantage for
unilateral ECT ($\chi^2 = 9.25$, $p < 0.001$).

Even among the studies finding approximate global equivalence
for the two methods on objective measures, there are large differences
that favor bilateral ECT in certain clinically important subgroups.
Thus, Cronin et al. (1970) found that 6 bilateral ECTs reduced depression scale scores in endogenous depressives by 72 percent as compared
with 35 percent for unilateral ECT, and Strömgren (1973) found a

statistically significant advantage for bilateral ECT in relieving depression in patients over age 44.

Considering its marked cognitive advantages over bilateral ECT, right-unilateral ECT is used far less widely than might be expected. A 1976 survey of its members conducted by the American Psychiatric Association Task Force on Electroconvulsive Therapy (APA, 1978) revealed that 75 percent used bilateral ECT exclusively and that fewer than 10 percent of all patients received unilateral ECT. In a 1975–1976 survey of ECT usage in New York City, Asnis et al. (1978) reported that 83 percent of the respondents used bilateral ECT exclusively. In Great Britain, Gill and Lamborn (1979) found that 50 percent of the senior psychiatric consultants preferred bilateral ECT; Pippard and Ellam's (1981) survey 2 years later found that 80 percent of all clinicians "rarely or never" used unilateral ECT. Unilateral ECT is probably most widely used in the Scandinavian countries, but even there only 25 percent of the Danish centers (Heshe and Roeder, 1976) and 50 percent of the Swedish centers (Fredericksen and d'Elia, 1979) used unilateral ECT exclusively at the time they were surveyed.

The many studies demonstrating therapeutic equivalence for unilateral and bilateral ECT have been reviewed by d'Elia and Raotma (1975) and Fink (1979). Contrary data have been less well-publicized (Abrams, 1986), however, and the following selective review describes in more detail each of the random assignment, double-blind, controlled studies that report a statistically significant advantage for bilateral over different types of unilateral ECT (or, in one instance, for flurothyl over unilateral ECT).

Strain et al. (1968) assigned 96 hospitalized depressives to right-unilateral or bilateral ECT and assessed the outcome under double-blind conditions. Forty percent of the right-unilateral ECT group required 10 or more treatments, compared with 17 percent of the bilateral group. The bilateral ECT group improved substantially more on the two Clyde mood scale factors found to be the most valid indicators of depression—*unhappy* and *dizzy*—and the right-unilateral ECT group required an average of 1 extra treatment and a stay of 2 days longer in the hospital.

Abrams and Taylor (1974) treated 30 melancholics with either 1 bilateral ECT, 2 right-sided unilateral ECTs, or 1 right- followed by 1 left-sided unilateral ECT each treatment session. On assessment by Hamilton rating scale 4 bilaterally induced seizures produced the same therapeutic effect as 8 seizures induced by either of the 2 unilateral methods over the same period of time.

In a different sample of patients, Abrams and Taylor (1976) assigned 20 melancholics to receive 6 seizures either with bilateral placement or 2 sets of unilateral electrodes separately and simultaneously applied to both sides of the head. After 6 treatments the bilateral ECT group exhibited significantly lower depression scale scores, and 91 percent of the patients in the left-right unilateral group went on to receive additional treatments, compared with only one-third of the bilateral group.

Reichert et al. (1976) assigned 50 patients with varied diagnoses to unilateral or bilateral ECT and found a significant advantage for the latter method at several points during the treatment course on a self-rated mood scale. Significantly more patients in the unilateral group also required an additional course of ECT within 6 months after terminating treatment.

Heshe et al. (1978) treated 51 endogenous depressives with either right-unilateral or bilateral ECT and rated their global outcome 1 week and 3 months after the treatment course. At the 1-week rating more than one-third of the right-unilateral ECT patients were scored "unimproved" compared with none in the bilateral group (exact $p = 0.01$). No differences were found at 3 months. For patients over age 60, more than 50 percent of those given unilateral ECT were rated "unimproved" at 1 week, compared with none in the bilateral group (exact $p = 0.003$), and at 3 months 75 percent of the unilateral ECT patients were rated "unimproved" compared with 30 percent of the bilateral ECT group (exact $p = 0.003$).

Abrams et al. (1983) assigned 51 melancholics to right-unilateral or bilateral ECT and monitored all treatments by EEG. Hamilton Depression Scale scores after 6 ECTs were reduced by 81 percent in the bilateral group compared with only 56 percent in the right-unilateral group. Moreover, right-unilateral ECT patients required an average of about 3 more treatments, more often required a course of treatment in excess of 9 ECTs, and were more frequently switched to the alternate form of treatment by a psychiatrist who was blind to treatment assignment.

Malitz et al. (1986) assigned 52 primary major depressives to right-unilateral or bilateral ECT, both administered with just-above-threshold stimulation. Hamilton Depression Scale scores obtained before treatment and after the sixth and the final ECT showed much greater improvement with bilateral than right-unilateral ECT (70 percent improvement for bilateral ECT after the full course, compared with only 37 percent with right-unilateral ECT), a result also confirmed when global outcome ratings were used to divide patients into treatment *responders* and *nonresponders* (right-unilateral ECT was associated with a strikingly high nonresponse rate of 34 percent). Despite the low-dose electrical stimulation, EEG seizure duration was the same in both groups and similar to that usually reported for conventional bilateral ECT.

Gregory et al. (1985) treated 60 depressives with either bilateral, right-unilateral, or sham ECT. Both genuine methods were superior to sham ECT, an advantage that appeared after the second bilateral ECT but not until after the fourth unilateral ECT. Moreover, unilateral ECT patients required significantly more treatments after their sixth than did those in the bilateral group.

Crowe et al. (in press) assigned 23 patients with major depressive disorder to right-unilateral or bilateral ECT administered either 3 or 5 times a week. Assessments on the Hamilton and Carroll depression scales after 8 ECTs revealed a significantly better therapeutic effect for bilateral ECT. After the eighth ECT patients in the unilateral group also went on to receive significantly more additional treatments than those in the bilateral group. Seizure duration monitored by EEG was the same for both groups.

Although not a random-assignment study, the recent report of Tandon et al. (in press) is of interest because it was prospective and assessed outcome blindly. These authors studied 46 medication-resistant depressives who had received bilateral (the first 30 patients) or right-unilateral (the next 16 patients) ECT with blind weekly evaluations performed on the Hamilton scale during the treatment course. After 5 treatments bilateral ECT induced a 57 percent improvement compared with only 19 percent in the right-unilateral group. Global assessments after the full course of ECT showed 72 percent of the bilateral group to be fully recovered, compared with 32 percent of the unilateral group. This advantage for bilateral ECT was also observed when seizure length was equivalent for the 2 methods.

Sebag-Montefiore (1974) assigned 104 primary depressives to unilateral ECT or flurothyl-induced seizures and found a significant advantage for the latter method after 4 seizures. This paper is included here because flurothyl-induced seizures are therapeutically equal to those obtained with bilateral ECT (Fink et al., 1961; Laurell, 1970).

Thus, 9 methodologically sound studies report a statistically significant therapeutic advantage for bilateral over various forms of unilateral ECT in depression, and 1 study shows such an advantage for flurothyl. Of 14 controlled trials in depression completed since d'Elia and Raotma's (1975) paper, (Abrams and Taylor, 1974; Abrams and Taylor, 1976; Reichert et al., 1976; Heshe et al., 1978; Weeks et al., 1980; Fraser and Glass, 1980; Abrams et al., 1983; Horne et al., 1985; Gregory et al., 1985; Weiner et al., 1986; Malitz et al., 1986; Welch et al., 1982; Crowe et al., in press; Tandon et al., in press), 8 favor bilateral ECT.

The results of sham ECT studies are also instructive: of 12 comparisons of the efficacy of genuine versus sham ECT in the treatment of depression (Ulett et al., 1956; Harris and Robin, 1960; Robin and Harris, 1962; Wilson et al., 1963; McDonald et al., 1966; Lambourne and Gill, 1978; Freeman et al., 1978; Johnstone et al., 1980; West, 1981; Brandon et al., 1984; Ghangadar et al., 1982; Gregory et al., 1985) 11 used bilateral placement as the active treatment and found an advantage for genuine ECT; the single study that compared right-unilateral ECT with sham ECT (Lambourn and Gill, 1978) found no such advantage. Finally, meta-analysis, a statistical method for integrating the results from diverse studies on a single topic, has been used to review the unilateral versus bilateral ECT literature. Although Janicak et al. (1985) and Pettinati et al. (1986) both used meta-analytic procedures to arrive at the conclusion that the two electrode placements were equally effective in treating depressed patients, Overall and Rhoades (1986, 1987) reanalyzed both studies using three different meta-analytic techniques, each of which revealed statistical significance in favor of bilateral ECT in the relief of depression.

In sum, therefore, several points seem clear:

1. For many depressed patients right-unilateral and bilateral ECT appear to be therapeutically interchangeable.
2. For some patients, right-unilateral ECT produces less improvement in depression than bilateral ECT and requires more treatments to achieve the same outcome.
3. A few patients who do not respond to even substantial numbers of unilateral ECTs (e.g., 10 to 20 treatments) may nevertheless achieve a remission when switched to bilateral ECT (Price, 1981; Abrams et al., 1983).
4. Confusion and memory-loss consequent to right-unilateral ECT are much less than for bilateral ECT and may be clinically indetectable.

The following considerations may help to account for the discrepant findings among the various studies reviewed (Abrams, 1986a, 1986b).

Diagnosis. Endogenous depression (melancholia) constitutes the prime indication for ECT and is the diagnostic group most likely to show between-group differences in any treatment comparisons. For example, as cited earlier, Cronin et al., (1970) found bilateral ECT to induce substantially more improvement than right-unilateral ECT in melancholics but not in reactive depressives. Unfortunately, many comparisons of unilateral and bilateral ECT do not specify the proportion of melancholics in their samples, or report the treatment results separately for this diagnostic group.

Age. As previously noted, in her 1973 monograph, Strömgren reported a statistically significant advantage for bilateral over unilateral ECT in patients over 44 years of age, a result later confirmed by Heshe et al. (1978) for patients over age 60. In the recent meta-analytic review cited earlier by Pettinati et al. (1986) a trend was uncovered for older patients to show a larger bilateral > right-unilateral ECT advantage.

Sex. The same meta-analytic review found an even stronger trend for men to exhibit larger bilateral > right-unilateral ECT differences than women. Sackeim et al. (1987b) reported that the seizure threshold is about 50 percent higher in men than in women.

Electrical dosage. The study reporting the largest bilateral > right-unilateral ECT advantage (Malitz et al., 1986) used the lowest electrical dosage, as determined by a titration procedure that resulted in just-above-threshold stimulation.

Interelectrode distance for unilateral ECT. The original suggestion by d'Elia and Raotma (1975) that smaller interelectrode distances for unilateral placements resulted in a smaller therapeutic effect was also examined in the meta-analytic study of Pettinati et al. (1986). The effect was significant: a larger bilateral > unilateral advantage occurred in studies using smaller interelectrode distances for unilateral ECT.

Relevance of technique. Is the therapeutic advantage sometimes reported for bilateral ECT simply a result of poor technique in administering unilateral ECT, so that inadequate seizures and a reduced therapeutic effect are obtained? That is, would monitoring of seizures in those studies reporting an advantage for bilateral ECT have revealed shorter, incomplete, or abortive seizures in the unilateral ECT groups and thus a reduced effect? This is a plausible but untenable argument. The reasoning would of course apply primarily to the earlier studies reviewed by Abrams (1972) and d'Elia and Raotma (1975), as seizure monitoring was not a routine part of ECT when those studies were conducted. But virtually all of these studies showed *equal* therapeutic effects of bilateral and unilateral ECT on blindly obtained objective outcome measures, so that inadequate technique with unilateral ECT can hardly have played a role in the investigators' concomitant clinical impressions that bilateral ECT was somehow more effective.

In a hypothesis published in 1986 (Abrams, 1986a), I tried to explain how age, gender, electrical dosage, and unilateral ECT inter-electrode distances might interact to influence the likelihood of finding a therapeutic advantage for bilateral ECT. Seizure threshold and intracerebral current density both vary with changes in each of these factors and are themselves related (a sufficient quantity of electricity, or charge, must enter the brain in order to exceed the seizure threshold; therefore, reducing electrical dosage has the same effect on obtaining seizures as increasing the threshold). Seizure threshold increases with age and is higher in men than in women (Sackeim et al., 1987c). Intracerebral current densities are reduced with smaller inter-electrode distances (Weaver et al., 1976), and of course, with low-dose stimulation. Relevant in this context is the report that seizure threshold is higher with bilateral than unilateral ECT (Sackeim et al., 1986), requiring a larger electrical charge to be introduced into the brain to elicit seizures with the former method.

What effect does the intensity of the electrical stimulus have on the seizure and the therapeutic effect of ECT in depression? Evidence for a therapeutic effect of the stimulus was found by Ottosson (1960) in a comparison of the clinical efficacy of moderately and markedly suprathreshold stimuli. On all measures of improvement the markedly suprathreshold group fared better—a difference that was statistically significant only for the improvement in depression score per second of seizure discharge in patients who received four or fewer treatments. Abrams and Taylor (1976) found that conventional bilateral ECT was significantly more effective in relieving depression than simultaneous left- and right-sided unilateral ECT. They interpreted their findings in terms of differential intracerebral distribution of the stimulating currents and resultant seizure activity and proposed that the therapeutic differences observed were due to greater diencephalic (specifically, hypothalamic) stimulation with bilateral ECT. Robin and De Tissera (1982) compared high and low energy brief pulse ECT and found a significantly greater therapeutic effect for high energy stimulation at every post-ECT assessment interval. Evidence for greater cerebral stimulation with bilateral than unilateral ECT comes from Swartz and Abrams (1984) who demonstrated that bilateral ECT releases more prolactin into the bloodstream than unilateral ECT, a finding confirmed by Papakostas et al. (1984) and by Swartz (1985) in a sample of women. Observations (Abrams and Swartz, 1985) that the electrical stimulus can release prolactin in the absence of an observable motor or EEG seizure, and that multiple electrical stimuli tend to release more prolactin than single ones, provide further evidence for a physiological effect of the stimulus current.

The electrical stimulus might contribute to the therapeutic effect of ECT by a direct effect on the brain by either influencing the intensity or the generalization of the induced seizure activity, or both. Ottosson's (1960) finding of a greater therapeutic effect per seizure second with markedly rather than with moderately suprathreshold stimulation, albeit only in patients who received small numbers of treatments, suggests that the larger electrical stimulus acted by affecting the intensity or generalization of the induced seizure activity. More intense or completely generalized seizures are followed by greater immediate postictal EEG suppression: Ottosson's (1960) comparison of seizures with and without lidocaine modification showed that lidocaine-modified seizures often failed to terminate in the usual EEG phase of electrical silence (postictal suppression). Postictal EEG suppression is greater with bilateral than with unilateral ECT (Small et al., 1970; Abrams et al., 1973; Weiner et al., 1986), presumably because the larger charge of electricity bilateral ECT introduces into the brain results in more intense or generalized seizures. Greater seizure generalization with bilateral ECT is also suggested by the recent finding of Swartz and Larson (1986) that the correlation between each pair of four separate estimates of seizure duration (motor activity, heart rate, and two EEG measures) was significantly greater with bilateral than with unilateral ECT, by the report of fewer missed or abortive seizures with bilateral than unilateral ECT (Pettinati and Nilsen, 1985), and by the finding that bilateral ECT is associated with a greater cardiac response than unilateral ECT (Lane et al., in preparation). Of course, the previously cited data on the different prolactin-releasing effects of bilateral and unilateral ECT can also be interpreted in terms of seizure generalization.

Seizure intensity or generalization and differences in intracerebral current densities are reflected in the interictal as well as in the immediate postictal EEG. There are several reports of accentuation of unilateral ECT-induced EEG slowing ipsilateral to the treated hemi-sphere (Martin et al., 1965; Zamora and Kaelbling, 1965; Sutherland et al., 1969; Abrams et al., 1970; Volavka et al., 1972); less well-known is the documented tendency for left-hemispheric accentuation of EEG slowing after bilateral ECT (Green, 1957; Marjerrison et al., 1975; Abrams et al., 1970; Volavka et al., 1971; Abrams et al., 1987; Weiner et al., in preparation). This differential lateralization of EEG slowing with unilateral and bilateral ECT is age-related, with increasing age associated with a relative reduction of left versus right hemisphere frequencies (Volavka et al., 1972). Moreover, as noted in Chapter 4, Abrams et al. (1987) have recently documented a relationship between the direction of ECT-induced lateral EEG symmetry change and clinical response such that the greater the abundance of left-relative to right-hemispheric slowing induced by ECT, the greater the percentage drop in depression scale score. The findings have been generally supported in the topographic multichannel EEG studies of Weiner et al. (in preparation).

Sackeim et al. (1987a) have suggested that the degree to which the electrical stimulus exceeds the seizure threshold may be critical for the fully developed therapeutic effect of a given treatment. I suggested (Abrams, 1986b) that the seizure and the electrical stimulus both contribute to the therapeutic activity of ECT in depression. Once a seizure with well-developed polyspike (tonic) and polyspike-and-slow-wave (clonic) phases occurs its therapeutic effect does not depend on its duration, but on how intense, complete, or well-generalized throughout the brain the seizure activity is. At substantially suprathreshold levels of stimulation the therapeutic effect attributable to the electrical stimulus is dwarfed by the effects of the fully generalized seizure. With reduced electrical dosage or elevated seizure threshold, however, therapeutic effects of the stimulus emerge. Under these circumstances bilateral ECT introduces more electrical charge into a larger and differently distributed volume of brain than unilateral ECT, resulting in more efficient seizure generalization, greater diencephalic stimulation, a relative decrease of left versus right hemisphere EEG frequencies, and more rapid or complete relief of depression. Common to both views of the therapeutic role of the electrical stimulus, however, is the notion that increasing the stimulus charge with unilateral ECT should result in an increased therapeutic effect; indeed, data from two studies now in progress (H. Sackeim, personal communication; Abrams and Swartz, 1986) suggests that this is indeed the case.

Discussion

It is a cornerstone of scientific psychiatry that an intimate relationship exists between brain function and behavior. In many ways, modern psychiatry can be viewed as the study of the abnormal aspects of this relationship, which is also subsumed under the rubric *behavioral neurology*. In this context it would certainly be unexpected if two treatment methods, unilateral and bilateral ECT, with such different effects on various parameters of cerebral activity, nevertheless had identical effects on the melancholic syndrome, which is surely another manifestation of brain (dys)function.

In their influential review, d'Elia and Raotma (1975) concluded that unilateral ECT was "the treatment of choice in endogenous depression," a sentiment subsequently echoed in various ways by other reviewers and investigators (American Psychiatric Association, 1978; Squire, 1982; Strömgren, 1984; Horne et al., 1985). The present review suggests that such assertions are premature and do not consider all of the available data. A more appropriate focus would attempt to elucidate the precise clinical differences between the two methods so that a fuller understanding might be provided of their relative risks and benefits. Such an assessment is now more critical than ever, due to recent reports of persistent amnesia with bilateral ECT (Squire, 1986; Weiner et al., 1986). An accurate understanding of the relative therapeutic effects of the two methods is no less important than that for their amnesic effects, for if a patient who might have recovered with bilateral ECT commits suicide after receiving unilateral ECT (Gambill and McLean, 1983), any cognitive advantages of the latter method are rendered moot.

Clinical Recommendations

The pronounced cognitive advantages of unilateral over bilateral ECT have been extensively documented (Chapter 9) and constitute nothing less than a mandate for using this method in preference to bilateral ECT wherever clinically feasible (Abams and Fink, 1984). Such a policy is rendered even more compelling by the recent evidence alluded to earlier that bilateral ECT, but not unilateral ECT, can produce deficits in autobiographical memory that persist at least 6 months post-ECT (Weiner et al., 1986; Squire et al., 1985). Unilateral ECT administered with substantially suprathreshold, brief-pulse, square-wave stimuli should be given an initial trial in every patient for whom ECT is prescribed, with the following exeptions:

1. Melancholic patients who are severely agitated, delusional, or suicidal.
2. Patients in acute mania.
3. Patients in catatonic stupor.
4. Patients with concomitant medical conditions whose high-risk status mandates the fewest possible anesthesia inductions.

If 4 to 6 unilateral ECTs do not elicit a substantial degree of improvement a switch should be made to bilateral ECT. Conversely, once a patient in categories 1–3 above has shown a substantial response to initial treatment with 3 to 4 bilateral ECTs the patient may be switched to unilateral ECT for the remainder of the treatment course.

9

Memory and Cognitive Functioning After Electroconvulsive Therapy

Several aspects of cerebral functioning are affected for varying durations by ECT, depending, in part, on the number and frequency of the induced seizures, the anatomical placement of the stimulating electrodes, and the wave-form and charge of the electrical stimulus. During the immediate postictal period, patients experience a period of *confusion* and *neurological dysfunction*, occasionally progressing to *delirium*, that results from the combined effects of atropine premedication, barbiturate narcosis, electrical stimulation, and the induced seizure. After the postictal confusion has cleared, two specific types of memory impairment can be demonstrated: a *retrograde amnesia* for events preceding the seizure, and an *anterograde amnesia* for events following it. *Nonmemory cognitive impairment* is also readily detectable in the interictal period using various modern neuropsychological procedures. Finally, patients may experience *subjective memory dysfunction* that may or may not be objectively detectable. Studies of the various aspects of ECT-induced disruption of functioning naturally divide themselves into those conducted during the immediate postictal period and those conducted after full alertness and orientation have been reestablished.

Confusion

Although the imprecise term confusion as generally applied to ECT subsumes mainly disorientation, a patient recovering consciousness from ECT understandably exhibits multiform abnormalities of *all* aspects of thinking, feeling, and behaving, including disturbed memory, impaired comprehension, automatic movements, a dazed facial expression, and motor restlessness. The term *disorientation* is also misleading as its "time, place, and person" components are actually memories, some recent (e.g., age and date), and some remote (e.g., name). True orientation, that is, the ability to properly locate one's self in space and time solely by environmental cues, has not been studied with regard to ECT.

Lunn and Trolle (1949) studied 21 patients during a 2-hour post-ECT period at intervals of 10, 30, 60, and 120 minutes. Personal orientation items of *name* and *marital state* were most resistant to the effects of ECT. At the 10-minute assessment interval 90 percent of the patients could give their name, while only 10 percent could give their age, nicely demonstrating a temporal gradient of retrograde amnesia because a lifetime elapses between the learning of these two variables. Improvement in all functional areas was rapid but only reached 100 percent accuracy by the end of the 2-hour interval for items testing agnosia, visual perception, and apraxia. At the same test interval, 5 items of time orientation were responded to with less than 60-percent accuracy. Daniel and Crovitz' (1986) observation of a close correspondence between the curves for postical recovery of these orientation items and the temporal resolution of retrograde amnesia reported by Cronholm and Lagergren (1959) is consistent with the view that conventional tests of orientation simply measure memory.

Wilcox (1955) administered various tests of intellectual functioning at 15, 30, and 45 minutes post-ECT in 51 patients and confirmed Lunn and Trolle's (1949) results, reporting that memory for *name* was present in 97 percent of the observations made immediately upon awakening, but that memory for *time* was often still impaired when tested 45 minutes later. Mowbray (1959) studied the recovery of consciousness after ECT in 30 patients by a method of continuous systematic interrogation from the period of postical stupor to the reestablishment of full consciousness. Again, memory for *name* was present almost immediately, followed in short order by *address, marital status,* and *birthplace,* whereas memory for *age, year,* and *date* was not restored until an average elapsed time of slightly more than 45 minutes. Similar results were obtained by later investigators (Lancaster et al., 1958; Daniel and Crovitz, 1986).

The temporal gradient for memories affected during the postictal recovery period was demonstrated in a different way by Rochford and Williams (1962), who asked patients emerging from ECT to name a series of simple common objects, the names of which are acquired at different ages in childhood. Whereas a *comb* (a word usually learned by 4 years of age) could be named by about 90 percent of patients shortly after being able to give their own names, the *teeth* of the comb (not learned until about 11 years of age) could not be named until 12 minutes later.

Relation to Treatment Electrode Placement

Early workers were unanimous in describing less postictal confusion after unilateral than bilateral ECT (Goldman, 1949; Bayles et al., 1950; Blaurock et al., 1950; Impastato and Pacella, 1952; Liberson, 1953; Liberson et al., 1956; Thenon, 1956; Lancaster et al., 1958; Cannicott, 1962; Impastato and Karliner, 1966), although their reports can be faulted for lack of a systematic methodology and for confounding the effects of electrode placement with stimulus type (usually brief-pulse). Numerous subsequent investigators have used the time required post-ECT for the return of full orientation to more precisely measure the confusion induced by different treatment techniques (Gottlieb and Wilson, 1965; Valentine et al., 1968; Halliday et al., 1968; Sutherland et al., 1969; d'Elia, 1970; Fraser and Glass, 1980; Daniel and Crovitz, 1986). With the exception of the study of Gottlieb and Wilson (1965), their results confirm the earlier observations that reorientation occurs more rapidly after right-unilateral ECT than after bilateral ECT. Moreover, investigators including a left-unilateral ECT group for comparison reported that this method, along with bilateral ECT, was associated with *slower* reorientation or more postictal confusion than right-unilateral ECT (Halliday et al., 1968; Sutherland et al., 1969; Cronin et al., 1970; d'Elia, 1970). A similar advantage for right-unilateral ECT is obtained when patients emerging from ECT are required to recall words or sentences learned shortly before the seizure (Lancaster et al., 1958; Cannicott and Waggoner, 1967; Valentine et al., 1968).

Most recently, Sackeim et al. (1986b) studied time to reorientation in a sample of depressives receiving brief-pulse right-unilateral or bilateral ECT with stimulus charge titrated to just-above-threshold levels. With this low-dosage technique, recovery of full orientation was rapid in both treatment groups, but significantly more so after right-unilateral (mean = 8.6 minutes) than after bilateral ECT (mean = 26.7 minutes). Spontaneous respirations also returned significantly earlier after unilateral than bilateral ECT.

Relation to Electrical Stimulus

In addition to assigning patients randomly to unilateral or bilateral electrode placements, two groups of investigators also split assignment by stimulus type: sine-wave or brief-pulse (Valentine et al., 1968; Daniel and Crovitz, 1986). The method of statistical analysis employed by Valentine et al. (1968) does not permit a precise separation of the effects on postictal reorientation of the two treatment variables. Reorientation, however, always occurred earlier after brief-pulse than after sine-wave stimulation. Daniel and Crovitz (1986) used analysis of variance to separate treatment effects, and found that full orientation was regained significantly earlier after brief-pulse than after sine-wave stimulation, an effect separate from the equally significant advantage described earlier for unilateral over bilateral electrode placement. In neither of these studies is it possible to determine whether stimulus *type* (sine-wave versus brief-pulse) or stimulus *intensity* (electrical charge delivered) is the critical intervening variable with regard to postictal confusion.

Neurological Dysfunction

Transient neurological abnormalities, including aphasias, apraxias, and agnosias, were noted by early clinicians to occur during the immediate postictal phase following bilateral ECT (Hemphill, 1940; Kalinowsky, 1945; Gallinek, 1952; Kane, 1963), but were never systematically investigated. Jargon aphasia has been reported after left-unilateral ECT (Gottlieb and Wilson, 1965), as have other dysphasias (Pratt et al., 1971; Annet et al., 1974; Clyma, 1975), all generally resolving within 30 minutes after treatment. The only systematic study is that of Kriss et al. (1978), who performed neurological examinations on 29 dextral patients before and immediately after each of 62 left- or right-unilateral ECTs. Asymmetrical motor responses observed during the seizure usually consisted of more intense clonic movements of the musculature contralateral to the stimulated hemisphere, despite the induction of a generalized, bilateral seizure. Following the seizure, and before recovery of consciousness, upper limb reflexes ipsilateral to the treated hemisphere generally returned first. Limb strength tested after the return of consciousness revealed upper limb weakness or flaccid paresis contralateral to the treated side in 80 percent of the observations, with a gradual return to normal over the ensuing 15 minutes. Motor and visual inattention contralateral to the treated side also occurred, as well as corresponding tactile inattention. All patients receiving left-sided ECT showed signs of dysphasia (dysnomia) immediately afterward. Overall, patients took longer to respond and to open their eyes after left- than right-unilateral ECT, supporting claims for the major role played by the dominant hemisphere in the maintenance and manifestation of consciousness. Anosognosia (unawareness or denial of impairment) was profound and striking after right-unilateral ECT, even after patients had become fully alert and cooperative. All of these neurological abnormalities resolved within about 20 minutes post-ECT.

Delirium

Although postictal (*emergence*) delirium (see Chapter 6) regularly occurs in patients receiving ECT (Fink, 1979; Abrams and Essman, 1982) it has received scant attention in the literature. Sackeim et al. (1983) described two patients who manifested transient postictal delirium after bilateral and right-unilateral ECT (but not after left-unilateral ECT), exhibiting agitation, restlessness, clouded sensorium, disorientation, and failure to respond to commands. Based on these cases and on a proposed similarity to acute confusional states occurring after right middle cerebral artery infarction, these authors proposed that postictal delirium reflected a primary disruption of right-sided cerebral systems with resultant increased neurometabolic activity. Daniel (1985) reported the contradictory case of a patient who developed postictal delirium after bilateral but not after right-unilateral ECT, and claimed that the syndrome was nonspecific. The report of postictal delirium in a fully dextral man who received left-unilateral ECT (Leechuy and Abrams, 1987) suggested that it is premature to attribute this syndrome exclusively to right hemisphere mechanisms. In fact, in a study of the postictal phase in which patients are randomly assigned to receive either left- or right-unilateral ECT or bilateral ECT, the occurrence of postictal delirium was evenly divided among the three types of electrode placement (Leechuy, Kohlhaas, and Abrams, in press).

Effects on Memory

The principal side-effect of ECT, bearing primary responsibility for its continued lack of full acceptance among laity and professionals alike, has always been the disturbance it causes in memory functioning. Even this statement, however, is only partially correct because there is no monolithic entity "ECT" per se, but only specific types of ECT, such as *sine-wave bilateral ECT* or *brief-pulse unilateral ECT*. This is no mean point, for as will be discovered later in this chapter, it is quite possible (even usual) to administer a fully therapeutic course of treatment with brief-pulse unilateral ECT without incurring *any* measurable degree of amnesia. Nonetheless, in large measure the history of ECT research has been characterized by attempts to reduce the undesirable and unnecessary effects of this treatment on memory, while retaining its beneficial action on depression and other psychiatric syndromes. This research spans two broad eras of about 25 years each. The first, roughly extending from the introduction of bilateral ECT in 1938 to the spreading acceptance of unilateral ECT in the early 1960s, attempted to characterize the amnesic effects of bilateral ECT, often (but by no means always) using tasks and methodologies that were conceptually simple by today's standards. The second, extending to the present, has concentrated mainly on demonstrating the differential effects on memory of bilateral, right-unilateral and left-unilateral ECT, employing more rigorous methodology (e.g., random assignment, blind assessment, and untreated control groups) and increasingly sophisticated and precise neuropsychological measures often developed for the study of lateralized hemispheric processes.

The results of the first era of investigation have been summarized or reviewed by several authors (Campbell, 1960; Williams, 1966; Cronholm, 1969; Dornbush, 1972; Dornbush and Williams, 1974; Fink, 1979) and will generally be referred to here only in abbreviated form or for historical clarification. The second era of investigation, particularly the past decade, provides the most important clinical and theoretical data, and will be covered in more detail.

In assessing the literature on ECT-induced memory loss a distinction must be made between *learning* and *retention* (Cronholm and Ottosson, 1961; Harper and Wiens, 1975). This is because the depressive syndrome (specifically, melancholia), either through attentional–motivational deficits or some more integral biological dysfunction, generally impairs the ability to acquire new information, and the relief of this syndrome by ECT tends to reverse this impairment. [For example, the ability to learn nonsense syllables increases remarkably throughout a course of ECT (Thorpe, 1959)]. Thus, a standard "memory" test, such as the Wechsler Memory Scale (Wechsler, 1945), is variously estimated to contain only 13 to 22 percent of memory-specific variance (Cannicott and Waggoner, 1967; Zung, 1968; Harper and Wiens, 1975), and predominantly measures new learning, or *acquisition*. Investigators studying the effects of ECT using the Wechsler Memory Scale (and other similar instruments such as the Babcock or Gresham inventories) may incorrectly conclude simply that ECT improves memory. The same holds true for paired-associate learning tasks, also widely used to study ECT-induced amnesia. The real memory variable of interest in the context of ECT is, of course, *retention*: the ability to *recognize*, *relearn*, or *recall* (in order of increasing difficulty) previously learned material (Ottosson, 1968; Dornbush and Williams, 1974). Impaired retention for material learned prior to a disruptive event (in this case, ECT) constitutes retrograde amnesia; impaired retention of material learned after a disruptive event constitutes anterograde amnesia. Anterograde amnesia is tested under conditions in which patients are required to learn new material (*immediate memory*) and then to recognize or recall it after a timed interval has elapsed (*delayed memory*). The difference between immediate and delayed memory constitutes the hypothetical variable *forgetting* (Cronholm and Ottosson, 1961), and it is precisely differences in forgetting induced by ECT that should be of primary interest to investigators. Naturally, forgetting (or decay) is inherent to all memories, and it is therefore necessary to design studies that control for normal forgetting, or baseline decay, when investigating the effects of ECT on retention. Unfortunately, only a few investigators (e.g., Zinkin and Birtchnell, 1968; d'Elia, 1970) have done so.

Retrograde Amnesia

Cronholm and Lagergren (1959) tested the ability of endogenous depressives (among others) to recall a number learned 5, 15, and 60 seconds before a single bilateral ECT; recall was better the greater the interval between learning and ECT, clearly demonstrating what later would be called the temporal gradient of retrograde amnesia and supporting the "consolidation" hypothesis of memory formation. In a more complex design, Cronholm and Molander (1961) used 3 sets of verbal and nonverbal paired associate tasks to test learning, and then retention 6 hours later, on the day prior to the first ECT. This procedure was repeated with parallel test forms of equal difficulty on the next day, but with ECT administered 1 hour after learning. On all 3 tests (word pairs, figure pairs, and letter–symbol pairs), performance 6 hours after learning was much worse following the interposition of ECT, consistent with a significant adverse effect of bilateral ECT on retention of recently learned material. Miller (1970) found a similar retrograde disruption of verbal paired-associates learned 30 minutes prior to bilateral ECT. Daniel and Crovitz (1983a,b) analyzed the raw data from nine published studies of ECT-induced retrograde amnesia and found that material presented 20 to 60 minutes before ECT was recalled better than that presented up to 10 minutes before ECT, and that recall of material learned prior to ECT was more difficult in the immediate postictal period (up to 22 minutes post-ECT) than 23 minutes or more afterwards.

Although such studies of very recently learned material are of theoretical importance in precisely defining the nature of ECT-induced retrograde amnesia, they do not evaluate retention of memories acquired some time prior to ECT, and it is disturbed memory for such past events that is of major concern to patients, their families, and their physicians. Studies of the effects of ECT on autobiographical and other remote memories are therefore of primary clinical relevance. The first such study was reported by Janis (1950), who obtained extensive anamneses concerning early schooling, travel, employment, and other life experiences from 19 patients scheduled to have ECT as well as from control subjects. Four weeks after a mean course of 17 bilateral ECTs, every patient exhibited deficits for some of the previously reported memories, whereas such deficits rarely occurred in controls. Five of the ECT patients continued to show such deficits in autobiographical memory over a 10- to 14-week follow-up period. For reasons that are unclear, this excellent study was mostly discounted or ignored, perhaps because its results were inconsistent with the prevalent clinical view of the time that ECT simply did not cause long-term or persistent memory loss (Kalinowsky and Hoch, 1952), except, perhaps, in patients with preexisting marked histrionic personalities (Stengel, 1951), or because Janis himself felt that the observed memory deficits were related more to the patient's emotional state than to any lasting cerebral effects of ECT.

In any case, almost 20 years elapsed before any formal attempt was made to study this problem again (Strain et al., 1968). These authors studied the effects of right-unilateral and bilateral ECT on several tasks, including scores derived from a Personal Data Sheet that included 25 questions pertaining to personal experiences from the remote past, and 25 questions about the recent events leading up to and including the index hospitalization. Both treatment groups exhibited significant retrograde amnesia (that was worse for bilateral than unilateral ECT) for personal memory data 36 hours after the last ECT received. Ten days after the last treatment both groups still showed significant impairment, although between-treatment differences had disappeared by this time. A 1-year follow-up study unfortunately did not include assessment of the personal memory items (Bidder et al., 1970), although Brunschwig et al. (1971) alluded to persistent deficits in personal memory scores after 1 year in an abstract devoted to methodological issues in the assessment of post-ECT memory changes. In any even, no untreated group had been included to control for "normal" forgetting.

In a comprehensive follow-up study of memory and nonmemory cognitive impairment 1 week and 4 and 7 months after right-unilateral or bilateral ECT, Weeks et al. (1980) included a 28-item personal remote memories schedule modeled after the one used by Strain et al. (1968). One week after a course of ECT personal memory recall was no different from before starting treatment; moreover, there were no differences between ECT patients and a matched no-ECT control group for the number of personal memory items recalled at either of the longer follow-up intervals.

Squire et al. (1981) asked 10 depressed patients who were scheduled to receive bilateral ECT, and 7 drug-treated depressed controls, a series of personal history questions covering events in their lives occurring from 1 week to 20 years previously and ranging from naming the teachers in their first six grades to reporting everything they could remember about the day of hospitalization for their present admission. Shortly after ECT there was a marked reduction in the number of autobiographical facts that could be recalled, although about 7 months later there was no difference between ECT and control subjects for the total number of items correctly recalled. On closer examination, however, it became clear that ECT patients performed substantially worse than controls on the more recent memory items, especially those pertaining to the day of admission. Moreover, the ECT patients were less likely than controls to recognize omitted information when reminded of it by the examiners, and although this unrecognized information was mainly from recent time periods, half of the ECT patients denied recognizing some material about remote events that they had spontaneously recalled during the initial interview. In contrast, the 7 control subjects never failed to recognize such information.

Perhaps the most specific demonstration of persistent retrograde amnesia for autobiographical information after ECT is that of Weiner et al. (1986), who employed a personal memory questionnaire that was constructed from an individualized inventory of a number of items relevant to the patient's own life experiences, concentrating on the several years prior to the time of testing and including such items as last birthday, last New Year's Eve, favorite television program, last overnight trip out of town, and last movie seen. The questionnaire was administered prior to ECT, 2 to 3 days after a course of ECT, and 6 months later, to a sample of depressed patients who had been randomly assigned to receive unilateral or bilateral ECT with either brief-pulse or sine-wave stimulation. Shortly after ECT, all patients except those receiving brief-pulse unilateral ECT were significantly impaired in the recall of these personal memory items. More importantly, only patients who had received bilateral ECT (regardless of stimulus type) continued to exhibit significant deficits on this questionnaire 6 months later, which might have involved the recent or remote past.

Bilateral ECT also impairs retention of nonautobiographical memories. In order to avoid the sampling bias introduced by the fact that questions about the remote past tend to sample a greater time interval and to be more general than questions about the recent past, Squire et al. (1975) developed a test in which subjects were asked to recognize the names of television programs that had been broadcast nationally between 6 and 11 PM for a single season between 1957 and 1972. After 5 bilateral ECTs amnesia occurred for the names of programs broadcast 1 to 3 years before treatment but not for programs broadcast 4 to 17 years before treatment, demonstrating a temporal gradient of retrograde amnesia in very long-term memory and confirming the nineteenth century proposition that the susceptibility of a memory to disruption is proportional to its age. The amnesia for recently broadcast television programs, as well as that for public events of an overlapping time period, gradually subsided during the weeks after treatment and was not detectable after 7 months (Squire et al., 1981). Pre-ECT performance for the entire 15-year period was not significantly poorer than in controls, demonstrating little or no effect of depressive illness on the retention of memories (in contrast to the previously described adverse effect of depression on new learning). Moreover, the fact that amnesia could occur for material learned 3 years, but not 4 years, previously suggests that the process of consolidation of memories continues for years. (In the same study, a group of 8 depressed patients who had received a course of right-sided ECT showed no impairment in memory for past television programs, even as early as 1 hour after the fifth treatment.)

The study of Weeks et al. (1980) included a Famous Personalities test that required subjects to identify 50 names of famous or obscure personalities from the 1930s to the 1970s. Although no significant change in scores on this task was observed 1 week after ECT, the ECT group scored significantly lower than the no-ECT controls at the 4-month follow-up testing. By 7 months, this difference had disappeared.

EFFECTS OF ELECTRODE PLACEMENT

Retrograde amnesia for test items learned prior to treatment is less pronounced after unilateral than bilateral ECT. Lancaster et al. (1958) found that a test sentence given immediately before the first ECT was more readily recalled 15 minutes after the fourth right-unilateral ECT than after the fourth bilateral ECT, and Cannicott and Waggoner (1967) reported that 4 words learned immediately before ECT were more readily recalled 30 minutes after right-unilateral than after bilateral ECT. Valentine et al. (1968) found that free recall of verbal paired-associates learned 10 minutes before treatment was much more impaired after bilateral than after right-unilateral ECT when sinusoidal current was used. Zinkin and Birtchnell (1968) also found a right-unilateral ECT advantage 2 to 3 hours after treatment for recognition of pictures of common objects (e.g., shoe) learned 2 to 3 minutes before ECT. d'Elia (1970) reported a similar right-unilateral versus bilateral ECT advantage in the recall 5 hours after ECT of paired-associates and biographical facts learned 1 hour pretreatment.

The reduced retrograde amnesic effects of right-unilateral ECT compared with bilateral ECT occur regardless of whether identification of the test items learned prior to ECT (in this case, verbal paired-associates) is accomplished by recognition, relearning, or recall (Costello et al., 1970). A substantial and similar advantage for right-unilateral over bilateral ECT, although not statistically significant, was also reported by Valentine et al. (1968), Sutherland et al. (1969) and Fleminger et al. (1970). In a never-to-be-confirmed study, Wilson and Gottlieb (1967) provided the only contrary data in the literature, reporting *less* retrograde amnesia after bilateral than after right-unilateral ECT for the recall immediately upon regaining consciousness of 4 digits and a proverb learned 30 minutes before each of 6 treatments.

In their investigation of the effects of low-dose unilateral and bilateral ECT, Sackeim et al. (1986) tested patients 5 minutes after full post-ECT reorientation for the recall or recognition of words, geometric and nonsense shapes, and faces learned 15 minutes prior to the administration of ECT. The recall and recognition of words and the recognition of geometric and nonsense shapes were all significantly better after right-unilateral than after bilateral ECT; no between-group differences occurred on the facial recognition task. The effects of ECT on these memory variables was also examined over the course of treatment, revealing the interesting finding that neither method was associated with cumulative impairment of retrograde memory. In fact, bilateral ECT, but not unilateral ECT, was associated with a significant cumulative *improvement* of nonsense shape recognition that was entirely attributable to the patients who showed marked improvement over the treatment course.

EFFECTS OF THE STIMULUS

Daniel et al. (1983) studied retrograde amnesia in a sample of depressives who had been radnomly assigned to right-unilateral or bilateral ECT administered with either brief-pulse or sine-wave stimuli. Twenty-four hours after the fifth ECT retrograde amnesia for events occurring 30 minutes before treatment was significantly greater with sine-wave than with brief-pulse ECT, regardless of the electrical energy delivered (sine-wave ECT delivered significantly more joules of electrical energy than did brief-pulse ECT). This provocative finding suggests that the reduced amnesic effects of brief-pulse, square-wave therapy are inherent to the stimulus configuration itself, rather than to its reduced electrical intensity when compared with sine-wave stimuli. This study also confirmed prior reports of lesser retrograde amnesia after right-unilateral than after bilateral ECT.

EFFECTS OF SEIZURE DURATION

In the same study, Daniel et al. (1983) found no correlation between seizure duration and retrograde amnesia. Miller et al. (1985), however, studied recall 20 minutes and 4 hours after each of 6 right-unilateral ECTs of verbal paired-associates and block designs that had been learned 20 minutes before each treatment and found that seizure duration correlated modestly but significantly with retrograde amnesia for block designs, but not verbal paired-associates, at both retesting intervals ($r = 0.4$ and 0.5, respectively).

Anterograde Amnesia

A series of deceptively simple studies on memory function in endogenous depressives before and after ECT were conducted by Cronholm and his associates at Stockholm's Karolinska Institute during the late 1950s (Cronholm and Molander, 1957; 1961; Cronholm and Blomquist, 1959; Cronholm and Ottosson, 1960; 1961). These investigators introduced a procedure requiring patients to recall verbal and nonverbal materials immediately after presentation and then again after a delay of 3 hours. The immediate memory score was taken as a measure of *learning ability*, the delayed memory score as a measure of *retention*, and the difference between them a measure of *forgetting*. Testing intervals and conditions varied among the substudies, but their overall conclusion was that endogenous depression was associated with an impairment of learning ability (but not retention), and that this learning impairment was reversed by the clinical improvement caused by ECT, which itself impaired retention but not learning ability. This retention deficit, however, was no longer detectable 1 month later (Cronholm and Molander, 1964). Thus, ECT converted a disorder (melancholia) characterized by poor learning and normal retention into one characterized by normal learning and poor retention (Ottosson, 1968).

In a study that was sophisticated for its time, Korin, Fink, and Kwalwasser (1956) examined the ability of patients over a course of 12 bilateral ECTs to learn and then recall word lists after either an interpolated nonsense-syllable learning task, or a 10-minute rest period filled by reading a popular magazine. Compared with untreated controls, patients showed sharp and significant retention decrements throughout the treatment course under both delayed-recall conditions, but more markedly so after the interpolated learning task. Scores under both conditions returned to baseline 1 week post-ECT and surpassed it 2 weeks later. In this study, no relation was found between anterograde amnesia and clinical improvement.

The severity of the anterograde amnesia induced by bilateral ECT depends, in part, on how long ECT precedes the new learning. Squire et al. (1976) tested the ability of patients to recognize material learned up to 1 hour after ECT or 3 hours after ECT and found retention significantly better under the latter condition. Squire and Miller (1974) demonstrated that ECT had less of an effect on the ability to retain memory contents over short retention intervals (e.g., 30 minutes) than over long ones (e.g., 24 hours), perhaps because after ECT, forgetting occurs more rapidly than normal. And, when learning occurs 6 to 10 hours after treatment, immediate retention can be normal, but delayed retention as tested 24 hours later can be markedly impaired (Squire and Chace, 1975). This means that patients who have recovered the ability to retain some newly learned material over 30 minutes or so, and who appear normal on casual observation, may nevertheless be markedly amnesic as demonstrated by their inability to reproduce that material the next day (Squire, 1982).

EFFECTS OF ELECTRODE PLACEMENT

Often included in reviews of ECT-induced anterograde amnesia (e.g., Price, 1982; Daniel and Crovitz, 1983), but actually more appropriately considered studies of learning, are the many investigations of the effects of left- or right-unilateral and bilateral ECT that employ the Wechsler Memory Scale (or similar memory inventories) or paired-associate learning tasks without a delayed recall condition (Martin et al., 1965; Zamora and Kaelbling, 1965; Cohen et al., 1968; Levy, 1968; Sutherland et al., 1969; Cronin et al., 1970; Fleminger et al., 1970a, 1970b; Fromholt et al., 1973). Without exception, these studies show greater impairment in verbal learning after bilateral or left-unilateral ECT than after right-unilateral ECT. Moreover, several studies using these and other verbal tasks actually find an *improvement* in verbal learning after right-unilateral ECT (Martin et al., 1965; Zamora and Kaelbling, 1965; Sutherland et al., 1969; Costello et al., 1970; Strömgren et al., 1976).

The following investigators specifically studied anterograde amnesia. Halliday et al. (1968) used verbal and nonverbal learning tasks with a 30-minuted delayed recall condition to assess anterograde amnesia after left- and right-unilateral and bilateral ECT. No differences in delayed recall were found between right-unilateral and bilateral ECT; left-unilateral ECT was associated with the greatest recall decrement among the three methods. Zinkin and Birtchnell (1968) assessed delayed recall after 5, 20, and 60 minutes in their picture-recognition task and found anterograde amnesia to be significantly worse after bilateral than after right-unilateral ECT. d'Elia (1970) used the Cronholm and Molander (1957) memory battery to study anterograde amnesia after right-unilateral and bilateral ECT. Calculating before and after ECT *change* scores for the variables of forgetting and delayed recall, he was unable to demonstrate increased verbal forgetting with either method, although delayed recall scores were significantly lower after bilateral ECT. The importance of this study lies in the fact that changes in forgetting before and after ECT are arguably the most appropriate measure of anterograde amnesia induced by this treatment. This is also the only comparison of the verbal anterograde amnesic effects of right-unilateral and bilateral ECT to account for baseline decay when assessing retention differences.

Dornbush, Abrams, and Fink (1971) examined the short-term (18 seconds) and long-term (3 hours) retention of verbal and visual memory in endogenous depressives with delayed recall tasks presented before and 24 hours after 4 to 5 treatments. Short-term auditory verbal memory was tested by asking the patients to recall nonsense consonant trigrams (e.g., DLG) presented by tape at intervals of 0, 6, 12, and 18 seconds after learning, with retention intervals filled with an interposed rote task (number reading) to prevent rehearsal. Neither method impaired trigram learning (the 0-second interval) and unilateral ECT did not affect retention at any of the other test intervals. Bilateral ECT, however, significantly impaired retention at the 6-second interval and thereafter, presumably by disrupting the "holding" period required for transfer of information from short-term to long-term memory store. A visuospatial short-term memory task with low verbal encodability was devised that required patients to reproduce the location of a circle on a straight line after the same filled retention intervals described earlier. Neither unilateral nor bilateral ECT impaired retention at any of the filled intervals, but immediate retention at 0 seconds was significantly better with unilateral than bilateral ECT (performance improved with the former and worsened with the latter). This result suggests that this task may require the time-dependent, sequential processing skills of the left hemisphere (Horan, Ashton, and Minto, 1980). Longer-term verbal retention was also studied using the paired-associate subtest of the Wechsler Memory Scale presented in the usual 3 learning trials and then 3 hours later to measure delayed recall, a variable that was significantly impaired by bilateral but not right-unilateral ECT.

Fromholt et al. (1973) included a delayed recall task (the Logical Memory subtests of the Wechsler Memory Scale) in their comparison of the relative effects of right-unilateral and bilateral ECT on the Wechsler Memory Scale, and found that 6 right-unilateral ECTs were followed by better retention of the memory passages 20 minutes after learning, as well as by the higher Wechsler Memory Scale scores previously noted.

Squire and Slater (1978) also compared the effects of unilateral and bilateral ECT using the short-term retention tasks of Dornbush,

Abrams, and Fink (1971), adding an additional long-term (16–19 hours) verbal task of paragraph recall and a visual one requiring recall of the complex Rey-Osterreith geometric figure. These authors confirmed the reported impairment in short-term verbal memory retention after bilateral, but not unilateral ECT, as well as the advantage of unilateral over bilateral ECT in retention of visuospatial material. In addition, they reported that bilateral ECT (but not unilateral ECT) markedly reduced the number of paragraph segments retained after 16 to 19 hours, and that both methods impaired the ability to reproduce the Rey-Osterreith figure at the same interval, bilateral ECT significantly more so than unilateral ECT.

Using visually presented stimuli of systematically varying verbal encodability (low- and high-imagery nouns, pictures of common objects, geometric designs, and nonsense figures), and including no-ECT patient controls, normal controls, and a delayed recognition condition, Robertson and Inglis (1978) found that bilateral ECT induced similar retention deficits across all tasks, whereas the deficits after right-unilateral ECT rose with increasing nonverbal task mediation, reaching significance only for nonsense figures. Bilateral ECT induced significantly greater retention deficits than right-unilateral ECT for low- and high-imagery nouns and pictures of common objects, but not for geometric designs or nonsense figures. The results of this model study were interpreted by its authors to support Paivio's (1969; 1971) dual-encoding model of verbal learning

> that specifies those stimulus and task attributes that vary the exent to which memory and learning depend upon symbolic (verbal) and imagery (nonverbal) encoding. Symbolic encoding is evoked by verbal and abstract stimuli and by demands for the sequential processing of information. The imagery system is evoked by concrete stimuli and by demands for parallel processing.

This portrayal of the mechanisms or processes involved in information acquisition and retention clearly overlaps with the material-specific view (verbal versus nonverbal) of human cerebral asymmetry; the symbolic and imagery systems relate strongly to the left and right hemispheres. It finds support in the later study of Horan, Ashton, and Minto (1980) who demonstrated in 2 separate samples that right-unilateral ECT, but not bilateral ECT, significantly improved performance on a relatively pure sequential processing task—the Knox Cube Imitation test. These authors suggest that right-unilateral ECT suppression of right hemisphere interference allowed the left hemisphere's sequential processing mode to operate more efficiently. Such reasoning can explain a variety of otherwise puzzling reports that right-unilateral ECT *improves* verbal memory performance (Martin et al., 1965; Zamora and Kaelbling, 1965; Sutherland et al., 1969; Costello et al., 1970; Strömgren et al., 1976). The findings of Zinkin and Birtchnell (1968) and Halliday et al. (1968) that bilateral and left-unilateral ECT caused greater difficulty than right unilateral ECT on visual recognition tasks of relatively high verbal encodability likewise fit the model, as does Williams' (1973) demonstration that patients receiving right-unilateral, but not bilateral, ECT more frequently recognized nominal than pictorial representations of pictures of common objects learned before treatment, and Ashton and Hess' (1976) report that right-unilateral and bilateral ECT induced equivalent retrograde amnesia for complex geometric forms of low verbal encodability. In the same vein, Weeks et al. (1980) included a delayed recall task that required patients to remember 9 pictorially presented common objects after a 10-minute interval that was filled with another memory task. One week after a course of treatment patients receiving bilateral ECT recalled significantly fewer items than those receiving right-unilateral ECT, a difference that was no longer apparent 4 and 7 months post-ECT.

Sackeim et al. (1986b) included measures of delayed recall to test anterograde effects of low-dose ECT (separate analyses for unilateral and bilateral groups were not presented in this report), and included a normal control group for comparison. Prior to the first ECT, after the seventh ECT and 4 days after the last ECT of their course, patients were tested for their performance on verbal and nonverbal (faces) paired-associate learning tasks; 4 hours later recognition memory for these pairs was tested again, providing a measure of delayed recall. At the pretreatment session patients performed significantly worse than controls on immediate recognition memory (learning), but did not exhibit a greater rate of forgetting over the 4-hour delay, confirming the work of earlier investigators (e.g., Cronholm and Ottosson, 1961). Although there was a significant reduction in immediate recognition memory scores after the seventh ECT compared with baseline, 4 days after the last ECT no such deficit could be demonstrated. In contrast, delayed memory scores were reduced following both the seventh and final treatments, also supporting the claim of earlier workers that ECT had different effects on the acquisition and retention of information (Cronholm and Ottosson, 1961).

The study of Miller et al. (1985) of right-unilateral ECT described earlier in the retrograde amnesia section also included a delayed recall condition in which patients learned verbal and nonverbal material 4 hours post-ECT and were tested for recall 20 hours later. As for retrograde amnesia, anterograde amnesia for block designs, but not verbal paired-associates, significantly correlated with seizure duration—the longer the seizure, the greater the forgetting.

Anterograde amnesia for recently learned material diminishes fairly rapidly after ECT. Squire, Shimamura, and Graf (1985) presented word lists to patients 45 minutes, 60 minutes, 85 minutes, and 9 hours after 4 or 5 ECTs, testing retention by recognition of the words 15 minutes after each presentation. After bilateral ECT, retention was initially no better than chance, but increased to about 80 percent correct recognition by the 9-hour test interval (a control group of depressed patients not receiving ECT obtained a mean of 95 percent correct answers). Patients receiving unilateral ECT were not significantly impaired on this test, obtaining 80 to 90 percent correct answers at all test intervals.

Nonmemory Cognitive Effects

Neuropsychological issues of lateralized hemispheric specialization of function that were raised by the introduction of unilateral ECT stimulated most of the studies of ECT-induced nonmemory cognitive impairment reviewed in this section. Earlier studies have been reviewed elsewhere (e.g., Campbell, 1960; Fink, 1979; Price, 1982) and are difficult to assess as they were not blind, often contained mixed diagnostic groups, and frequently tested patients after much longer courses of ECT (e.g., 20 or more) than would be given today. In general, however, impairments in various perceptual and psychomotor performance tasks were observed immediately after bilateral ECT, recovering to pretreatment levels or better by about 2 weeks after the last seizure.

McAndrew, Berkey, and Matthews (1967) were the first to use lateralized neuropsychological tests to study the effects of left- or right-unilateral ECT and bilateral ECT in a small sample of depressives (only 8 in each group). Cognitive functions generally improved after ECT, and they found no differences among or within the

3 treatment groups for performance on Halstead categories, finger tapping, sandpaper roughness discrimination, maze coordination, the grooved pegboard, finger agnosia, and the WAIS similarities, vocabulary, digit span, block design, and picture arrangements subtests. It is doubtful, however, that their sample was large enough to permit them to detect an existing real difference among the methods. A tendency was observed for improvement in performance on hemisphere-related tasks to occur following unilateral stimulation of that hemisphere.

Using a similar battery of tasks to study patients randomly assigned to receive either left- or right-unilateral ECT, Small et al. (1972) found that 5 right-unilateral ECTs improved performance on a number of right-hemisphere Halstead subtests, but the reverse was not true for left-unilateral ECT. In an extension of this study that included a bilateral ECT group, Small et al. (1973) found that all 3 electrode placements were associated with improved performance on nonverbal cognitive tasks.

Annett et al. (1974) employed naming and visual discrimination tasks administered before and 30 minutes after left- or right-unilateral ECT, and found that although left-unilateral ECT impaired naming ability, right-unilateral ECT did not impair visual discrimination. Berent et al. (1975) found significant impairment on a verbal task 5 hours after a single left-unilateral ECT, and significant impairment on a nonverbal task after right-unilateral ECT under the same conditions. Interestingly, this latter degree of nonverbal impairment was similar to that observed after 5 ECTs in an earlier study from the same laboratory (Cohen et al., 1968), whereas the verbal impairment consequent to 5 left-unilateral ECTs in that study had been much greater than that observed by Berent et al. (1975) after a single treatment. This observation led these authors to suggest that the left hemisphere was more susceptible than the right to the cumulative effects of a series of ECT.

Kronfol et al. (1978) studied the effects of left- and right-unilateral ECT on verbal and nonverbal tests after both a single ECT and a course of 8 treatments. The neuropsychological measures were chosen to be relatively hemisphere-specific on the basis of prior studies in patients with lateralized brain damage, and had all been developed in the neuropsychology laboratory of A. L. Benton at the University of Iowa. They included left hemisphere tasks of Digit Sequence Learning, Controlled Word Association, Sentence Repetition, and the Token Test, and right hemisphere tasks of Form Sequence Learning, Judgement of Line Orientation, Three-Dimensional Constructional

Praxis, and Facial Recognition. Despite considerable variability in right- and left-hemisphere task performance observed after single ECTs given with either treatment method, the statistically significant and clinically relevant findings of this study are limited to the observations that 8 left-unilateral ECT impaired performance on 1 left hemisphere task and 8 right-unilateral ECT improved performance on 1 right hemisphere task. The most striking aspect of this study is the absence of systematic lateralized hemispheric effects of either left- or right-sided unilateral ECT even when carefully studied by a highly trained research neuropsychologist using sophisticated and well-validated measures. Although the relatively meager results obtained are indeed consonant with several other studies demonstrating a decline in left-hemisphere task performance after left-unilateral ECT (Cronin et al., 1970; d'Elia and Raotma, 1975; Berent et al., 1975) and an improvement in right hemisphere task performance after right-unilateral ECT (McAndrew et al., 1967; Small et al., 1972; Dornbush, Abrams, and Fink, 1971; Horan, Ashton, and Minto, 1980), they are likewise dissonant with studies showing that right-unilateral ECT improves performance on some left hemisphere tasks (Zamora and Kaelbling, 1965; Martin et al., 1965; Cannicott and Waggoner, 1967; Halliday et al., 1968; Costello et al., 1970; Fromholt et al., 1973; Strömgren et al., 1976) and impairs performance on right hemisphere tasks (Cohen et al., 1968; Robertson and Inglis, 1978), and that left-unilateral ECT improves performance on right hemisphere tasks (Small et al., 1973).

In fact, the findings by Kronfol et al. (1978) that right-unilateral ECT improved performance on 3 "right-hemisphere" tasks (Form Sequence Learning, Three-Dimensional Constructional Praxis, and Judgement of Line Orientation, with only the last reaching statistical significance) suggests that these tasks may demand substantial sequential processing by the left hemisphere (Robertson and Inglis, 1978). This is clearly the case for the Form Sequence Learning task, and anyone taking the Judgement of Line Orientation test can readily testify that it requires an iterative, and therefore sequential, mental matching of the pair of test lines with each pair in the array of choices. The Three-Dimensional Construction Praxis task does not, at first blush, seem to require sequential processing, but it is notably the only one of the tasks to show impairment after left hemisphere lesions. Weeks et al. (1980) also included a variety of nonmemory cognitive tasks in their study and found significant improvement in choice reaction time and visual perceptual analysis 1 week after a course of ECT.

Recently, Taylor and Abrams (1985) studied primarily nonmemory neuropsychological functioning in a sample of 37 melancholic patients who were randomly assigned to receive either right-unilateral ECT or bilateral ECT. Patients were examined prior to ECT and again 48 to 72 hours after their sixth ECT on an extensive test battery that included evaluation of neurological soft signs, aphasia testing, the Mini-Mental State examination (Folstein et al., 1975), tachistoscopically presented verbal and nonverbal materials, and a variety of tasks selected from the Halstead–Reitan (Reitan, 1955) and Luria–Nebraska (Golden et al., 1978) test batteries. Test protocols were scored blindly and assigned global, hemispheric, and regional cortical impairment scores. In this sample, 6 ECTs with either electrode placement did not significantly increase global cognitive impairment scores, nor were increases in regional hemispheric cortical impairment scores observed after right-unilateral ECT. Bilateral ECT worsened only the right temporal lobe score; this, coupled with a nonsignificant improvement in the same score induced by right-unilateral ECT, led to the study's only real cognitive difference between electrode placements.

Intelligence Quotient (IQ)

Intelligence quotient tests are mixed neuropsychological test batteries that contain only modest numbers of memory-related items. The Wechsler Memory Scale, although not specifically an IQ test, correlates very highly with the Wechsler–Bellevue and Wechsler Adult Intelligence Scales (WAIS), so it should come as no surprise that the older literature shows that bilateral ECT does not impair (and may improve) performance on these and similar instruments (Huston and Strother, 1948; Fisher, 1949; Stieper, Williams, and Duncan, 1951; Foulds, 1952; Summerskill, Seeman, and Meals, 1952). More recently, Squire et al. (1975) demonstrated that the verbal IQ of the WAIS, including the arithmetic subtest, which is considered to be particularly sensitive to cerebral dysfunction, was the same before ECT as 1 hour after 6 bilateral ECTs.

Follow-up Studies

Squire and Chace (1975) examined memory functions in a retrospective follow-up study of patients who had received courses of right-unilateral or bilateral ECT 6 to 9 months earlier and in control patients who had never received ECT. To maximize test sensitivity, 1-day and 2-week intervals were interposed between learning and retention, and assessments of memory functions were made with 6 different tests of new learning and remote memory capacity. No objective evidence for persisting memory impairment (e.g., the ability to learn and retain) could be found on any of the tests.

The Squire et al. (1981) study reviewed earlier was part of a larger, prospective, follow-up study of retrograde amnesia induced by bilateral ECT. In addition to the autobiographical memory items already discussed, the authors included tests of recognition and recall of public events and recall of previously broadcast television programs, all administered before ECT, 1 week after completion of treatment, and about 7 months later. At this latter test interval, no persistent deficits could be demonstrated in the recognition or recall of the public events or television program items. As already noted, strong evidence for persistent memory loss was limited to personal events that had occurred a few days or weeks prior to treatment.

The study by Weeks et al. (1980) was also the first controlled, prospective study of enduring nonmemory cognitive deficits in depressed patients after right-unilateral and bilateral ECT. One week after a course of ECT patients did not exhibit any cognitive worsening compared with their pretreatment performance; indeed, they improved significantly on certain tasks. Compared with the performance of non-ECT treated depressives and with matched normal controls, on a comprehensive test battery, ECT caused no impairment at 4 or 7 months posttreatment. There was a significant cognitive advantage for right-unilateral ECT versus bilateral ECT at 1 week posttreatment (right unilateral ECT patients were actually quite similar to controls on many tasks), that was no longer present at 4 and 7 weeks.

A subsequent long-term follow-up study of nonmemory cognitive functions after ECT confirmed these results. Abrams and Taylor (1985) examined 13 patients before ECT, 1 day after 6 right-unilateral or bilateral ECTs, and 30 days, 6 months, 1 year, and 2 years after completion of a treatment course, comparing their scores on a global impairment index (calculated from a comprehensive cognitive test battery) with that of a sample of age-equated normal controls. Patients exhibited significantly more global cognitive impairment than controls at baseline and 1 day after 6 ECTs, but were no different from controls at the 30-day, 6-month and 1- to 2-year follow-up intervals. Within patients, global impairment scores were reduced (but not significantly) from baseline levels 1 day after 6 ECTs, with further reductions observed during the follow-up period, so that 1 to 2 years later impairment scores were very significantly reduced below pre-ECT levels. (As no significant cognitive differences were found between right-unilateral and bilateral ECT in this sample, or in a much larger one studied with the same battery—Taylor and Abrams, 1985—the two groups were combined for analysis.)

Subjective Memory Dysfunction

In one of the Cronholm and Ottosson (1963) studies of immediate and delayed recall and retention after ECT, patients were asked 1 week after a course of treatment whether they felt their memory was worse, unchanged, or better. The experience of relief from depression was associated with a subjective sense of improved memory and correlated with improved performance on the immediate recall (learning) tasks but not on retention, and with verbal, but not visuospatial, performance.

Although, as noted earlier, Squire and Chace (1975) could not detect objective evidence of impaired learning, retention, or remote memory 6 to 9 months after right-unilateral or bilateral ECT, 63 percent of the bilaterally treated sample complained of impaired memory since their treatment, compared with 30 percent of the right-unilateral group (and 17 percent of the no-ECT controls). The authors interpreted the patients' subjective experiences in terms of their expectation that they might suffer long-term memory difficulties.

Subsequently, Squire et al. (1979) developed a new self-rating instrument for assessing subjective memory functioning after ECT, requiring subjects to rate themselves on a continuum from "worse than ever before" to "better than ever before" on 18 items reflecting recognition, recall, retention, comprehension, concentration, and alertness. These authors found persistent complaints of memory impairment in some patients as long as 6 months after an average course of 11 bilateral ECT. These complaints closely resembled those occurring 1 week after treatment had ended, but were sharply different qualitatively from those observed prior to ECT, suggesting to the authors that the patient's experience of altered memory 6 months after the course of bilateral ECT could not be attributed solely to illness variables (e.g., depressed mood, low self-esteem). Freeman, Weeks, and Kendell (1980) examined a nonsystematically obtained sample of patients who complained of persistent cognitive dysfunction a mean of 10 years after having had a course of ECT, most with bilateral electrode placement. These patients generally performed as well as no-ECT controls on most subtests of a battery of 19 memory and non-memory cognitive tasks, but were significantly impaired on several tasks, a few even scoring in the organic impairment range. The authors concluded that a small subgroup of patients receiving ECT might suffer permanent memory impairment.

In a 3-year follow-up study of the Squire et al. (1979) sample, Squire and Slater (1983) found that patients who had received bilateral ECT generally felt that they had difficulty remembering events from about 6 months before ECT to 2 months afterward. In fact, about 50 percent of the patients who had received bilateral ECT felt that their memory had never returned to normal. Again, the pattern of memory complaints much more closely resembled the one reported 1 week after ECT when patients were amnesic than of that prior to treatment, when they were depressed (prior to their course of ECT 3 years earlier, these patients had already had difficulty remembering the events of the preceding 5 months). Right-unilateral ECT was generally not associated with the subjective experience of memory impairment.

Summary

A remarkable amount has been learned in the past decade about the effects of ECT on memory, and the day is now past when the physician administering bilateral ECT can blithely assure his patient that "the memory-loss will only be temporary." True, many who receive bilateral ECT will not complain of persistent dysmnesia, either because none exists or because they are characteristically the ones with the highly favorable therapeutic responses, who are likewise known for their denial-prone personality structure and the development of anosognosia after treatment (Fink et al., 1959; Kahn and Fink, 1959). Although more studies are needed to confirm and extend those of essentially two investigators and their associates (see review of Squire, 1986), the data now at hand are adequate to provide patients a more accurate and reasonable indication of what to expect with bilateral ECT: at best, transient memory disturbances for events immediately before and after the course of treatment, clearing within a few weeks; at worst, significant memory deficits for a period extending from at least 6 months (and perhaps longer) before ECT to 2 months afterward, which may persist objectively for at least 6 months (and perhaps longer), and subjectively for several years later. In addition, *all* patients receiving bilateral ECT will experience permanent memory-loss (anterograde amnesia) for some events occurring during the course of treatment, especially on treatment days. Patients can be assured, however, that no permanent effects on memory *functioning* will occur (that is, the ability to learn and retain new information), and that nonmemory cognitive functions, including *intelligence* and its components of reasoning, judgement, comprehension, abstract thinking, and so on, as well as visual-motor and perceptual skills, will also be unaffected and will likely seem improved in comparison to their pretreatment status.

The situation with right-unilateral ECT is quite different. Patients can be assured that little or no retrograde or anterograde memory disturbance will occur during or immediately following the treatment course, and that whatever dysmnesia does occur will be transient and probably undetectable, 6 months later. The most striking finding in this context in recent years has been the even more benign effects on memory that result when right-unilateral ECT is administered with brief-pulse stimulation (Weiner et al., 1986). Among all stimulus and electrode combinations, only patients receiving brief pulse, right-unilateral ECT were found to be no different from untreated controls on every measure of retrograde (including autobiographical) and anterograde amnesia studied, either 2 or 3 days after a treatment course, or 6 months later. This was most apparent in the very sensitive Personal Memory Recall questionnaire that included, among other items, recent outstanding experiences as well events of the current hospitalization: all groups except controls and brief-pulse right-unilateral ECT patients exhibited significant levels of impairment when tested 2 to 3 days after ECT. Of equal importance, of course, is the fact that in this study, patients receiving brief-pulse right-unilateral ECT had just as good a clinical response as those assigned to other treatment combinations. Even the subtantial cognitive advantages of brief-pulse stimulation, however, can be rendered transitory by employing excessively high electrical dosages (Squire and Zouzounis, 1986.)

At this point it is unclear what proportion of patients receiving brief-pulse right-unilateral ECT can be expected to recover fully from their depressive illness without experiencing any short- or long-term memory-loss, but the study of Weiner et al. (1986) suggests that it may be substantial, thus truly heralding a new era for this "beleaguered and maligned treatment modality."

10

Neurochemical Correlates of Electroconvulsive Therapy

By searching through the literature on neurochemical correlates of induced convulsions, the dearth of human ECT studies in contrast to the staggering wealth of ECS trials in rodents immediately stands out, yet it is far from clear just how helpful such normal animal data may be in explicating mechanisms of ECT's action in depressed patients. Discrepant results abound (Lerer, in press), and the few observations that are consistently replicable—a reduction in beta-adrenergic receptors and an increase in serotonin-2 receptors are two frequently cited examples—may yet defy interpretation, e.g., ECS and antidepressant drugs affect serotonin-2 receptors in *opposite* directions (Kellar and Stockmeier, 1986). Although repeated ECS clearly results in major functional changes in a variety of rodent brain neurochemical and neurotransmitter systems, there is presently no direct way to determine whether ECT produces similar changes in humans. As Lerer and Sitaram (1983) and Cowen (1986) point out, however, neuroendocrine responses to ECT in humans can be used to indirectly probe its mechanisms of action because many anterior pituitary hormones are under the control of brain monoamine pathways. Likewise, amine precursors or blockers of specific neurotransmitters can be administered to patients receiving ECT to demonstrate the relevance, or lack of it, of that particular pathway to the therapeutic response.

The present chapter will briefly review and summarize the relevant ECS literature in animals and then examine in detail whatever human studies have been done. For those readers who, like most of us, are unaccustomed to thinking in neuropharmacological terms, the following brief glossary may be helpful.

Receptors are molecules on the surfaces of cells that bind to specific *ligands* (neurotransmitters, drugs, or hormones), resulting in an intracellular alteration of ion transport, enzyme activation, protein synthesis, or neurotransmitter release that eventuates in a biological response (Cooper et al., 1986). Receptors may be *postsynaptic* or *presynaptic*; the latter are also known as *autoreceptors*. Ligands that increase receptor sensitivity (equivalent to increasing the action per receptor) are said to *up-regulate* them; *down-regulation* refers to inhibition of receptor sensitivity. The same ligand may regulate both the presynaptic and postsynaptic receptor at different doses. Thus, low-dose clonidine stimulates the presynaptic, and high-dose clonidine the postsynaptic, noradrenergic receptor. Multiple receptors have been demonstrated for a number of ligands—for example, the four types of noradrenergic receptors (alpha-1, alpha-2, beta-1, beta-2)—each with a different cellular locus and biological response. Measurement of the number and sensitivity of receptors is usually accomplished by *radioligand binding* techniques in which a tissue's receptors are saturated with an isotopically labeled ligand and then examined radiographically. There are basically two types of ECS animal studies—behavioral and neurochemical—although both have the goal of elucidating neurotransmitter correlates of induced seizures. Behavioral studies typically examine those motor responses that are more or less neurotransmitter-specific (e.g., apomorphine-induced stereotypy—a postsynaptic dopaminergic phenomenon), whereas neurochemical studies directly assay intracellular neurotransmitter kinetics (synthesis, turnover, and release) as well as receptor changes. Monoaminergic systems have been the most widely studied to date, followed by the cholinergic, GABAergic, and endorphinergic systems.

A notable difference between ECS and ECT administration in most of the pre-1980s animal studies has been the higher frequency and often the number of ECS given: 1 or 2 seizures daily for 1 to 2 weeks has been the standard (often referred to as *repeated* or *chronic* ECS). More recently, the importance of an induction schedule more closely resembling the administration of ECT in humans has been recognized (Lerer and Sitaram, 1983), and alternate-day (*spaced* ECS) schedules have been increasingly adopted. Although much of the repeated ECS data has been confirmed in spaced ECS studies (Vetulani, 1986), albeit sometimes with a significantly smaller effect, the possibility exists that the passage of time, at least as much as the number of seizures, determines the full neurochemical effect of an

ECS, suggesting that even wider spacing of seizures may be experimentally informative and perhaps clinically desirable.

Dopamine

Animal Studies

Dopamine-mediated animal behaviors (hyperactivity, stereotypies) are generally increased by ECS administered daily, whether given alone or in combination with compounds (L-dopa, apomorphine) known to increase postsynaptic dopaminergic functioning (Modigh, 1975; Green et al., 1977; Deakin et al., 1981; Grahame-Smith, 1984), which are observations that are interpreted as manifestations of increased postsynaptic dopamine receptor sensitivity. The administration of clonidine at doses sufficient to stimulate the noradrenergic postsynaptic receptor augments this effect (Modigh, 1975), whereas depletion of brain norepinephrine attenuates it (Green and Deakin, 1980). The dopamine autoreceptor is also affected by ECS, but in the opposite direction: a decreased sensitivity is reported (Chiodo and Antelman, 1980; Serra et al., 1981). Functionally, however, both receptor effects results in increased locomotor activity.

These behavioral responses, which characterize dopamine receptors, have not been supported by observations of either significant ECS-induced changes in brain dopamine concentration, synthesis, or turnover, or direct neurochemical measurements using radioligand binding techniques (Lerer and Sitaram, 1983). The anatomical site studied (striatum) and the particular radioligand employed (^{3}H-spiperone) however, may not have been optimal for reflecting the effects of ECS.

Human Studies

Neuroendocrine probes are one method that has been used to study dopaminergic mechanisms of ECT in humans (Checkley, 1980; Cowen, 1986). For example, pituitary hormone responses before and after ECT to drugs that have known stimulatory effects on central monoaminergic systems can reflect ECT-induced changes in receptor functioning. In such studies, care must be taken to choose hormones that are not altered in depressive illness, or changes in hormonal responses that are due to relief from depression may be interpreted incorrectly as reflecting changes in receptor sensitivity. Both growth hormone and prolactin responses have been studied, with the former increasing and the latter decreasing in response to dopaminergic stimulation.

The dopamine agonist, apomorphine, has been used to probe receptor changes induced by ECT with rather contradictory results. Although Balldin et al. (1982) failed to find any systematic effects of a course of ECT on the growth hormone response to intravenous apomorphine (some patients showed an increased response, but others showed a decreased response), they did find a consistent (although not significant) ECT-induced increase in apomorphine suppression of serum prolactin in depressed subjects. Christie et al. (1982) conducted a similar trial in depressives, but reported virtually opposite results: a substantial and systematic (but not significant) ECT-induced increase in the growth hormone response to apomorphine, but no effect on apomorphine-induced prolactin suppression. Costain et al. (1982) included a sample of drug-treated depressives in their study in order to control for the effects of clinical improvement and found a substantial *and* significant increase in the growth hormone response to apomorphine after a course of ECT but not after antidepressant drug therapy. [In fact, amitriptyline *reduced* the growth hormone response to apomorphine (Cowen et al., 1984).]

Balldin et al. (1980, 1981, 1982) have also examined dopaminergic effects of ECT in parkinsonian patients who had become partially resistant to L-dopa therapy and who exhibited the "on–off" phenomenon. L-dopa therapy was continued during the trial. A marked improvement in parkinsonian symptoms after ECT was observed in 8 of 12 patients treated, with the best improvement occurring in those patients who had been on L-dopa the longest. Since these patients presumably had the least sensitive receptors, the study provides considerable support for the hypothesis that ECT increases postsynaptic dopamine receptor sensitivity. Moreover, in contrast to the sample of depressives described earlier, a course of ECT in these parkinsonian patients significantly enhanced apomorphine-induced suppression of serum prolactin.

The prolactin response to ECT may provide information on dopaminergic changes itself. Pituitary prolactin release is under tonic dopaminergic inhibitory control, and any changes in peak or total prolactin released over a course of ECT may reflect changes in the sensitivity of pituitary dopamine receptors. Whalley et al. (1982) observed a systematic (but not significant) fall in prolactin response from the first to the second to the last ECT, Deakin et al. (1983) found a significantly smaller release of prolactin after the last than after the first ECT (an effect that did not occur with sham treatments), and Abrams and

Swartz (1985; 1986) demonstrated a systematic fall in peak prolactin elevations across a course of ECT in two different samples of depressed patients, a finding confirmed by Aperia et al. (1985) and Haskett et al. (1985). [Coppen et al. (1980) provide the only contradictory data: their small sample of depressives ($n = 5$) showed a significant *increase* in plasma prolactin concentrations after a course of ECT.] In sum, however, these observations suggest that repeated seizures increase the sensitivity of the pituitary dopamine receptor.

Growth hormone levels, which may more closely reflect dopaminergic effects on hypothalamic, rather than pituitary, receptors, do not appear to change with ECT (Yalow et al., 1968; Ryan et al., 1970; O'Dea et al., 1978; Arato et al., 1980; Whalley et al., 1982; Deakin et al., 1983; Linnoila et al., 1984), although contradictory data exist (Aperia et al., 1986). A possible.explanation for the generally negative growth hormone studies is that dopamine-stimulated growth hormone secretion may involve alpha-2 receptors, which are down-regulated by ECS in animal studies (Modigh et al., 1984).

Several investigators have investigated presynaptic (intracellular) dopaminergic effects of ECT by studying cerbrospinal fluid levels of the dopamine metabolite homovanillic acid before and after a course of ECT (Nordin, Ottosson, and Roos, 1971; Jori et al., 1975; Abrams et al., 1976; Härnryd et al., 1979; Hoffman et al., 1985; Aberg-Wistedt, 1986). Only one study (Jori et al., 1975) demonstrated a significant increase of this metabolite after a course of ECT, and this was for baseline levels only—no increase was observed for its accumulation after probenecid, a drug given to block metabolite transport out of the cerebrospinal fluid and thereby provide a measure of dopamine turnover. It is probably unrealistic to expect cerebrospinal fluid studies to contribute significantly to defining mechanisms of action of ECT that presumably depend on effects at relevant sites in the brain since cerebrospinal fluid metabolite levels reflect the global effects of neurochemical activity throughout the CNS.

Serotonin

Animal Studies

Repeated ECS increases the hyperactivity to rats following the administration of a monoamine-oxidase inhibitor in combination with the serotonin precursor, L-tryptophan (Evans et al., 1976), enhances head-twitching that is induced by another serotonin precursor, 5-hydroxy-tryptophan (Lebrecht and Nowak, 1980), and enhances the hyper-thermic response to the serotonin agonist chlorophenylpiperazine (Vetulani et al., 1981). As noted earlier for the dopamine receptor, chemical lesioning of ascending brain norepinephrine pathways abol-ishes the ECS-induced increases in serotonin-mediated behaviors (Green and Deakin, 1980). In view of the fact that repeated ECS does not increase the brain content or the synthesis rate of serotonin, these findings are consistent with the interpretation (Grahame-Smith et al., 1978) that ECS increases postsynaptic serotonin receptor sensitivity. Identification of ECS-induced serotonin receptor changes by radioli-gand binding has been complicated by the characterization of two receptor types with different responsiveness to ECS. The serotonin-1 receptor exhibits no change in response to ECS (Vetulani et al., 1981; Lerer and Belmaker, 1982), whereas serotonin-2 receptor sensitivity markedly increases in the cortex following ECS (Kellar et al., 1981; Vetulani et al., 1981), suggesting that the ECS-enhanced motor behav-iors previously described are mediated by serotonin-2 receptors (Green, 1986).

Human Studies

Thyrotrophin-releasing hormone (TRH) stimulates the release of pro-lactin from the pituitary, and there is evidence that this action may be mediated by serotonin. Coppen et al. (1980) found that a course of ECT significantly increased the peak prolactin response to intravenous TRH in a sample of severely depressed patients, all of whom recov-ered. As baseline prolactin levels with or without TRH were no different from age- and sex-matched controls, the authors concluded that ECT may act to increase postsynaptic serotonin receptor sensitiv-ity in humans as well as rodents.

Linnoila et al. (1984) studied the urinary excretion of serotonin and its major metabolite, 5-hydroxyindoleacetic acid, in 6 depressed patients receiving ECT. Electroconvulsive therapy significantly reduced the urinary output of both compounds across the overall sample, as well as for each patient individually—a finding the authors interpreted in terms of enhanced efficiency of serotonergic transmission.

Studies of 5-hydroxyindoleacetic acid levels in cerebrospinal fluid after ECT have shown inconsistent results. Several investigators have found no increase in the levels of this metabolite (Cooper et al., 1968; Nordin, Ottosson, and Roos, 1971; Abrams et al., 1976; Härnryd et al.,

1979; Aberg-Wistedt, 1986), whereas others have reported significant increments (Jori et al., 1975; Hoffman et al., 1985; Rudorfer et al., 1986).

Norepinephrine

Animal Studies

Following clonidine administration rodents exhibit sedation and hypoactivity that are attributed to stimulation of the presynaptic alpha-2 adrenoreceptor (Heal et al., 1981). Daily ECS attenuates this clonidine-induced sedation, but not the similar behavioral sedation induced by the beta adrenoreceptor antagonist propranolol, which suggests specific mediation of this response by the alpha-2 adrenoreceptor.

Repeated ECS increases both presynaptic norepinephrine turnover (Kety et al., 1967; Modigh, 1976) and norepinephrine uptake into brain slices (Hendley, 1976; Minchin et al., 1983). Repeated or spaced ECS also consistently reduces beta-adrenoreceptor density in the rodent cortex and hippocampus (Lerer, 1984; Kellar and Stockmeier, 1986)—areas in which the beta-1 receptor subtype predominates—presumably as a compensatory presynaptic receptor down-regulation in response to ECS-induced norepinephrine axon activation and increased neurotransmitter availability in the synaptic cleft (Kellar and Stockmeier, 1986). Serotonergic mediation may be required for this response to ECS as Green (1986) was able to abolish it by lesioning the ascending serotonergic pathways.

Repeated ECS in rats increases the density in the cortex and hippocampus of ^{3}H-prazosin binding sites (Vetulani et al., 1983), which are believed to be identical to the alpha-1 adrenoreceptor. Reversal of clonidine-induced sedation by ECS has already been noted earlier as a presynaptic alpha-2 adrenoreceptor effect; Ebstein et al. (1983) have provided the supporting data that repeated ECS attenuates clonidine-induced inhibition of norepinephrine release in cortical synaptosomal preparations. The alpha-2 adrenoreceptor as identified by its ligand ^{3}H-clonidine is down-regulated by repeated ECS (Vetulani, 1986), but only after several weeks of repeated seizures and not in every laboratory (Kellar and Stockmeier, 1986). Moreover, it is unclear whether this is primarily a presynaptic or postsynaptic effect. It seems reasonable to hypothesize, however, that ECS acts to enhance the availability of norepinephrine at postsynaptic sites by simultaneously up-regulating presynaptic alpha-1 receptors and down-regulating postsynaptic alpha-2 adrenoreceptors (Vetulani, 1984; Lerer, in press).

Human Studies

Dopaminergic effects on growth hormone release have already been described, and there is evidence for an even greater role of noradrenergic mechanisms (Checkley et al., 1984). The alpha-2 receptor agonist clonidine is a known releaser of growth hormone in humans and was used by Slade and Checkley (1980) to study the effects of ECT. These authors infused clonidine intravenously in depressed patients before and after a course of ECT and failed to find any growth hormone response at either test session. These authors also found no growth hormone response to infusions of the alpha-2 receptor agonist, methylamphetamine, but they did observe a significant increase in the cortisol response to this drug, presumably via release of pituitary ACTH—a response that may be mediated by alpha-1 adrenoreceptors because no effects of alpha-2 agonists were observed (Cowen, 1986). [The repeatedly observed ability of a course of ECT to lower elevated plasma cortisol levels in depressed patients is believed to be due to a nonspecific reduction in stress-induced ACTH release associated with relief of depression (Swartz and Chen, 1985.)]

Acetylcholine

Acetylcholine is released acutely during electrically induced seizures in animals and humans (Fink, 1966), but there is scant evidence for any cumulative changes in turnover or synthesis of this neurotransmitter (Lerer, in press). Postsynaptically, however, repeated (but not single) ECS induces small but consistent reductions in cortical muscarinic receptor density (Lerer, 1985). It also reverses the cortical binding effects of chronic atropine administration; however, contradictory data exists (Atterwill, 1980).

Gamma-Amino Butyric Acid (GABA)

Animal Studies

Repeated ECS increases GABA concentrations in the hippocampus, cortex, striatum, and hypothalamus, an effect that is blocked by subconvulsant doses of the GABA-agonist, bicuculline (Green et al., 1977b and 1982; Bowdler and Green, 1982). No ECS-induced changes in cortical ³H-GABA binding have been observed (Deakin et al., 1981). Immediately following ECS, however, there is an almost total inhibition of GABA synthesis and a marked inhibition of GABA release—findings that are difficult to integrate with the notion that ECS-induced increases in brain GABA concentrations might be causally related to the concomitant increase in seizure threshold so consistently observed (Green, 1986).

Endorphins and Enkephalins

Animal Studies

Following repeated ECS, met-enkephalin concentrations are increased in the caudate nucleus, hippocampus, hypothalamus, and limbic system (Green et al., 1977; Hong et al., 1979; Kanamatsu et al., 1986), dynorphin concentrations are increased in limbic and basal ganglia structures and variably affected in the hippocampus (Przewlocki et al., 1981; Kanamatsu et al., 1986), and beta-endorphin concentrations in the hypothalamus are unchanged. Repeated ECS enhances the acute effects of morphine and releases endogenous opioids, and some of the behavioral, neuroendocrine, and EEG effects of ECS in rodents can be completely or partially blocked or reversed by the opiate antagonist, naloxone—observations that are consistent with the view that ECS increases postsynaptic receptor sites for opioid peptides (Swartz and Dunbar, 1983; Holaday et al., 1986; Lerer, in press). [An intriguing related finding of Tortella and Long (1985) is that cerebrospinal fluid obtained following seizures in rats reduced seizure activity in naive rats, an effect that was blocked by naloxone.]

Human Studies

The possibility that ECT exerts its therapeutic effects through endorphinergic mechanisms is suggested by observations that both ECT and beta-endorphin release prolactin in humans. Three studies (Papakostas et al., 1985; Haskett et al., 1985; Turner, Ur, and Grossman, 1987), however, have now failed to demonstrate any effect of the potent and specific opiate antagonist, naloxone, on the prolactin response to ECT, suggesting that an intermediary (e.g., serotonin) is responsible for opioid-induced prolactin release.

Conclusions

It should be clear from this brief review that no coherent general neurotransmitter or receptor theory of the action of ECT is yet possible. The broad suggestions that ECT exerts its beneficial effects in depression through hypothalamic mechanisms (Abrams and Taylor, 1976; Fink and Ottosson, 1980) are not specific enough to be heuristic. What is sorely needed now are systematic applications to human ECT studies of the variegated findings of the ECS investigations in animals that employ neurotransmitter precursors and receptor ligands to enhance or block synaptic transmission in specific systems, with depression score changes as the dependent variable.

11
Patients' Attitudes, Legal Issues, and Informed Consent

Doctors who give ECT have shown remarkably little interest in their patients' views of the procedure and its effects on them, and only recently has this topic received any consideration in the literature. Gomez (1975) was the first to examine the incidence and severity of subjectively experienced side effects of ECT in an attempt to understand why, in her words, "many patients and their relatives view the prospect of ECT with horror." She interviewed 96 patients, most of them depressed, 24 hours after each treatment for a total of 500 consecutive treatments, of which 420 were given with bilateral electrode placement. The self-reported incidence of side-effects was remarkably low: muscle-pain topped the list at 8.2 percent, with subjective memory impairment and headache occurring only about 3 percent of the time. Surprisingly, subjective complaints were no less frequent in patients receiving unilateral than bilateral ECT. The aspect of ECT most disliked by patients who were interviewed after they had received 3 or 4 ECTs related primarily to fear—most frequently a fear of permanent impairment of memory or intellectual abilities, followed about equally by fear of entering the ECT room, fear of death or serious damage, and the apprehension experienced while simply waiting to receive treatment. A quarter of the sample expressed no special fear or dislike of ECT.

Hillard and Folger (1977) administered a questionnaire to patients receiving ECT on two different state mental hospital wards and found that attitudes toward this treatment were significantly more favorable on the ward in which ECT was more frequently given, despite the fact that neither hospital made any effort to brief patients beforehand on the safety or therapeutic aspects of ECT.

Freeman and Kendell (1980) conducted a systematic study of the experiences and attitudes toward ECT among 166 patients who had received treatment from 1 to 6 years earlier. Almost one-half of the patients either had no particular feelings prior to receiving their first ECT or were reassured and pleased that treatment was about to begin. Specifically, a large majority (77 to 90 percent) had no fears at all about becoming unconscious, losing bladder control, receiving electricity, having the seizure, or experiencing brain damage as a result of the treatment. More than 80 percent of the patients said that having ECT was no worse than a visit to the dentist and 50 percent actually preferred the ECT; nevertheless, only 65 percent reported that they would be willing to have it again. One-half of the patients felt that memory impairment was the worst side-effect and 30 percent felt their memory had never returned to normal afterward. Only 1.2 percent, however, felt that the treatment had worked by making them forget their problems. Only about 20 percent fully understood what the treatment involved; most had no idea or only a partial understanding (presumably as a result of the combined cognitive effects of the disorder for which they were treated and the treatment itself). Many patients could not recall ever having signed consent for ECT, did not regard the process as particularly important, and were quite willing to relinquish the responsibility to others (90 percent of the patients said that either the consent procedures had been adequate or were satisfied to defer to the doctor's recommendation); it was the authors' strong impression that most patients would agree to almost anything a doctor suggested.

Hughes et al. (1981) used the same questionnaire to interview 72 patients who received ECT for severe mental illness; 83 percent said they had improved and 81 percent were willing to have ECT again. Slightly more than half thought a visit to the dentist was more distressing. Almost half reported memory impairment after treatment, and 18 percent said it was still present when interviewed. Half said they had received no explanation of the treatment and 28 percent could not remember signing the consent form; nevertheless, only about 10 percent thought the consent procedure should be changed and most thought the decision about ECT should be left to the doctors.

Similar results to the preceding two studies were reported by Kerr et al. (1982), who also found that more than 50 percent of their patients denied ever having had the procedure explained to them.

A prospective study of patients' attitudes regarding ECT was conducted by Baxter et al. (1986) in the community of Berkeley,

California. More than 50 percent of patients who were about to have ECT for the first time were concerned about memory loss, having a seizure, or sustaining brain damage, and about 25 percent were worried about the anesthesia, the possibility of pain, and the use of electricity. After a course of ECT, most of these patients felt that they had received adequate information to decide about having the treatment, were helped by it, and their decision to have it had been a good one. In contrast, patients who had received ECT in the past (some of them presumably without modern anesthesia techniques) were more frightened about the treatment and pessimistic about its outcome, although all consented to a new course of ECT.

In view of the fact that most of the several hundred patients interviewed in these studies and in a review by Freeman and Cheshire (1986) had rather positive views about ECT and did not find the treatment especially frightening, upsetting, painful, or unpleasant, how is it possible to account for the widespread negative public image of ECT (Frankel, 1982; Consensus Development Conference, 1985) and the recent spate of legislative restrictions on its use (Winslade et al., 1984)? I believe there are several contributory factors, which I will discuss as follows.

Abuse of ECT

Fink (1983) points out that professional concerns about ECT are hardly new, citing the critical 1947 report of the Group for the Advancement of Psychiatry (which began with the introductory statement "In view of the reported promiscuous and indiscriminate use of electroshock therapy, your Committee on Therapy decided to devote its first meeting to an evaluation of the role of this type of therapy in psychiatry."). In 1972 Dr. Milton Greenblatt, then the Commissioner of Mental Health for the State of Massachusetts, organized a Task Force to Study and Recommend Standards for the Administration of Electro-Convulsive Therapy (Frankel, 1973). This Task Force was created in response to local allegations about the excessive use of ECT, particularly for outpatient maintenance therapy, by one or two zealous practitioners, as exemplified in an article by Regestein et al. (1975) entitled "A case of prolonged, reversible dementia associated with abuse of electroconvulsive therapy." These authors described in detail the appalling (but apparently ultimately reversible) cognitive consequences in a 57-year-old woman who had received a "maintenance" ECT every Saturday morning *for more than 2 years*. They also briefly described the devastating effects of a similar treatment schedule on an executive, concluding with the statement that "the ready insurance payments for any number of ECT further encourage errors in judgement concerning the efficacy of such treatment." [Basing their recommendations in part on the clinical manuals of Abrams and Fink (1969) and Salzman (1970), the Task Force responded with a series of carefully worded recommendations that limited, among other things, the number of ECTs to be given in a single treatment course and constrained the use of outpatient and maintenance ECT.] Indeed, concerns over the "potential for misuse and abuse of ECT and the desires to ensure the protection of patient's rights" were central to a recent U.S. Government-sponsored conference to assess the place of ECT in medical practice (National Institutes of Health, 1985).

The Anti-ECT Lobby

Among those offering their opinions at this conference, as well as at another one earlier in the year (Electroconvulsive Therapy: Clinical and Basic Research Issues, New York Academy of Sciences, January 16–18, 1985), were members of lay groups such as the Mental Patient Law Project, the Citizen's Commission on Human Rights (sponsored by the Church of Scientology), the Network Against Psychiatric Assault, and the International Network for Alternatives to Psychiatry, as well as several indefatigable individual crusaders against the use of ECT. Anyone who was present at these meetings can readily testify that the term *vocal minority* aptly describes this loose coalition of expatients, civil libertarians, religious cultists, consumer advocates, and medical opportunists,—a consortium virtually unopposed by any equivalent pro-ECT patient advocacy groups. The reasons for this imbalance are obvious: the majority of patients (variously estimated at about 50,000 to 100,000 each year) that are well-satisfied with the ECT they received are hardly motivated to influence public opinion on the subject—they are too busy getting on with their lives and would probably prefer not to be reminded of their illness *or* its treatment.

The resultant disproportionate effectiveness of the anti-ECT lobby is amply demonstrated by the history of the introduction and passage of the highly restrictive Assembly Bill 4481 for legislating ECT usage in California (Moore, 1977). A junior student at the University of Massachusetts, who was also a member of the Network Against

Psychiatric Assault, wrote the bill while participating in a special study project at the University of California. A northern California Assembly-man, John Vasconcellos, was then found who was willing to present the bill which passed both houses of the legislature with only one dissenting vote, and was signed into law by then-Governor Ronald Reagan, who later claimed, under criticism, that he "had no respect for the type of people who had supported the Vasconcellos law," but had signed the bill at the end of the legislative session when he had had more than 100 legislative actions to consider (Bennett, 1983). AB 4481 was successfully challenged by Gary Aden, M.D., an officer of the International Psychat-ric Association for the Advancement of Electrotherapy, and was re-placed by the somewhat less restrictive AB 1032, which remains in force at this time. Interestingly, although the availability of ECT steadily declined during the 7 years after the enactment of AB 1032, there was little year-to-year variation in its use: approximately 1.12 persons per 10,000 population per year received ECT during this period (Kramer, 1985), a figure that is just below the range of the national average of 1.3 to 4.6 per 10,000 when sampled in 1978 (Fink, 1979) and the 1.6 to 2.8 per 10,000 estimated by Thompson and Blaine for 1975 and 1980, but less than the reported 2.42 patients per 10,000 population who received ECT in Massachusetts from 1977 to 1980 (Kramer, 1985).

Inadequate Consent Procedures

Psychiatrists have lagged behind other medical specialists in develop-ing and promulgating the doctrine of informed consent for medical procedures. This is likely to have resulted in large measure from the nature of the patients treated, whose frequent impairments of percep-tion, judgement, and reasoning often require others, including their physicians, to make decisions for them. A stream of recent articles (Salzman, 1977; Culver et al., 1980; Gilbert, 1981; Frankel, 1982; Senter et al., 1984; Winslade et al., 1984), however, makes it abund-antly clear that the laggard must now catch up. In fact, there is no longer any choice in the matter, as state after state introduces mental health legislation with the same three recurrent themes: 1) voluntary patients may not receive involuntary treatment; 2) likewise for compe-tent patients, even if involuntary; and 3) involuntary, incompetent patients may only receive involuntary treatment under court order (or, in some states, in the presence of a documented real and immediate threat to life or limb).

Misrepresentation of ECT in the Media

Although the depiction of ECT in the 1940s movie *The Snake Pit* was accurate for that time, the portrayal of electricity stiffening MacMurphy's body in *One Flew Over the Cuckoo's Nest* was not because the nature of ECT had been completely transformed by modern anesthesia techniques long before the latter movie was filmed. Nevertheless, for reasons known only to themselves, both the director of the movie and the author of the book on which it was based deliberately presented a false image of the treatment to the public. It is difficult to estimate the extent of the adverse effects such portrayals as this (and television specials such as the ABC News closeup *Madness and Medicine*, shown on May 26, 1977, or the Oprah Winfrey show of April 22, 1987) have on prospective candidates for ECT, or on state legislators.

Whether public opinion is less easily swayed by such misrepresentations than many have feared, or such inaccurate portrayals are effectively countered by more balanced media presentations, recent public surveys have revealed an unexpectedly over-all positive attitude toward ECT (Kalayam and Steinhart, 1981; Baxter et al., 1986). Nevertheless, media-induced negative attitudes presumably played an influential role in November 1982, when the citizens of Berkeley, California, approved by referendum a city ordinance that made administering ECT a misdemeanor punishable by a fine of $500 or 6 months in prison, or both (Bennett, 1983). (This ordinance was subsequently reversed by the County Superior Court on a technical point of law.)

Realistic Fears of Memory-Loss

As described in Chapter 9, there is substantial subjective and objective support for long-term, perhaps even permanent, memory loss in some patients who receive sine-wave bilateral ECT. Considering the appropriately high social and individual value placed on intact memory function it is readily understandable that fears of ECT-induced memory loss are paramount among a majority of candidates for and recipients of this treatment. The facile reassurance by generations of psychiatrists (including myself) that such memory-loss was "only temporary" not only occasionally proved inaccurate but served to inculcate a deserved sense of distrust among patients whose personal experience proved otherwise.

Legal Considerations

Frankel (1982) has pointed out that the introduction of civil rights concerns into the mental health controversy over the medicolegal and ethical aspects of ECT has transformed

> what might have been a narrow medical debate into a political challenge involving litigation and legislation, while jurists and legislators largely unfamiliar with ECT have been drawn into the debate.

Although there is understandably great interest and concern over the issue of procedural constraints on civil commitment (e.g., Stone, 1977; APA, 1978; Frankel, 1982), this is a problem that does not directly impinge upon the administration of ECT, which comes into play only *after* a patient's legal status has been determined. At this point, there are two major ethical and legal concerns: the competency of a patient to consent to treatment and the components of valid informed consent.

Competency

The general issue of legal competency is enormously complex and far beyond the scope of this volume. Roth et al. (1977), from the Law and Psychiatry Program at Western Psychiatric Institute, have pointed out the dearth of legal guidance on the question of competency to consent to medical treatment. They note that a person may at the same time be considered competent for some legal purposes and incompetent for others, a person is not judged incompetent merely because of the presence of mental illness, the consent to treatment of an incompetent person does not validly authorize a physician to perform such treatment, and a physician who does not take reasonable steps to obtain legal authorization for treating an incompetent patient who refuses treatment may be held liable. These authors agree that although there is no single valid test for competency,

> It has been our experience that competency is presumed so long as the patient modulates his or her behavior, talks in a comprehensible way, remembers what he or she is told, dresses and acts so as to appear to be in meaningful communication with the environment, and has not been declared legally incompetent.

The ability of a patient to understand the risks, benefits, and alternatives to treatment (including no treatment at all), however, is becoming increasingly the commonly applied standard of competence for consenting to ECT. Interestingly, although the critical element of this "test" of competence is the patient's ability to comprehend the elements that the law presumes to be a part of treatment decision-making, such decision-making need not be *rational* to be legally acceptable. This is exemplified by the patient of Roth et al. (1977) who fully understood the nature of the ECT that was being offered to her, but accepted it because she hoped it would kill her.

The right to refuse treatment, of course, is implicit in the concept of competency. Even committed psychotic patients who are deemed by the law to require continued involuntary psychiatric hospitalization and treatment may refuse ECT, as shown by *N.Y. City Health and Hospitals Corp. v. Stein.* Paula Stein had been committed to Bellevue Hospital by court order to receive whatever course of treatment the psychiatric staff deemed advisable, including ECT, regardless of her consent and without the necessity of prior judicial approval. Because of a recently introduced state Mental Hygiene Law, however, the hospital attempted nonetheless to obtain the patient's consent and when this was not forthcoming, petitioned the court to authorize treatment. In a landmark decision the court denied the petition, concluding that although

> she is sufficiently mentally ill to require further retention . . . that determination does not imply that she lacks the mental capacity to knowingly consent or withhold her consent to electroshock therapy . . . It does not matter whether this court would agree with her judgement; it is enough that she is capable of making a decision, however unfortunate that decision may prove to be.

Informed Consent

The criterion of the ability of the patient to understand the nature of the treatment being offered is, of course, fully consistent with the doctrine of informed consent (Meisel et al., 1977). One of the two 1960 landmark cases of the informed consent doctrine, *Mitchell v. Robinson*, involved a psychiatric patient who had sustained spinal fractures as a result of ECT. Even though the patient's consent had been obtained, and the physician was not deemed negligent in the performance of the procedure, the court nevertheless ruled the consent invalid (and the physician liable) because he had not adequately informed the patient beforehand of the hazards of treatment.

Meisel et al. (1977) pointed out that in order for consent to treatment to be valid the patient must be able to act voluntarily, the patient must be provided with a particular amount of information concerning the treatment (specifically, its risks, benefits, and alternatives), have the capacity to understand the information provided (that is, the patient must be competent), and actually make a decision regarding the treatment (although consent may sometimes be implied by the patient's passive acceptance of the treatment).

Conclusions

It was apparent from the testimony from the floor at the NIMH Consensus Development Conference that the anti-ECT sentiment derived almost entirely from two kinds of patients: those who had received involuntary ECT and those who had received ECT voluntarily but without sufficient warning about the possibility of persistent memory impairment. Psychiatrists who wish to continue having ECT available to them as a therapeutic modality should therefore do three things: 1) discontinue the use of sine-wave devices in favor of those administering a brief-pulse, square-wave stimulus; 2) refrain from giving involuntary ECT except under court order; and 3) carefully inform potential ECT candidates and their families about the possibility, however infrequent, of permanent memory loss after ECT, especially with bilateral electrode placement. Moreover, all patients should be started on substantially suprathreshold unilateral ECT unless their clinical condition is so severe as to warrant bilateral ECT at the outset (Abrams and Fink, 1984). Following these simple guidelines will help defuse the ECT controversy and ensure the continued availability of ECT for the many patients who are likely to benefit from no other form of treatment.

In obtaining consent for ECT the physician should present the advantages and disadvantages of the proposed treatment in sufficient detail to permit the patient a truly informed choice, without either exaggerating the potential benefits (e.g., promising favorable results) or unduly alarming the patient with a litany of every conceivable risk, no matter how remote. A good relationship with both patient and family is essential in this process, which is ultimately based on personal trust. Of particular help are videotapes that have recently become available that portray the rationale and procedures of ECT in a straightforward and unbiased fashion (Baxter and Liston, 1986; Frankel, 1986; Ries, 1987). A clearly written, concise consent form is also required, one that can be readily comprehended by patients who have only a limited ability to focus their attention. An example prepared by Dr. Max Fink (Fink, 1979) provides an excellent model that can be modified to suit the needs of a particular physician or institution.

References

Abbott, R. J., and Loizou, L. A. Neuroleptic malignant syndrome. *Brit. J. Psychiatry 148*:47–51, 1986.

Aberg-Wistedt, A., Martensson, B., Bertilsson, L., and Malmgren, R. Electroconvulsive therapy effects on cerebrospinal fluid monoamine metabolites and platelet serotonin uptake in melancholia. *Convul. Ther. 2*:91–98, 1986.

Abiuso, P., Dunkelman, R., and Proper, M. Electroconvulsive therapy in patients with pacemakers. *J.A.M.A. 240*:2459–2460, 1978.

Abramczuk, J. A., and Rose, N. M. Pre-anaesthetic assessment and the prevention of post-ECT morbidity. *Br. J. Psychiatry 134*:582–587, 1979.

Abrams, R. Daily administration of unilateral ECT. *Am. J. Psychiatry 124*:384–386, 1967.

Abrams, R. Recent clinical studies of ECT. *Semin. Psychiatry 4*:3–12, 1972.

Abrams, R. Drugs in combination with ECT. In: M. Greenblatt (Ed.) *Drugs in Combination with Other Therapies.* Grune and Stratton, New York, pp. 157–164, 1975.

Abrams, R. Clinical prediction of ECT response in depressed patients. *Psychopharmacol. Bull. 2*:48–50, 1982.

Abrams, R. ECT and tricyclic antidepressants in the treatment of endogenous depression. *Psychopharm Bull. 18*:73–765, 1982.

Abrams, R. A hypothesis to explain divergent findings among studies comparing the efficacy of unilateral and bilateral ECT in depression. *Convul. Ther. 2*:253–257, 1986a.

Abrams, R. Is unilateral electroconvulsive therapy really the treatment of choice in endogenous depression? *Ann. N.Y. Acad. Sci. 462*:50–55, 1986b.

Abrams, R. ECT in schizophrenia. *Convul. Ther. 3*:169–170, 1987.

Abrams, R., and Essman, W. B. *Electroconvulsive Therapy: Biological Foundations and Clinical Applications.* Spectrum Publications, New York, 1982.

Abrams, R., Essman, W. B., Taylor, M. A., and Fink, M. Concentration of 5-hydroxyindoleacetic acid, homovanillic acid and tryptophan in the cerebrospinal fluid of depressed patients before and after ECT. *Biol. Psychiatry 11*:85–90, 1976.

Abrams, R., and Fink, M. *Convulsive Therapy: Methods and Applications.* New York Medical College, New York, 1969.

Abrams, R., and Fink, M. Clinical experiences with multiple electroconvulsive treatments. *Compr. Psychiatry 13*:115–122, 1972.

Abrams, R., and Fink, M. The present status of unilateral ECT: Some recommendations. *J. Affective Disord. 7*:245–247, 1984.

Abrams, R., and Swartz, C. M. ECT and prolactin release: Effects of stimulus parameters. *Convul. Ther. 1*:115–119, 1985a.

Abrams, R., and Swartz, C. M. ECT and prolactin release: Relation to treatment response in melancholia. *Convul. Ther. 1*:38–42, 1985b.

Abrams, R., and Swartz, C. M. ECT and prolactin release. Paper presented at C.I.N.P., Puerto Rico, December 17, 1986.

Abrams, R., and Taylor, M. A. Anterior bifrontal ECT: A clinical trial. *Br. J. Psychiatry 122*:587–590, 1973.

Abrams, R., and Taylor, M. A. Unipolar and bipolar depressive illness: Phenomenology and response to electroconvulsive therapy. *Arch. Gen. Psychiatry 30*:320–321, 1974.

Abrams, R., and Taylor, M. A. Catatonia: A prospective study. *Arch. Gen. Psychiatry 33*:579–581, 1976a.

Abrams, R., and Taylor, M. A. Diencephalic stimulation and the effects of ECT in endogenous depression. *Br. J. Psychiatry 129*:482–485, 1976b.

Abrams, R., and Taylor, M. A. Mania and schizo-affective disorder, manic type: A comparison. *Am. J. Psychiatry 133*:1445–1447, 1976c.

Abrams, R., and Taylor, M. A. Differential EEG patterns in affective disorder and schizophrenia. *Arch. Gen. Psychiatry 36*:1355–1358, 1979.

Abrams, R., and Taylor, M. A. Importance of schizophrenic symptoms in the diagnosis of mania. *Am. J. Psychiatry 138*:658–661, 1981.

Abrams, R., and Taylor, M. A. A prospective follow-up study of cognitive functions after ECT. *Convul. Ther.1*:4–9, 1985.

Abrams, R., Taylor, M. A., Faber, R., Ts'o, T., Williams, R, and Almy, G. Bilateral versus unilateral ECT: Efficacy in melancholia. *Am. J. Psychiatry 140*:463–465, 1983.

Abrams, R., Taylor, M. A., and Volavka, J. ECT-induced EEG asymmetry and therapeutic response in melancholia: Relation to treatment electrode placement. *Am. J. Psychiatry 144*:327–329, 1987.

Abrams, R., and Volavka, J. Electroencephalographic effects of convulsive therapy. In: R. Abrams and W. B. Essman (Eds.) *Electroconvulsive*

Therapy: Biological Foundations and Clinical Applications. Spectrum Publications, New York, pp. 157–167, 1982.

Abrams, R., Volavka, J., Dornbush, R., Roubicek, J., and Fink, M. Lateralized EEG changes after unilateral and bilateral electroconvulsive therapy. *Dis. Nerv. Syst. 31*:28–33, 1970.

Abrams, R., Volavka, J., and Fink, M. EEG seizure patterns during multiple unilateral and bilateral ECT. *Compr. Psychiatry 14*:25–28, 1973.

Ackermann, R. F., Engel, J., Jr., and Baxter, L. Positron emission tomography and autoradiographic studies of glucose utilization following electroconvulsive seizures in humans and rats. *Ann. NY Acad. Sci. 462*:263–269, 1986.

Addersley, D. J., and Hamilton, M. Use of succinylcholine in ECT. *Br. Med. J. 1*:195–197, 1953.

Addonizio, G., and Susman, V. Neuroleptic malignant syndrome and use of anesthetic agents. *Am. J. Psychiatry 143*:127–128, 1986.

Aird, R. B., Straut, L. A., Pace, J. W., Hrenoff, M. K., and Bowditch, S. C. Neurophysiologic effects of electrically induced convulsions. *Arch. Neurol. Psychiatry 75*:371–378, 1956.

Albala, A. A., Greden, J. F., Tarika, J., and Carroll, B. J. Changes in serial dexamethasone suppression tests among unipolar depressive receiving electronconvulsive treatment. *Biol. Psychiatry 16*:551–560, 1981.

Alexopoulos, G. S., and Frances, R. J. ECT and cardiac patients with pacemakers. *Am. J. Psychiatry 137*:1111–1112, 1980.

Alexopoulos, G. S., Shamoian, C. J., Lucas, J., Weiser, N., and Berger, H. Medical problems of geriatric psychiatric patients and younger controls during electroconvulsive therapy. *J. Am. Geriatr. Soc. 32*:651–654, 1984.

Alexopoulos, G. S., Young, R. C., and Shamoian, C. A. Unilateral electroconvulsive therapy: An open clinical comparison of two electrode placements. *Biol. Psychiatry 19*:783–787. 1984b.

Allen, R. E., and Pitts, F. N., Jr. ECT for depressed patients with lupus erythematosus. *Am. J. Psychiatry 135*:367–368, 1978.

American Psychiatric Association. *Electroconvulsive Therapy.* Task force report 14, Washington, D.C., 1978, p. 167.

American Psychiatric Association. *Petition to Reclassify ECT Devices.* Appendix G, Washington, D.C., April 1982, pp. G1–G7.

Ames, D., Burrows, G., Davies, B., Maguire, K., and Norman, T. A study of the dexamethasone suppression test in hospitalized depressed patients. *Br. J. Psychiatry 144*:311–313, 1984.

Ananth, J., Samra, D., and Kolivakis, T. Amelioration of drug-induced Parkinsonism by ECT. *Am. J. Psychiatry 136*:1094, 1979.

Annett, M., Hudson, P. T., and Turner, A. Effects of right and left unilateral ECT on naming and visual discrimination analyzed in relation to handedness. *Br. J. Psychiatry 124*:260–264, 1974.

Anton, A. H., Uy, D. S., and Redderson, C. L. Autonomic blockade and the cardiovascular and catecholamine response to electroshock. *Anesth. Analg.* 56:46–54, 1977.

Aperia, B. Hormone pattern and post-treatment attitudes in patients with major depressive disorder given electroconvulsive therapy. *Acta Psychiatr. Scand.* 73:271–274, 1986.

Aperia, B., Thoren, M., and Wetterberg, L. Prolactin and thyrotropin in serum during electronconvulsive therapy in patients with major depressive illness. *Acta Psychiatr. Scand.* 72:302–308, 1985.

Arana, G. W., Baldessarini, R. J., and Ornsteen, M. The dexamethasone suppression test for diagnosis and prognosis in psychiatry. Commentary and review. *Arch. Gen. Psychiatry* 42:1193–1204, 1985.

Arato, M., Erdos, A., Kurcz, M., Vermes, I., and Fekete, M. Studies on the prolactin response induced by electroconvulsive therapy in schizophrenics. *Acta Psychiatr. Scand.* 61:239–44, 1980.

Ashton, R., and Hess, N. Amnesia for random shapes following unilateral and bilateral electroconvulsive shock therapy. *Percept. Mot. Skills* 42:669–70, 1976.

Asnis, G. Parkinson's disease, depression, and ECT: A review and case study. *Am. J. Psychiatry* 134:191–195, 1977.

Asnis, G. M., Fink, M., and Saferstein, S. ECT in metropolitan New York hospitals: A survey of practice, 1975–1976. *Am. J. Psychiatry* 135:479–482, 1978.

Asnis, G. M., and Leopold, M. A. A single-blind study of ECT in patients with tardive dyskinesia. *Am. J. Psychiatry* 135:1235–1237, 1978.

Atterwill, C. K. Lack of effect of repeated electroconvulsive shock on ^{3}H spiroperidol and [3]H 5-hydroxytryptamine binding and cholinergic parameters in rat brain. *J. Neurochem.* 35:729–734, 1980.

Avery, D., and Lubrano, A. Depression treated with imipramine and ECT: The DeCarolis study reconsidered. *Am. J. Psychiatry* 136:559–562, 1979.

Babigian, H. M., and Guttmacher, L. B. Epidemiologic considerations in electroconvulsive therapy. *Arch. Gen. Psychiatry* 41:246–253, 1984.

Babington, R. G., and Wedeking, P. W. Blockade of tardive seizures in rats by electroconvulsive shock. *Brain Res.* 88:141–144, 1975.

Bagadia, V. N., Abhyankar, R. R., Doshi, J., Pradhan, P. V., and Shah, L. P. A double blind controlled study of ECT vs chlorpromazine in schizophrenia. *J. Assoc. Physicians India.* 31:637–640, 1983.

Balldin, J., Bolle, P., Eden, S., Eriksson, E., and Modigh, K. Effects of electroconvulsive treatment on growth hormone secretion induced by monoamine receptor agonists in reserpine-pretreated rats. *Psychoneuroendocrinology* 5:329–337, 1980.

Balldin, J., Granerus, A. K., Lindstedt, G., Modigh, K., and Walinder, J.

Predictors for improvement after electroconvulsive therapy in parkinsonian patients with on-off symptoms. *J. Neural Transm.* 52:199–211, 1981.

Balldin, J., Granerus, A. K., Lindstedt, G., Modigh, K., and Walinder, J. Neuroendocrine evidence for increased responsiveness of dopamine receptors in humans following electroconvulsive therapy. *Psychopharmacology* 76:371–376, 1982.

Barbour, G. L., and Blumenkrantz, M. J. Videotape aids informed consent decision. *J.A.M.A.* 240:2741–2742, 1978.

Barker, J. C., and Baker, A. A. Deaths associated with electroplexy. *J. Ment. Sci.* 105:339–348, 1959.

Barton, J. L. ECT in depression: The evidence of controlled studies. *Biol. Psychiatry* 12:687–695, 1977.

Barton, J. L., Mehta, S., and Snaith, R. P. The prophylactic value of ECT in depressive illness. *Acta Psychiatr. Scand.* 49:386–392, 1973.

Bates, W. J., and Smeltzer, D. J. Electroconvulsive treatment of psychotic self-injurious behavior in a patient with severe mental retardation. *Am. J. Psychiatry 139*:1355–1356, 1982.

Baxter, L. R., Jr., and Liston, E. H. Informed ECT for patients and families with Dr. Max Fink (videotape review). *Convul. Ther.* 2:301–303, 1986.

Baxter, L. R., Roy-Byrne, P., Liston, E. H., and Fairbanks, L. Informing patients about electroconvulsive therapy: Effects of a videotape presentation. *Convul. Ther.* 2:25–29, 1986.

Bayles, S., Busse, E. W., and Ebaugh, F. G. Square waves (BST) versus sine waves in electroconvulsive therapy. *Am. J. Psychiatry 107*:34–41, 1950.

Bennett, A. E. Electroshock and Berkeley. *Biol. Psychiatry 18*:609–610, 1983.

Berent, S., Cohen, B. D., and Silverman, A. Changes in verbal and nonverbal learning following a single left or right unilateral electroconvulsive treatment. *Biol. Psychiatry 10*:95–100, 1975.

Berg, S., Gabriel, A. R., and Impastato, D. J. Comparative evaluation of the safety of chlorpromazine and reserpine used in conjunction with ECT. *J. Neuropsychiatry 1*:104–107, 1959.

Bergman, P. S., Gabriel, A. R., Impastato, D. J., and Wortis, S. B. EEG changes following ECT with the Reiter apparatus. *Conf. Neurol. 12*:347–351, 1952.

Bergsholm, P., Gran, L., and Bleie, H. Seizure duration in unilateral electroconvulsive therapy. The effect of hypocapnia induced by hyperventilation and the effect of ventilation with oxygen. *Acta Psychiatr. Scand.* 69:121–128, 1984.

Berson, S. A., and Yalow, R. S. Radioimmunoassay of ACTH in plasma. *J. Clin. Invest.* 47:2725–2751, 1968.

Bidder, T. G., and Strain, J. J. Modifications of electroconvulsive therapy. *Compr. Psychiatry 11*:507–517, 1970.

Bidder, T. G., Strain, J. J., and Brunschwig, L. Bilateral and unilateral ECT: Follow-up study and critique. *Am. J. Psychiatry 127*:737–745, 1970.

Blachly, P., and Gowing, D. Multiple monitored electroconvulsive treatment. *Compr. Psychiatry 7*:100–109, 1966.

Blachly, P. H., and Semler, H. J. Electroconvulsive therapy of three patients with aortic valve prostheses. *Am. J. Psychiatry 124*:233–236, 1967.

Blaurock, M. F., Lorimer, F. M., Segal, M. M., and Gibbs, F. A. Focal electroencephalographic changes in unilateral electric convulsive therapy. *Arch. Neurol. Psychiatry 64*:220–226, 1950.

Bodley, P. O., and Fenwick, P. B. C. The effect of electroconvulsive therapy on patients with essential hypertension. *Br. J. Psychiatry 112*:1241–1249, 1966.

Bolwig, T. G. The influence of electrically induced seizures on deep brain structures. In: B. Lerer, R. D. Weiner, and R. H. Belmaker (Eds.). *ECT: Basic Mechanisms.* John Libbey, London, pp. 132–138, 1984.

Bolwig, T. G., Hertz, M. M., and Holm-Jensen, J. Blood–brain barrier during electroshock seizures in the rat. *Eur. J. Clin. Invest. 7*:95–100, 1977.

Bourne, H. Convulsion dependence. *Lancet 2*:1193–1196, 1954.

Bourne, H. Convulsion dependence and rational convulsion therapy. *J. Indian Med. Profession 3*:1–6, 1956.

Bowdler, J. M., and Green, A. R. Regional rat brain benzodiazepine receptor number and gamma-aminobutyric acid concentration following a convulsion. *Br. J. Pharmacol. 76*:291–298, 1982.

Boyd, D. A., and Brown, D. W. Electroconvulsive therapy in mental disorders associated with childbearing. *J. Missouri Med. 45*:573–579, 1948.

Braasch, E. R., and Demaso, D. R. Effect of electroconvulsive therapy on serum isoenzymes. *Am. J. Psychiatry 137*:625–626, 1980.

Bracha, S., and Hess, J. P. Death occurring during combined reserpine-electroshock treatment. *Am. J. Psychiatry 113*:257, 1956.

Brandon, S. The history of shock treatment. In: R. L. Palmer (Ed.) *Electroconvulsive Therapy: An Appraisal.* Oxford University Press, New York, pp. 3–10, 1981.

Brandon, S., Cowley, P., McDonald, C., Neville, P., Palmer, R., and Wellstood-Eason, S. Electroconvulsive therapy: Results in depressive illness from the Leicestershire trial. *Br. Med. J. 288*:22–25, 1984.

Brandon, S., Cowley, P., McDonald, C., Neville, P., Palmer, R., and Wellstood-Eason, S. Leicester ECT trial. Results in schizophrenia. *Br. J. Psychiatry 146*:177–183, 1985.

Breggin, P. R. Electroconvulsive therapy for depression [letter]. *N. Engl. J. Med. 303*:1305–1306, 1980.

Bridenbaugh, R. H., Drake, F. R., and O'Regan, T. J. Multiple monitored electroconvulsive treatment of schizophrenia. *Compr. Psychiatry 13*:9–17, 1972.

Brill, N. Q., Crumpton, E., Eiduson, S., Grayson, H. M., Hellman, L. I., and Richards, R. A. Relative effectiveness of various components of electroconvulsive therapy. *Arch. Neurol. Psychiatry 81*:627-635, 1959.

Brockman, R. J., Brockman, J. C., Jacobsohn, N., Gleser, G. C., and Ulett, G. A. Changes in convulsive threshold as related to type of treatment. *Confin. Neurol. 16*:97-104, 1956.

Brodersen, P., Paulson, O. B., Bolwig, T. G., Rogon, Z. E., Rafaelsen, O. J., and Lassen, NA. Cerebral hyperemia in electrically induced epileptic seizures. *Arch. Neurol. 28*:334-338, 1973.

Bross, R. Near fatality with combined ECT and reserpine. *Am. J. Psychiatry 113*:933, 1957.

Brown, G. L. Parkinsonism, depression, and ECT. *Am. J. Psychiatry 132*:1084, 1975.

Brown, G. L., Wilson, W. P., and Green, R. L., Jr. Mental aspects of Parkinsonism and their management. In: S. J. Bern (Ed.) *Parkinson's Disease—Rigidity, Akinesia, Behavior, vol. 2, Selected Communications on Topic.* Verlag Hans Huber, pp. 265-278, 1973.

Brunschwig, L., Strain, J. J., and Bidder, T. G. Issues in the assessment of post-ECT memory changes. *Br. J. Psychiatry 119*:73-74, 1971.

Calloway, S. P., Dolan, R. J., Jacoby, R. J., and Levy, R. ECT and cerebral atrophy. A computed tomographic study. *Acta Psychiatr. Scand. 64*:442-445, 1981.

Campbell, D. The psychological effects of cerebral electroshock. In: H. J. Eysenck (Ed.) *Handbook of Abnormal Psychology: An Experimental Approach.* Pitnam Medical Publishing Co., Ltd., London, pp. 611-633, 1960.

Cannicott, S. M. Unilateral electro-convulsive therapy. *Postgrad. Med. J. 38*:451-459, 1962.

Cannicott, S. M., and Waggoner, R. W. Unilateral and bilateral electroconvulsive therapy. *Arch. Gen. Psychiatry 16*:229-232, 1967.

Caplan, G. Electrical convulsion therapy in the treatment of epilepsy. *J. Ment. Sci. 92*:784, 1946.

Carlson, G. A., and Goodwin, F. R. The stages of mania. *Arch. Gen. Psychiatry 28*:221-228, 1973.

Carney, M. W., and Sheffield, B. F. Depression and Newcastle scales. Their relationship to Hamilton's scale. *Br. J. Psychiatry 121*:35-40, 1972.

Carney, M. W. P., Roth, M., and Garside, R. F. The diagnosis of depressive syndromes and the prediction of E.C.T. response. *Br. J. Psychiatry 111*:659-674, 1965.

Carney, M. W. P., and Sheffield, B. F. The effects of pulse ECT in neurotic and endogenous depression. *Br. J. Psychiatry 125*:91-94, 1974.

Carter, C. Neurological considerations with ECT. *Convul. Ther. Bull. 2*:6-19, 1977.

Cerletti, U. Old and new information about electroshock. *Am. J. Psychiatry* *107*:87–94, 1950.

Cerletti, U. Electroshock therapy. In: F. Marti-Ibanez, A. M. Sackler, and R. R. Sackler (Eds.): *The Great Physiodynamic Therapies in Psychiatry.* Hoeber-Harper, New York, pp. 91–120, 1956.

Cerletti, U., and Bini, L. Un nuevo metodo di shockterapie "L'elettro-shock". *Boll. Acad. Med. Roma 64*:136–138, 1938.

Chacko, R. C., and Root, L. ECT and tardive dyskinesia: Two cases and a review. *J. Clin. Psychiatry 44*:265–266, 1983.

Chapman, A. H. Aortic dacron graft surgery and electroshock: Report of a case. *Am. J. Psychiatry 117*:937, 1961.

Charatan, F. B., and Oldham, A. J. Electroconvulsive treatment in pregnancy. *J. Obstet. and Gynecol. of the British Empire 61*:665–667, 1954.

Chatrian, G. E., and Petersen, M. C. The convulsive patterns provoked by Indoklon, Metrazol and electroshock: Some depth electrographic observations in human patients. *Electroencephalogr. Clin. Neurophysiol. 12*:715–725, 1960.

Checkley, S. A. Neuroendocrine tests of monoamine function in man: A review of basic theory and its application to the study of depressive illness. *Psychol. Med. 10*:35–53, 1980.

Checkley, S. A., Meldrum, B. S., and McWilliam, J. R. Mechanism of action of ECT: Neuroendocrine studies. In: B. Lerer, R. D. Weiner, and R. H. Belmaker (Eds.) *ECT: Basic Mechanisms.* John Libbey, London, pp. 101, 1984.

Chiodo, L. A., and Antelman, S. M. Electroconvulsive shock: Progressive dopamine autoreceptor subsensitivity independent of repeated treatment. *Science 210*:799–801, 1980.

Christie, J. E., Whalley, L. J., Brown, N. S., and Dick, H. Effect of ECT on the neuroendocrine response to apomorphine in severely depressed patients. *Br. J. Psychiatry 140*:268–273, 1982.

Ciraulo, D., Lind, L., Salzman, C., Pilon, R., and Elkins, R. Sodium nitroprusside treatment of ECT-induced blood pressure elevations. *Am. J. Psychiatry 135*:1105–1106, 1978.

Clinical Research Centre Division of Psychiatry. The Northwick Park ECT trial: Predictors of response to real and simulated ECT. *Brit. J. Psychiatry 144*:227–237, 1984.

Clyma, E. A. Unilateral electroconvulsive therapy: How to determine which hemisphere is dominant. *Br. J. Psychiatry 126*:372–379, 1975.

Coffey, C. E., Weiner, R. D., McCall, W. V., and Heinz, E. R. Electroconvulsive therapy in multiple sclerosis: A magnetic resonance imaging study of the brain. *Convul. Ther. 3*:137–144, 1987.

Cohen, B. D., Noblin, C. D., Silverman, A. J., and Penick, S. B. Functional asymmetry of the human brain. *Science 162*:475–477, 1968.

Cooper, A. J., Moir, A. T., and Guldberg, H. C. The effect of electroconvulsive shock on the cerebral metabolism of dopamine and 5-hydroxy-tryptamine. *J. Pharm. Pharmacol. 20*:729–730, 1968.

Cooper, J. R., Bloom, F. E., and Roth, R. H. *The Biochemical Basis of Neuropharmacology, 5th Edition.* Oxford University Press, New York, 1986.

Coppen, A., Abou-Saleh, M. T., Milln, P., Bailey, J., Metcalfe, M., Burns, B. H., and Armond, A. Lithium continuation therapy following electroconvulsive therapy. *Br. J. Psychiatry 139*:284–287, 1981.

Coppen, A., Milln, P., Harwood, J., and Wood, K. Does the dexamethasone suppression test predict antidepressant treatment success? *Br. J. Psychiatry 146*:294–296, 1985.

Coppen, A., Rao, V. A., Bishop, M., Abou-Saleh, M. T., and Wood, K. Neuroendocrine studies in affective disorders. Part 2. Plasma thyroid-stimulating hormone response to thyrotropin-releasing hormone in affective disorders: Effect of ECT. *J. Affective Disord. 2*:317–320, 1980.

Coryell, W. Intrapatient responses to ECT and tricyclic antidepressants. *Am. J. Psychiatry 135*:1108–1110, 1978.

Coryell, W. Hypothalamic-pituitary-adrenal axis abnormality and ECT response. *Psychiatry Res. 6*:283–291, 1982.

Coryell, W., Pfohl, B., and Zimmerman, M. Outcome following electroconvulsive therapy: A comparison of primary and secondary depression. *Convul. Ther. 1*:10–14, 1985.

Coryell, W., and Zimmerman, M. The dexamethasone suppression test and ECT outcome: A six-month follow-up. *Biol. Psychiatry 18*:21–27, 1983.

Coryell, W., and Zimmerman, M. Outcome following ECT for primary unipolar depression: A test of newly proposed response predictors. *Am. J. Psychiatry 141*:862–867, 1984.

Costain, D. W., and Cowen, P. J. ECT and the growth hormone response to apomorphine [letter]. *Br. J. Psychiatry 141*:213, 1982.

Costain, D. W., Cowen, P. J., Gelder, M. G., and Grahame-Smith, D. G. Electroconvulsive therapy and the brain: Evidence for increased dopamine-mediated responses. *Lancet 2*:400–404, 1982.

Costello, C. G., Belton, G. P., Abra, J. C., and Dunn, B. E. The amnesic and therapeutic effects of bilateral and unilateral ECT. *Br. J. Psychiatry 116*:69–78, 1970.

Coull, D. C., Crooks, J., Dingwall-Fordyce, I., Scott, A. M., and Weir, R. D. Amitriptyline and cardiac disease: Risk of sudden death identified by monitoring system. *Lancet 2*:590–591, 1970.

Cowen, P. J. Neuroendocrine responses as a probe into the mechanisms of action of electroconvulsive therapy. *Ann. NY Acad. Sci. 462*:163–171, 1986.

Cowen, P. J., Braddock, L. E., and Gosden, B. The effect of amitriptyline treatment on the growth hormone response to apomorphine. *Psychopharmacology 83*:378–379, 1984.

Cronholm, B. Post-ECT amnesias. In: G. A. Talland and N. Waugh (Eds.) *The Pathology of Memory*. Academic Press, New York, pp. 81–89, 1969.

Cronholm, B., and Blomquist, C. Memory disturbances after electroconvulsive therapy: II. Conditions one week after a series of treatments. *Acta Psychiatr. Scand. 32*:18–25, 1959.

Cronholm, B., and Lagergren, A. Memory disturbances after electroconvulsive therapy. *Acta Psychiatr. Scand. 34*:283–310, 1959.

Cronholm, B., and Molander, L. Memory disturbances after electroconvulsive therapy: I. Conditions six hours after electroshock treatment. *Acta Psychiatr. Scand. 32*:280–306, 1957.

Cronholm, B., and Molander, L. Memory disturbances after electroconvulsive therapy: IV. Influence of an interpolated electroconvulsive shock on retention of memory material. *Acta Psychiatr. Scand. 36*:83–90, 1961.

Cronholm, B., and Molander, L. Memory disturbances after electroconvulsive therapy: V. Conditions one month after a series of treatments. *Acta Psychiatr. Scand. 40*:212–216, 1964.

Cronholm, B., and Ottosson, J.-O. Experimental studies of the therapeutic action of electroconvulsive therapy in endogenous depression. *Acta Psychiatr. Neurol. Scand. 35*:69–102, 1960.

Cronholm, B., and Ottosson, J.-O. Memory functions in endogenous depression before and after electroconvulsive therapy. *Arch. Gen. Psychiatry 5*:193–199, 1961a.

Cronholm, B., and Ottosson, J.-O. "Countershock" in electroconvulsive therapy. Influence on retrograde amnesia. *Arch. Gen. Psychiatry 4*:254–258, 1961b.

Cronholm, B., and Ottosson, J.-O. The experience of memory function after electroconvulsive therapy. *Br. J. Psychiatry 109*:251–258, 1963a.

Cronholm, B., and Ottosson, J.-O. Ultrabrief stimulus technique in electroconvulsive therapy. I. Influence on retrograde amnesia of treatments with the Elther ES electroshock apparatus, Siemens Konvulsator III and of lidocaine-modified treatment. *J. Nerv. Ment. Dis. 137*:117–123, 1963b.

Cronin, D., Bodley, P., Potts, L., Mather, M. D., Gardner, R. K., and Tobin, J. C. Unilateral and bilateral ECT: A study of memory disturbance and relief from depression. *J. Neurol. Neurosurg. Psychiatry 33*:705–711, 1970.

Cropper, C. F. J., and Hughes, M. Cardiac arrest (with apnoea) after E.C.T. *Br. J. Psychiatry 110*:222–225, 1964.

Crow, T. J., and Johnstone, E. C. Controlled trials of electroconvulsive therapy. *Ann. NY Acad. Sci. 462*:12–29, 1986.

Crowe, R. R. Current concepts. Electroconvulsive therapy—a current perspective. *N. Engl. J. Med. 311*:163–167, 1984.

Crowe, R. R., Bushnell, L., Shaw, D., Pfohl, B., and Varney, N. Daily vs. alternate-day electroconvulsive therapy. *Am. J. Psychiatry*, in press.

Culver, C. M., Ferrell, R. B., and Green, R. M. ECT and special problems of informed consent. *Am. J. Psychiatry 137*:586–591, 1980.

D'Elia, G. Unilateral electroconvulsive therapy. *Acta Psychiatr. Scand. 215*:5–98, 1970.

D'Elia, G., and Perris, C. Seizure and post-seizure electroencephalographic pattern. *Acta Psychiatr. Scand. 215*:9–29, 1970.

D'Elia, G., and Raotma, H. Is unilateral ECT less effective than bilateral ECT? *Br. J. Psychiatry 126*:83–89, 1975.

D'Elia, G., and Widepalm, K. Comparison of frontoparietal and temporoparietal unilateral electroconvulsive therapy. *Acta Psychiatr. Scand. 50*:225–232, 1974.

Daniel, W. F. ECT-induced hyperactive delirium and brain laterality. *Am. J. Psychiatry 142*:521–522, 1985.

Daniel, W. F., and Crovitz, H. F. Acute memory impairment following electroconvulsive therapy. 1. Effects of electrical stimulus waveform and number of treatments. *Acta Psychiatr. Scand. 67*:1–7, 1983a.

Daniel, W. F., and Crovitz, H. F. Acute memory impairment following electroconvulsive therapy. 2. Effects of electrode placement. *Acta Psychiatr. Scand. 67*:57–68, 1983b.

Daniel, W. F., and Crovitz, H. F. Disorientation during electroconvulsive therapy: Technical, theoretical, and neuropsychological issues. *Ann. NY Acad. Sci. 462*:293–306, 1986.

Daniel, W. F., Crovitz, H. F., Weiner, R. D., Swartzwelder, H. S., and Kahn, E. M. ECT-induced amnesia and postictal EEG suppression. *Biol. Psychiatry 20*:344–348, 1985.

Daniel, W. F., Weiner, R. D., and Crovitz, H. F. Autobiographical amnesia with ECT: An analysis of the roles of stimulus wave form, electrode placement, stimulus energy, and seizure length. *Biol. Psychiatry 18*:121–126, 1983.

Davidson, J., McLeod, M., Law-Yone, B., and Linnoila, M. Comparison of electroconvulsive therapy and combined phenelzine-amitriptyline in refractory depression. *Arch. Gen. Psychiatry 35*:639–644, 1978.

Deakin, J. F., Ferrier, I. N., Crow, T. J., Johnstone, E. C., and Lawler, P. Effects of ECT on pituitary hormone release: Relationship to seizure, clinical variables and outcome. *Br. J. Psychiatry 143*:618–624, 1983.

Deakin, J. F., Owen, F., Cross, A. J., and Dashwood, M. J. Studies on possible mechanisms of action of electroconvulsive therapy; effects of repeated electrically induced seizures on rat brain receptors for monoamines and other neurotransmitters. *Psychopharmacology 73*:345–349, 1981.

Dec, G. W., Stern, T. A., and Welch, C. The effects of electroconvulsive therapy on serial electrocardiograms and serum cardiac enzyme values: A prospective study of depressed hospitalized inpatients. *J.A.M.A. 253*:2525–2529, 1985.

DeCarolis, V., Gilberti, F., Roccatagliata, G., Rossi, R., and Venutti, G. Imipramine and electroshock in the treatment of depression: A clinical statistical analysis of 437 cases. *Dis. Nerv. Syst. 16*:29–42, 1964.

Decina, P., Malitz, S., Sackeim, H. A., Holzer, J., and Yudofsky, S. Cardiac arrest during ECT modified by beta-adrenergic blockade. *Am. J. Psychiatry 141*:298–300, 1984.

Decina, P., Guthrie, E. B., Sackeim, H. A., Kahn, D., and Malitz, S. Continuation ECT in the management of relapses of major affective episodes. *Acta Psychiatr. Scand. 75*:559–562, 1987a.

Decina, P., Sackeim, H. A., Kahn, D. A., Pierson, D., Hopkins, N., and Malitz, S. Effects of ECT on the TRH stimulation test. *Psychoneuroendocrinology 12*:29–34, 1987b.

Deglin, V. L. Kliniko-eksperimental'noe izuchenie unilateral'nykh elektrosudorozh-nykh pripadkov. *Zh Nevropatol. Psikhiatr. 73*:1609–21, 1973.

Deliyiannis, S., Eliakim, M., and Bellet, S. The electrocardiogram during electroconvulsive therapy as studied by radioelectrocardiography. *Am. J. Cardiol. 10*:187–192, 1962.

Demuth, G. W., and Rand, B. S. Atypical major depression in a patient with severe primary degeneration dementia. *Am. J. Psychiatry 137*:1609–1610, 1980.

Devanand, D. P., Decina, P., Sackeim, H. A., Hopkins, N., Novacenko, H., and Malitz, S. Serial DSTs: Initial suppressors and non-suppressors treated with ECT. *Abstracts Soc. Biol. Psychiatry*, 1986, pg. 256.

Dewald, P. A., Margolis, N. M., and Weiner, H. Vertebral fractures as complications of electroconvulsive therapy. *J.A.M.A. 154*:981–984, 1954.

Dornbush, R. L. Memory and induced ECT convulsions. *Semin. Psychiatry 4*:47–54, 1972.

Dornbush, R., Abrams, R., and Fink, M. Memory changes after unilateral and bilateral convulsive therapy (ECT). *Br. J. Psychiatry 119*:75–78, 1971.

Dornbush, R. L., and Williams, M. Memory and ECT. In: M. Fink, S. Kety, J. McGaugh, and T. Williams (Eds.): *Psychobiology of Convulsive Therapy*. V. H. Winston and Sons, Washington, D.C., pp. 199–205, 1974.

Douglas, C. J., and Schwartz, H. I. ECT for depression caused by lupus cerebritis: A case report. *Am. J. Psychiatry 139*:1631–1632, 1982.

Dressler, D. M., and Folk, J. The treatment of depression with ECT in the presence of brain tumor. *Am. J. Psychiatry 132*:1320–1321, 1975.

Dubovsky, S. L., Gay, M., Franks, R. D., and Haddenhorst, A. ECT in the presence of increased intracranial pressure and respiratory failure: Case report. *J. Clin. Psychiatry 46*:489–491, 1985.

Dunn, C. G., and Quinlan, D. Indicators of E.C.T. response and non-response in the treatment of depression. *J. Clin. Psychiatry 39*:620–622, 1978.

Durrant, B. W. Dental care in electroplexy. *Br. J. Psychiatry 112*:1173–1176, 1966.

Dysken, M., Evans, H. M., Chan, C. H., and Davis, J. M. Improvement of depression and parkinsonism during ECT: A case study. *Neuropsychobiology* 281–86, 1976.

Ebstein, R. P., Lerer, B., Shlaufman, M., and Belmaker, R. H. The effect of repeated electroconvulsive shock treatment and chronic lithium feeding on the release of norepinephrine from rat cortical vesicular preparations. *Cell. Mol. Neurobiol. 3*:191–201, 1983.

Egbert, L. D., and Wolfe, S. Evaluation of methohexital for premedication in electroshock therapy. *Anesth. Analg. 39*:416–419, 1960.

Egbert, L. D., Wolfe, S., Melmed, R. M., Deas, T. C., and Mullin, C. S., Jr. Reduction of cardiovascular stress during electroshock therapy by trimethaphan. *J. Clin. Exp. Psychopath. 20*:315–319, 1959.

El-Ganzouri, A. R., Ivankovich, A. D., Braverman, B., and McCarthy, R. Monoamine oxidase inhibitors: should they be discontinued preoperatively? *Anesth. Analg. 64*:592–596, 1985.

Elliot, D. L., Linz, D. H., and Kane, J. A. Electroconvulsive therapy: Pretreatment medical evaluation. *Arch. Intern Med. 142*:979–981, 1982.

Endler, N. S., and Persad, E. *Electroconvulsive Therapy: The Myths and the Realities.* Hans Huber, Toronto, in press.

Engle, J., Jr. The use of positron emission tomographic scanning in epilepsy. *Ann. Neurol. 15*:S180–S191, 1984.

Engle, J., Jr., Duhl, D. E., and Phelps, M. E. Patterns of human local cerebral glucose metabolism during epileptic seizures. *Science 218*:64–66, 1982.

Erman, M. K., Welch, C. A., and Mandel, M. R. A comparison of two unilateral ECT electrode placements: Efficacy and electrical energy considerations. *Am. J. Psychiatry 136*:1317–1319, 1979.

Essig, C. F. Frequency of repeated electroconvulsions and the acquisition rate of a tolerance-like response. *Exp. Neurol. 25*:571–574, 1969.

Evans, J. P., Grahame-Smith, D. G., Green, A. R., and Tordoff, A. F. Electroconvulsive shock increases the behavioural responses of rats to brain 5-hydroxytryptamine accumulation and central nervous system stimulant drugs. *Br. J. Pharmacol. 56*:193–199, 1976.

Faber, R. Dental fracture during ECT [letter]. *Am. J. Psychiatry 140*:1255–1256, 1983.

Feldman, M. J. A prognostic scale for shock therapy. *Psychol. Monogr. No. 327*, 1951.

Fink, M. Cholinergic aspects of convulsive therapy. *J. Nerv. Ment. Dis. 142*:475–484, 1966.

Fink, M. F. *Convulsive Therapy: Theory and Practice.* Raven Press, New York, 1979.

Fink, M. Missed seizure and the unilateral-bilateral electroconvulsive therapy controversy [letter]. *Am. J. Psychiatry 140*:198–199, 1983.

Fink, M. Meduna and the origins of convulsive therapy. *Am. J. Psychiatry 141*:1034–1041, 1984.

Fink, M. Neuroendocrine predictors of electroconvulsive therapy outcome: Dexamethasone suppression test and prolactin release. *Ann. NY Acad. Sci. 462*:30–36, 1986a.

Fink, M. Training in Convulsive Therapy. *Convul. Ther. 2*:227–229, 1986b.

Fink, M. Is ECT usage decreasing? *Conv. Ther. 3*:171–173, 1987.

Fink, M., Gujavarty, K., and Greenberg, L. Serial dexamethasone suppression tests in ECT. *Clin. Neuropharmacol. 9*:444–446, 1986.

Fink, M., and Johnson, L. Monitoring the duration of electroconvulsive therapy seizure: 'Cuff' and EEG methods compared. *Arch. Gen. Psychiatry 39*:1189–1191, 1982.

Fink, M., and Kahn, R. L. Relation of EEG delta activity to behavioral response in electroshock: Quantitative serial studies. *Arch. Neurol. Psychiatry 78*:516–525, 1957.

Fink, M., and Kahn, R. L. Behavioral patterns in convulsive therapy. *Arch. Gen. Psychiatry 5*:30–36, 1961.

Fink, M., Kahn, R. L., Karp, E., Pollack, M., Green, M., Alan, B., and Lefkowitz, H. J. Inhalant-induced convulsions; significance for the theory of the convulsive therapy process. *Arch. Gen. Psychiatry 4*:259–266, 1961.

Fink, M., Kahn, R. L., and Pollack, M. Psychological factors affecting individual differences in behavioral response to convulsive therapy. *J. Nerv. Ment. Dis. 128*:243–248, 1959.

Fink, M., and Ottosson, J. O. A theory of convulsive therapy in endogenous depression: Significance of hypothalamic functions. *Psychiatry Res. 2*:49–61, 1980.

Finner, R. W. Duration of conyulsion in electric shock therapy. *J. Nerv. Ment. Dis. 119*:530–537, 1954.

Fisher, K. A. Changes in test performance of ambulatory depressed patients undergoing E.C.T. *J. Gen. Psychol. 41*:195–232, 1949.

Fleminger, J. J., Horne, D. J., de L., Nair, N. P. V., and Nott, P. N. Differential effect of unilateral and bilateral ECT. *Am. J. Psychiatry 127*:430–436, 1970a.

Fleminger, J. J., Horne, D. J., de L., Nair, N. P. V., and Nott, P. N. Unilateral electroconvulsive therapy and cerebral dominance: Effect of right- and left-sided electrode placement on verbal memory. *J. Neurol. Neurosurg. Psychiatry 33*:408–411, 1970b.

Folstein, M. F., Folstein, S. W., and McHugh, P. R. "Mini Mental State", a practical method of grading the cognitive state of patients for the clinician. *J. Psychiatr. Res. 12*:189–198, 1975.

Forssman, H. Follow-up study of 16 children whose mothers were given electric convulsive therapy during gestation. *Acta Psychiatr. Neurol. Scand. 30*:437–441, 1955.

Foster, M. W., and Gayle, R. F. Dangers in combining Reserpine (Serpasil) with electroconvulsive therapy. *J.A.M.A. 159*:1520–1522, 1955.

Foulds, G. A. Temperamental differences in maze performance: II. The effect of distraction and of electroconvulsive therapy on psychomotor retardation. *Br. J. Psychol. 43*:33–41, 1952.

Frankel, F. H. Electro-convulsive therapy in Massachusetts: A task force report. *Mass. J. Ment. Health 3*:3–29, 1973.

Frankel, F. H. (Ed.): Report No. 14 of the American Psychiatric Association Task Force on Convulsive Therapy. APA, Washington, D.C., 1978.

Frankel, F. H. Medicolegal and ethical aspects of treatment. In: R. Abrams and W. B. Essman (Eds.) *Electroconvulsive Therapy: Biological Foundations and Clinical Applications.* Spectrum Publications, New York, pp. 245–258, 1982.

Frankel, F. H. Informed ECT for Health Professionals with Dr. Max Fink (videotape review). *Convul. Ther. 2*:303, 1986.

Fraser, R. M., and Glass, I. B. Unilateral and bilateral ECT in elderly patients. A comparative study. *Acta Psychiatr. Scand. 62*:13–31, 1980.

Frederiksen, S. O., and d'Elia, G. Electroconvulsive therapy in Sweden. *Br. J. Psychiatry 134*:283–287, 1979.

Freeman, C. P. L., Basson, J. V., and Crighton, A. Double-blind controlled trial of electroconvulsive therapy (E.C.T.) and simulated E.C.T. in depressive illness. *Lancet 1*:738–740, 1978.

Freeman, C. P. L., and Cheshire, K. E. Attitude studies on electroconvulsive therapy. *Conv. Ther. 2*:31–42, 1986.

Freeman, C. P., and Kendell, R. E. ECT: Patients' experiences and attitudes. *Br. J. Psychiatry 137*:8–16, 1980.

Freeman, C. P., Weeks, D., and Kendell, R. E. ECT: II: Patients who complain. *Br. J. Psychiatry 137*:17–25, 1980.

Freese, K. J. Can patients safely undergo electroconvulsive therapy while receiving monoamine oxidase inhibitors? *Conv. Ther. 3*:190–194, 1987.

Friedberg, J. Shock treatment, brain damage, and memory loss: A neurological perspective. *Am. J. Psychiatry 134*:1010–1014, 1977.

Friedel, R. O. The combined use of neuroleptics and ECT in drug resistant schizophrenic patients. *Psychopharm. Bull. 22*:928–930, 1986.

Friedman, E. Unidirectional electrostimulated convulsive therapy. I: The effect of wave form and stimulus characteristics on the convulsive dose. *Am. J. Psychiatry 99*:218–223, 1942.

Friedman, E., and Wilcox, P. H. Electrostimulated convulsive doses in intact humans by means of unidirectional currents. *J. Nerv. Ment. Dis. 96*:56–63, 1942.

Fromholt, P., Christensen, A. L., and Strömgren, L. S. The effects of unilateral and bilateral electroconvulsive therapy on memory. *Acta Psychiatr. Scand. 49*:466–478, 1973.

Funkenstein, D. H., Greenblatt, M., and Solomon, H. C. An autonomic nervous system test of prognostic significance in relation to electroshock treatment. *Psychosom. Med. 14*:347–362, 1952.

Gaitz, C. M., Pokorny, A. D., and Mills, M., Jr. Death following electroconvulsive therapy. *Arch. Neurol. Psychiatry 75*:493–499, 1956.

Galen, R. S., and Gambino, S. R. *Beyond Normality: The Predictive Value and Efficiency of Medical Diagnoses.* John Wiley and Son, New York, p. 17, 1975.

Gallineck, A. Organic sequelae of electric convulsive therapy including facial and body dysgnosias. *J. Nerv. Ment. Dis. 115*:377–393, 1952.

Gallineck, A., and Kalinowsky, L. B. Psychiatric aspects of multiple sclerosis. *Dis. Nerv. Syst. 19*:77–80, 1958.

Gambill, J. D., and McLean, P. E. Suicide after unilateral ECT in a patient previously responsive to bilateral ECT. *Psychiatr. Q. 55*:279–281, 1983.

Gassell, M. M. Deterioration after electroconvulsive therapy in patients with intracranial meningeoma. *Arch. Gen. Psychiatry 3*:504–506, 1960.

Geoghegan, J. J., and Stevenson, G. H. Prophylactic electroshock. *Am. J. Psychiatry 105*:494–496, 1949.

Gerst, J. W., Enderie, J. D., Staton, R. D., Barr, C. E., and Brumback, R. A. The electroencephalographic pattern during electroconvulsive therapy II. Preliminary analysis of spectral energy. *Clin. Electroencephalogr. 13*:251–256, 1982.

Ghangadhar, B. N., Kapur, R. L., and Kalyanasundaram, S. Comparison of electroconvulsive therapy with imipramine in endogenous depression: A double blind study. *Br. J. Psychiatry 141*:367–371, 1982.

Gibson, T. C., Leaman, D. M., Devors, J., and Lepeschkin, E. E. Pacemaker function in relation to electroconvulsive therapy. *Chest 63*:1025–1027, 1973.

Gilbert, D. T. Shock therapy and informed consent. *Illinois Bar Journal*, January:272–287, 1981.

Gill, D., and Lambourn, J. Indications for electric convulsion therapy and its use by senior psychiatrists. *Br. Med. J. 1*:1169–1171, 1979.

Glassman, A., Kantor, S. J., and Shostak, M. Depression, delusions and drug response. *Am. J. Psychiatry 132*:716–719, 1975.

Glassman, A. H., Perel, J. M., Shostak, M., Kantor, S. J., and Fleiss, J. L. Clinical implications of imipramine plasma levels for depressive illness. *Arch. Gen. Psychiatry 34*:197–204, 1977.

Golden, C. J., Hammeke, T. A., and Purisch, A. D. Diagnostic validity of a standardized neuropsychological battery derived from Luria's neuropsychological tests. *J. Consult. Clin. Psychol. 46*:1258–1265, 1978.

Goldman, D. Brief stimulus electric shock therapy. *J. Nerv. Ment. Dis.* *110*:36–45, 1949.

Gomez, J. Subjective side-effects of ECT. *Br. J. Psychiatry 127*:609–611, 1975.

Gordon, D. The electrical and radiological aspects of ECT. In: R. L. Palmer (Ed.) *Electroconvulsive Therapy: An Appraisal.* Oxford University Press, New York, pp. 79–96, 1981.

Gordon, D. Electro-convulsive therapy with minimum hazard. *Br. J. Psychiatry 141*:12–18, 1982.

Gottlieb, G., and Wilson, I. Cerebral dominance: Temporary disruption of verbal memory by unilateral electroconvulsive shock treatment. *J. Comp. Physiol. Psychol. 60*:368–370, 1965.

Grahame-Smith, D. G. The neuropharmacological effects of electroconvulsive shock and thier relationship to the therapeutic effect of electroconvulsive therapy in depression. *Adv. Biochem. Psychopharmacol. 39*:327–343, 1984.

Grahame-Smith, D. G., Green, A. R., and Costain, D. W. Mechanism of the antidepressant action of electroconvulsive therapy. *Lancet 1*:254–257, 1978.

Gran, L., Bergsholm, P., and Bleie, H. Seizure duration in unilateral electroconvulsive therapy. A comparison of the anaesthetic agents etomidate and Althesin with methohexitone. *Acta Psychiatr. Scand. 69*:472–483, 1984.

Gravenstein, J. S., Anton, A. H., Weiner, S. M., and Tetlow, A. G. Catecholamine and cardiovascular response to electroconvulsion therapy in man. *Br. J. Anaesth. 37*:833–839, 1965.

Green, A. R. Changes in gamma-aminobutyric acid biochemistry and seizure threshold. *Ann. NY Acad. Sci. 462*:105–119, 1986.

Green, A. R., and Deakin, J. F. Brain noradrenaline depletion prevents ECS-induced enhancement of serotonin- and dopamine-medicated behavior. *Nature 285*:232–233, 1980.

Green, A. R., Heal, D. J., and Grahame-Smith, D. G. Further observations on the effect of repeated electroconvulsive shock on the behavioral responses of rats produced by increases in the functional activity of brain 5-hydroxytryptamine and dopamine. *Psychopharmacology 52*:195–200, 1977.

Green, A. R., Sant, K., Bowdler, J. M., and Cowen, P. J. Further evidence for a relationship between changes in GABA concentration in rat brain and enhanced monoamine-mediated behavioural responses following repeated electroconvulsive shock. *Neuropharmacology 21*:981–984, 1982.

Green, M. A. Significance of individual variability in EEG response to electroshock. *J. Hillside Hosp. 6*:229–240, 1957.

Green, M. A. Relation between threshold and duration of seizures and electrographic change during convulsive therapy. *J. Nerv. Ment. Dis. 131*:117–120, 1960.

Green, R., and Woods, A. Effects of modified electro-convulsive therapy on the electrocardiogram. *Br. Med. J. 1*:1503–1505, 1955.

Greenbank, R. K. Aortic homograft surgery and electroshock: Case report. *Am. J. Psychiatry 115*:469, 1958.

Greenberg, L. B., and Gujavarty, K. The neuroleptic malignant syndrome: Review and report of three cases. *Compr. Psychiatry 26*:63–70, 1985.

Greenberg, L. B., Anand, A., Roque, C. T., and Grinberg, Y. Electroconvulsive therapy and cerebral venous angioma. *Convul. Ther. 2*:197–202, 1986.

Greenberg, L. B. Detection of prolonged seizures during electroconvulsive therapy: A comparison of electroencephalogram and cuff monitoring. *Convul. Ther. 1*:32–37, 1985.

Greenblatt, M., Grosser, G. H., and Wechsler, H. Differential response of hospitalized depressed patients in somatic therapy. *Am. J. Psychiatry 120*:935–943, 1964.

Gregory, S., Shawcross, C. R., and Gill, D. The Nottingham ECT study. A double-blind comparison of bilateral, unilateral and simulated ECT in depressive illness. *Br. J. Psychiatry 146*:520–524, 1985.

Grinspoon, L., and Greenblatt, M. Pharmacotherapy combined with other treatment methods. *Compr. Psychiatry 4*:256–262, 1963.

Griswold, R. L. Plasma adrenaline and noradrenaline in electroshock therapy in man and in rats. *J. Apl. Physiol. 12*:117–120, 1958.

Grunhaus, L., Zelnik, T., Albala, A. A., Rabin, D., Haskett, R., Zis, A. P., and Greden, J. Serial dexamethasone suppression tests in depressed patients treated only with electroconvulsive therapy. *J. Affect. Disorders 13*:233–240, 1987.

Gujavarty, K., Greenberg, L. B., and Fink, M. Electroconvulsive therapy and neuroloeptic medication in therapy-resistant positive-symptom psychosis. *Convul. Ther. 3*:185–195, 1987.

Guze, S. B. The occurrence of psychiatric illness in systemic lupus erythematosus. *Am. J. Psychiatry 123*:1562–1570, 1967.

Guze, B. H., Weinman, B., and Diamond, R. P. Use of ECT to treat bipolar depression in a mental retardate with cerebral palsy. *Convul. Ther. 3*:60–64, 1987.

Halliday, A. M., Davison, K., Browne, M. W., and Kreeger, L. C. A comparison of the effects on depression and memory of bilateral E.C.T. and unilateral E.C.T. to the dominant and non-dominant hemispheres. *Br.J. Psychiatry 114*:997–1012, 1968.

Hamilton, M. A rating scale for depression. *J. Neurol. Neurosurg. Psychiatry 23*:56–62, 1960.

Hamilton, M. Prediction of the response of depressions to ECT. In: R. Abrams and W. B. Essman (Eds.) *Electroconvulsive Therapy: Biological Foundations and Clinical Applications.* Spectrum Publications, New York, pp. 113–128, 1982.

Hamilton, M., Stocker, M. J., and Spencer, C. M. Post-ECT cognitive defect and elevation of blood pressure. *Brit. J. Psychiatry 135*:77–78, 1979.

Hamilton, M., and White, J. M. Factors related to the outcome of depression treated with ECT. *J. Ment. Sci. 106*:1031–1041, 1960.

Handforth, A. Postseizure inhibition of kindled seizures by electroconvulsive shock. *Exp. Neurol. 78*:483–491, 1982.

Hardman, J. B., and Morse, R. M. Early electroconvulsive treatment of a patient who had artificial aortic and mitral values. *Am. J. Psychiatry 128*:895–897, 1972.

Harms, E. The origin and early history of electrotherapy and electroshock. *Am. J. Psychiatry 111*:933–934, 1956.

Harnryd, C., Bjerkenstedt, L., Grimm, V. E., and Sedvall, G. Reduction of MOPEG levels in cerebrospinal fluid of psychotic women after electroconvulsive treatment. *Psychopharmacology 64*:131–4, 1979.

Harper, R. G., and Wiens, A. N. Electroconvulsive therapy and memory. *J. Nerv. Ment. Dis. 161*:245–254, 1975.

Harris, J. A., and Robin. A. A. A controlled trial of phenelzine in depressive reactions. *J. Ment. Sci. 106*:1432–1437, 1960.

Haskett, R. F., Zis, A. P., and Albala, A. A. Hormone response to repeated electroconvulsive therapy: Effects of naloxone. *Biol. Psychiatry 20*:623–633, 1985.

Hastings, D. W. Circular manic-depressive reaction modified by "prophylactic electroshock." *Am. J. Psychiatry 118*:258–260, 1961.

Hauser, W. A. Status epilepticus: Frequency, etiology, and neurological sequelae. *Adv. Neurol. 34*:3–14, 1983.

Heal, D. J., Akagi, H., Bowdler, J. M., and Green, A. R. Repeated electroconvulsive shock attenuates clonidine-induced hypoactivity in rodents. *Eur. J. Pharmacol. 75*:231–237, 1981.

Health Notice HN(82)18. Health Service Management, Psychiatric Services, Electro-convulsive Therapy: Equipment. DHSS Store, Health Publications Unit, May 1982.

Heath, E. S., Adams, A., and Wakeling, P. L. G. Short courses of ECT and simulated ECT in chronic schizophrenia. *Br. J. Psychiatry 110*:800–807, 1964.

Hemphill, R. E. Studies in certain pathophysiological and psychological phenomena in convulsive therapy. *J. Ment. Sci. 86*:799, 1940.

Hendley, E. D. Electroconvulsive shock and norepinephrine uptake kinetics in the rat brain. *Psychopharmacol. Commun. 2*:17–25, 1976.

Herrington, R. M., Bruce, A., and Johnstone, E. C. Comparative trial of L-tryptophan and E.C.T. in severe depressive illness. *Lancet 2*:731–734, 1974.

Heshe, J., and Roeder, E. Electroconvulsive therapy in Denmark. *Br. J. Psychiatry 128*:241–245, 1976.

Heshe, J., Roeder, E., and Theilgaard, A. Unilateral and bilateral ECT. A psychiatric and psychological study of therapeutic effect and side effects. *Acta Psychiatr. Scand. 275*:1–180, 1978.

Hicks, F. G. ECT modified by atracurium. Case report. *Convul. Ther. 3*:54–59, 1987.

Hill, G. E., Wong, K. C., and Hodges, M. R. Potentiation of succinylcholine neuromuscular blockage by lithium carbonate. *Anesthesiology 44*:439–442, 1976.

Hillard, J. R., and Folger, R. Patients' attitudes and attributions to electroconvulsive shock therapy. *J. Clin. Psychol. 33*:855–861, 1977.

Hinkle, P. E., Coffey, C. E., Weiner, R. D., Cress, M., and Christison, C. Use of caffeine to lengthen seizures in ECT. *Am. J. Psychiatry 144*:1143–1148, 1987.

Hobson, R. F. Prognostic factors in electric convulsive therapy. *J. Neurol. Neurosurg. Psychiatry 16*:275–281, 1953.

Hoffman, G., Linkowski, P., Kerkhofs, M., Desmedt, D., and Mendlewicz, J. Effects of ECT on sleep and CSF biogenic amines in affective illness. *Psychiatry Res. 16*:199–206, 1985.

Holaday, J. W., Tortella, F. C., Meyerhoff, J. L., Belenky, G. L., and Hitzemann, R. J. Electroconvulsive shock activates endogenous opioid systems: Behavioral and biochemical correlates. *Ann. NY Acad. Sci. 467*:249–255, 1986.

Holcomb, H. H., Sternberg, D. E., and Heninger, G. R. Effects of electroconvulsive therapy on mood, parkinsonism, and tardive dyskinesia in a depressed patient: ECT and dopamine systems. *Biol. Psychiatry 18*:865–873, 1983.

Hollender, M. H., and Steckler, P. P. Multiple sclerosis and schizophrenia: A case report. *Psychiatry Med. 3*:251–257, 1972.

Holmberg, G. The influence of oxygen administration on electrically induced convulsions in man. *Acta Psychiatr. Neurol. 28*:365–386, 1953a.

Holmberg, G. The factor of hypoxemia in electroshock therapy. *Am. J. Psychiatry 110*:115–118, 1953b.

Holmberg, G. Effect on electrically induced convulsions of the number of previous treatments in a series. *Arch. Neurol. Psychiatry 71*:619–623, 1954a.

Holmberg, G. Influence of sex and age on convulsions induced by electric shock treatment. *Acta Neurol. Psychiatr. 71*:619–623, 1954b.

Holmberg, G. The effect of certain factors on the convulsions in electric shock treatment. *Acta Psychiatr. Neurol. Scand. 98*:1–19, 1955.

Holt, W. L. Intensive maintenance EST. A clinical note concerning two unusual cases. *Int. J. Neuropsychiatry 1*:391–394, 1965.

Honcke, P., and Zahle, V. On the correlation between clinical and electroencephalographic observations in patients treated with electro-shock. *Acta Psychiatr. Neurol. Scand. Suppl. 47*:451–458, 1946.

Hong, J. S., Gillin, J. C., Yang, H. Y., and Costa, E. Repeated electroconvulsive shocks and the brain content of endorphins. *Brain Res. 177*:273–278, 1979.

Hood, D. D., and Mecca, R. S. Failure to initiate electroconvulsive seizures in a patient pretreated with lidocaine. *Anesthesiology 58*:379–381, 1983.

Horan, M., Ashton, R., and Minto, J. Using ECT to study hemispheric specialization for sequential processes, *Br. J. Psychiatry 137*:119–125, 1980.

Hordern, A., Burt, C. G., and Holt, N. F. *Depressive States*. Charles C. Thomas, Springfield, Ill., 1965.

Hordern, A., Holt, H. F., Burt, C. G., and Gordon, W. F. Amitriptyline in depressive cases. *Br. J. Psychiatry 109*:815–825, 1963.

Horne, R. L., Pettinati, H. M., Sugerman, A. A., and Varga, E. Comparing bilateral to unilateral electroconvulsive therapy in a randomized study with EEG monitoring. *Arch. Gen. Psychiatry 42*:1087–1092, 1985.

Hoyle, N. R., Pratt, R. T., and Thomas, D. G. Effect of electroconvulsive therapy on serum myelin basic protein immunoreactivity. *Brit. Med. J. 288*:1110–1111, 1984.

Hsiao, J. K., and Evans, D. L. ECT in a depressed patient after craniotomy. *Am. J. Psychiatry 141*:442–444, 1984.

Hughes, J. R. ECT during and after the neuroleptic malignant syndrome: Case report. *J. Clin. Psychiatry 47*:42–43, 1986.

Hughes, J., Barraclough, B. M., and Reeve, W. Are patients shocked by ECT? *J. R. Soc. Med. 74*:283–285, 1981.

Hughes, J., Wigton, R., and Jardon, F. Electroencephalographic studies in patients receiving electroshock treatment. *Arch. Neurol. Psychiatry 46*:748–749, 1941.

Hurwitz, T. D. Electroconvulsive therapy: A review. *Compr. Psychiatry 15*:303–314, 1974.

Hussar, A. E., and Pachter, M. Myocardial infarction and fatal coronary insufficiency during electroconvulsive therapy. *J.A..M.A. 204*:1004–1007, 1968.

Huston, P. E., and Strother, C. H. The effect of E.C.T. on mental efficiency. *Am. J. Psychiatry 104*:707, 1948.

Husum, B., Vester-Andersen, T., Buchmann, G., and Bolwig, T. G. Electroconvulsive therapy and intracranial aneurysm. Prevention of blood pressure elevation in a normotensive patient by hydralazine and propranolol. *Anaesthesia 38*:1205–1207, 1983.

Hyrman, V., Palmer, L. H., Cernik, J., and Jetelina, J. ECT: The search for the perfect stimulus. *Biol. Psychiatry 20*:634–635, 1985.

Imlah, N. W., Ryan, E., and Harrington, J. A. The influence of antidepressant drugs on the response to electroconvulsive therapy and on subsequent relapse rates. *Neuropsychopharmacology 4*:438–442, 1965.

Impastato, D. J. Tendon reflexes as a guide to the safe use of succinylcholine in medicine. *Can. Psychiatr. Assoc. J. 11*:67–77, 1966.

Impastato, D. J., and Almansi, R. The electrofit in the treatment of mental disease. *J. Nerv. Ment. Dis. 96*:395–409, 1942.

Impastato, D. J., Berg, S., and Pacella, B. L. Electroshock therapy: Focal spread technique. A new form of treatment of psychiatric illness. *Confin. Neurol. 13*:266–270, 1953.

Impastato, D. J., and Karliner, W. Control of memory impairment in EST by unilateral stimulation of the non-dominant hemisphere. *Dis. Nerv. Syst. 27*:182–188, 1966.

Impastato, D. J., and Pacella, B. L. Electrically produced unilateral convulsions. *Dis. Nerv. Syst. 13*:368–369, 1952.

Isaac, L., and Swanger, J. Alteration of electroconvulsive threshold by cerebrospinal fluid from cats tolerant to electroconvulsive shock. *Life Sci. 33*:2301–2304, 1983.

Jaeckle, R. S., and Dilsaver, S. C. Covariation of depressive symptoms, parkinsonism, and post-dexamethasone plasma cortisol levels in a bipolar patient: Simultaneous response to ECT and lithium carbonate. *Acta Psychiatr. Scand. 74*:68–72, 1986.

Janakiramaiah, N., Channabasavanna, S. M., and Murthy, N. S. ECT/chlorpromazine combination versus chlorpromazine alone in acutely schizophrenic patients. *Acta Psychiatr. Scand. 66*:464–470, 1982.

Janicak, P. G., Davis, J. M., Gibbons, R. D., Ericksen, S., Chang, S., and Gallagher, P. Efficacy of ECT: A meta-analysis. *Am. J. Psychiatry 142*:297–302, 1985.

Janis, I. L. Psychologic effects of electric convulsive treatments (post-treatment amnesias). *J. Nerv. Ment. Dis. 111*:359–382, 1950a.

Janis, I. L. Psychologic effects of electric convulsive treatments (changes in word association reactions). *J. Nerv. Ment. Dis. 111*:383–397, 1950b.

Janowsky, E. C., and Janowsky, D. S. What precautions should be taken if a patient on an MAOI is scheduled to undergo anesthesia? *J. Clin. Psychopharmacol. 5*:128–129, 1985.

Jauhar, P., Weller, M., and Hirsch, S. R. Electroconvulsive therapy for patient with cardiac pacemaker. *Br. Med. J. 1*:90–91, 1979.

Jeffries, B. F., Kishore, P. R. S., Singh, K. S., Ghatak, N. R., and Krempa, J. Postoperative computed tomographic changes in the brain. *Radiology 135*:751–753, 1980.

Jessee, S. D., and Anderson, G. F. ECT in the neuroleptic malignant syndrome: Case report. *J. Clin. Psychiatry 44*:186–188, 1983.

Johnson, L. C., Ulett, G. A., Johnson, M., Sineth, K., and Sines, J. O. Electroconvulsive therapy (with and without atropine). *Arch. Gen. Psychiatry 2*:324–336, 1960.

Johnstone, E. C., Deakin, J. F., Lawler, P., Frith, C. D., Stevens, M., McPherson, K., and Crow, T. J. The Northwick Park electroconvulsive therapy trial. *Lancet* 2:1317–1320, 1980.

Jones, G., and Callender, K. Northwick Park ECT trial (letter to the editor). *Lancet* 1:500–501, 1981.

Jones, R. M., and Knight, P. R. Cardiovascular and hormonal responses to electroconvulsive therapy. Modification of an exaggerated response in an hypertensive patient by beta-receptor blockade. *Anaesthesia* 36:795–799, 1981.

Jori, A., Dolfini, E., Casati, C., and Argenta, G. Effect of ECT and imipramine treatment on the concentration of 5-hydroxyindoleacetic acid (5HIAA) and homovanillic acid (HVA) in the cerebrospinal fluid of depressed patients. *Psychopharmacologia* 44:87–90, 1975.

Kahn, R. L., and Fink, M. Personality factors in behavioral response to electroshock therapy. *J. Neuropsychiatry* 1:45–49, 1959.

Kahn, R. L., and Fink, M. Prognostic value of Rorschach criteria in clinical response to convulsive therapy. *J. Neuropsychiatry* 1:242–245, 1960.

Kahn, R. L., Pollack, M., and Fink, M. Sociopsychologic aspects of psychiatric treatment in a voluntary mental hospital: Duration of hospitalization, discharge ratings and diagnosis. *Arch. Gen. Psychiatry* 1:565–574, 1959.

Kalayam, B., and Steinhart, M. J. A survey of attitudes on the use of electroconvulsive therapy. *Hosp. Community Psychiatry* 32:185–188, 1981.

Kalinowsky, L. B. Electric-convulsion therapy in schizophrenia. *Lancet* 2:1232–1233, 1939.

Kalinowsky, L. Organic psychotic syndromes occurring during electric convulsive therapy. *Arch. Neurol. Psychiatry* 53:269–273, 1945.

Kalinowsky, L. B. Epilepsy and convulsive therapy. *Res. Publ. Ass. Nerv. Ment. Dis.* 26:175–183, 1947.

Kalinowsky, L. B. The danger of various types of medication during electric convulsive therapy. *Am. J. Psychiatry* 112:745–746, 1956a.

Kalinowsky, L. B. Additional remarks on the danger of premedication in electric convulsive therapy. *Am. J. Psychiatry* 113:79–80, 1956b.

Kalinowsky, L. B. The history of electroconvulsive therapy. In: R. Abrams and W. B. Essman (Eds.) *Electroconvulsive Therapy: Biological Foundations and Clinical Applications.* Spectrum Publications, New York, pp. 1–6, 1982.

Kalinowsky, L. B. History of convulsive therapy. In: S. Malitz and H. Sackeim (Eds.) *Electroconvulsive Therapy: Clinical and Basic Research Issues. Ann. NY Acad. Sci.* 462:1–4, 1986.

Kalinowsky, L. B., Hippius, H., and Klein, H. E. *Biological Treatments in Psychiatry.* Grune and Stratton, New York, p. 267, 1982.

Kalinowsky, L., and Hoch, P. H. *Shock Treatment, Psychosurgery and Other*

Somatic Treatments in Psychiatry. Grune and Stratton, New York, 1952.

Kalinowsky, L. B., and Kennedy, F. Observations in electric shock therapy applied to problems of epilepsy. *J. Nerv. Ment. Dis.* 98:56–67, 1943.

Kanamatsu, T., McGinty, J. F., Mitchell, C. L., and Hong, J. S. Dynorphin- and enkephalin-like immunoreactivity is altered in limbic-basal ganglia regions of rat brain after repeated electroconvulsive shock. *J. Neuroscience* 6:644–649, 1986.

Kane, F. J. Transient neurological symptoms accompanying ECT. *Am. J. Psychiatry Feb.*:786–787, 1963.

Kantor, S. J., and Glassman, A. H. Delusional depressions: Natural history and response to treatment. *Brit. J. Psychiatry 131*:351–360, 1977.

Karliner, W. ECT for patients with CNS disease. *Psychosomatics 19*:781–783, 1978.

Katona, C. L. E., Aldridge, C. R., Roth, Sir M., and Hyde, J. The dexamethasone suppression test and prediction of outcome in patients receiving ECT. *Br. J. Psychiatry 150*:315–318, 1987.

Kaufman, K. R., Finstead, B. A., and Kaufman E. R. Status epilepticus following electroconvulsive therapy. *Mt. Sinai J. Med.* 53:119–122, 1986.

Kay, D. W., Fahy, T., and Garside, R. F. A seven-month double-blind trial of amitriptyline and diazepam in ECT-treated depressed patients. *Br. J. Psychiatry 17*:667–671, 1970.

Kellar, K. J., Cascio, C. S., Bergstrom, D. A., Butler, J. A., and Iadarola, P. Electroconvulsive shock and reserpine: Effects on beta-adrenergic receptors in rat brain. *J. Neurochemistry 37*:830–836, 1981.

Kellar, K. J., and Stockmeier, C. A. Effects of electroconvulsive shock and serotonin axon lesions on beta-adrenergic and serotonin-2 receptors in rat brain. *Ann. NY Acad. Sci. 462*:76–90, 1986.

Kendell, B., and Pratt, R. T. C. Brain damage and ECT. *Br. J. Psychiatry 143*:99–100, 1983.

Kendell, R. E., Cooper, J. E., Gourlay, A. J., and Copeland, J. R. M. Diagnostic criteria of American and British psychiatrists. *Arch. Gen. Psychiatry 25*:123–130, 1971.

Kerr, R. A., McGrath, J. J., O'Kearney, R. T., and Price, J. ECT: Misconceptions and attitudes. *Aust. NZ J. Psychiatry 16*:43–49, 1982.

Kety, S. S., Javoy, F., Thierry, A. M., Julou, L., and Glowinski, J. A sustained effect of electroconvulsive shock on the turnover of norepinephrine in the central nervous system of the rat. *Proc. Natl. Acad. Sci. 58*:1249–1250, 1967.

Kety, S. S., Woodford, R. B., Harmel, M. H., Freyhand, F. A., Appel, K. E., and Schmidt, C. F. Cerebral blood flow and metabolism in schizophrenia: The effects of barbiturate semi-narcosis, insulin coma and electroshock. *Am. J. Psychiatry 104*:765–770, 1948.

King, P. D. Clorpromazine and electroconvulsive therapy in the treatment of newly hospitalized schizophrenics. *J. Clin. Exp. Psychopathol.* *21*:101–105, 1960.

Kirstein, L., and Ottosson, J. -O. Experimental studies of electroencephalographic changes following electroconvulsive therapy. In: J.-O. Ottosson (Ed.) *Experimental Studies of the Mode of Action of Electroconvulsive Therapy, Acta Psychiat. Neuro. Scand. 145*:60–102, 1960.

Kitamura, T., and Page, A. J. Electrocardiographic changes following electroconvulsive therapy. *Eur. Arch. Psychiatry Neurol. Sci. 234*:147–148, 1984.

Klotz, M. Serial electroencephalographic changes due to electrotherapy. *Dis. Nerv. Syst. 16*:120–121, 1955.

Kolb, L. C., and Vogel, V. H. The use of shock therapy in 305 mental hospitals. *Am. J. Psychiatry 99*:90–100, 1942.

Kolbeinsson, H., Arnaldsson, O. S., Petursson, H., and Skulason, S. Computed tomographic scans in ECT-patients. *Acta Psychiatr. Scand. 73*:28–32, 1986.

Koo, J. Y., and Chien, C. P. Coma following ECT and intravenous droperidol: Case report. *J. Clin. Psychiatry 47*:94–95, 1986.

Korin, H., Fink, M., and Kwalwasser, S. Relation of changes in memory and learning to improvement in electroshock. *Confin. Neurol. 16*:88–96, 1956.

Kramer, B. A. Use of ECT in California, 1977–1983. *Am. J. Psychiatry 142*:1190–1192, 1985.

Kramer, B. A. Severe confusion in a patient receiving electroconculsive therapy and atenolol. *J. Nerv. Ment. Dis. 174*:562–563, 1986.

Kramer, B. A., Allen, R. E., and Friedman, B. Atropine and glycopyrrolate as ECT preanesthesia. *J. Clin. Psychiatry 47*:199–200, 1986.

Kraus, R. P., and Remick, R. A. Diazoxide in the management of severe hypertension after electroconvulsive therapy. *Am. J. Psychiatry 139*:504–505, 1982.

Kriss, A., Blumhardt, L. D., Halliday, A. M., and Pratt, R. T. Neurological asymmetries immediately after unilateral ECT. *J. Neurol. Neurosurg. Psychiatry 41*:1135–1144, 1978.

Kriss, A., Halliday, A. M., Halliday, E., and Pratt, R. T. Evoked potentials following unilateral ECT. II. The flash evoked potential. *Electroencephalogr. Clin. Neurophysiol. 48*:490–501, 1980.

Kronfol, Z., Hamsher, K. D., Digre, K., and Waziri, R. Depression and hemispheric functions: Changes associated with unilateral ECT. *Br. J. Psychiatry 132*:560–567, 1978.

Kurland, A. A., Turek, I. S., Brown, C. C., and Wagman, A. M. Electroconvulsive therapy and EEG correlates in depressive disorders. *Compr. Psychiatry 17*:581–589, 1976.

Kwentus, J. A., Hart, R. P., Calabrese, V., and Hekmati, A. Mania as a symptom of multiple sclerosis. *Psychosomatics 27*:729–731, 1986.

Kwentus, J. A., Schulz, S. C., and Hart, R. P. Tardive dystonia, catatonia, and electroconvulsive therapy. *J. Nerv. Ment. Dis. 172*:171–173, 1984.

Laird, D. M. Convulsive therapy in psychoses accompanying pregnancy. *N. Engl. J. Med. 252*:934–936, 1955.

Lambourn, J., and Gill, D. A controlled comparison of simulated and real ECT. *Br. J. Psychiatry 133*:514–519, 1978.

Lancaster, N. P., Steinert, R. R., and Frost, I. Unilateral electro-convulsive therapy. *J. Ment. Sci. 104*:221–227, 1958.

Lane, R. D., Zeitlin, S., Larson, G., Swartz, C. M., and Abrams, R. Differential cardiac response to right-unilateral and bilateral ECT. In preparation.

Langsley, D. G., Enterline, J. D., and Hickerson, G. X. Comparison of chlorpromazine and EST in treatment of acute schizophrenic and manic reactions. *Arch. Neurol. Psychiatry 81*:384–391, 1959.

Larson, G., and Swartz, C. M. Differences between first and second electroconvulsive treatments given in the same session. *Convul. Ther. 2*:191–196, 1986.

Larson, G., Swartz, C., and Abrams, R. Duration of ECT-induced tachycardia as a measure of seizure length. *Am. J. Psychiatry 141*:1269–1271, 1984.

Latey, R. H., and Fahy, T. J. Electroconvulsive therapy in the Republic of Ireland 1982: A summary of findings. *Br. J. Psychiatry 147*:438–439, 1985.

Laurell, B. Flurothyl convulsive therapy. *Acta Psychiatr. Scand. 213*:1, 1970.

Lazarus, A. Treatment of neuroleptic malignant syndrome with electroconvulsive therapy. *J. Nerv. Ment. Dis. 174*:47–49, 1986.

Lebensohn, Z. M., and Jenkins, R. B. Improvement of parkinsonism in depressed patients treated with ECT. *Am. J. Psychiatry 132*:283–285, 1975.

Lebrecht, U., and Nowak, J. Z. Effect of single and repeated electroconvulsive shock on serotonergic system in rat brain—II. Behavioral studies. *Neuropharmacology 19*:1055–61, 1980.

Lebrun-Grandie, P., Baron, J. C., Soussaline, R., Loch'h, C., Sastre, J., and Bousser, M. G. Coupling between regional blood flow and oxygen utilization in the normal human brain. *Arch. Neurol. 40*:230–236, 1983.

Leechuy, I., and Abrams, R. Postictal delirium (and recovery from melancholia) after left-unilateral ECT. *Convul. Ther. 3*:65–68, 1987.

Leechuy, I., Kohlhaas, J., and Abrams, R., Effects of ECT electrode placement on emergence delirium. *Am. J. Psychiatry*, in press.

Lehmann, L., and Liddell, J. Human cholinesterase (pseudocholinesterase): Genetic variants and their recognition. *Br. J. Anesth. 41*:235–244, 1969.

Lending, M., Slobody, L. B., and Mestern, J. Effect of convulsions on cerebrospinal fluid and plasma activity of glutamic oxalacetic transaminase and lactic dehydrogenase. *Neurology 9*:672–677, 1959.

Lerer, B. Electroconvulsive shock and neurotransmitter receptors: Implications for mechanism of action and adverse effects of electroconvulsive therapy. *Biol. Psychiatry 19*:361–383, 1984.

Lerer, B. Studies on the role of brain cholinergic systems in the therapeutic mechanisms and adverse effects of ECT and lithium. *Biol. Psychiatry 20*:20–40, 1985.

Lerer, B. Neurochemical and other neurobiological consequences of ECT: Implications for the pathogenesis and treatment of affective disorders. In: H. Meltzer (Ed.) *Psychopharmacology: The Third Generation of Progress*, Raven Press, New York, in press.

Lerer, B., and Belmaker, R. H. Receptors and the mechanism of action of ECT. *Biol. Psychiatry 17*:497–511, 1982.

Lerer, B., Jabotinsky-Rubin, K., Bannet, J., Ebstein, R. P. and Belmaker, R. H. Electroconvulsive shock prevents dopamine receptor supersensitivity. *Eur. J. Pharmacol. 80*:131–134, 1982.

Lerer, B., and Sitaram, N. Clinical strategies for evaluating ECT mechanisms— pharmacological, biochemical and psychophysiological approaches. *Prog. Neuropsychopharmacol. Biol. Psychiatry 7*:309–333, 1983.

Levy, L.A., Savit, J. M., and Hodes, M. Parkinsonism: Improvement by electroconvulsive therapy. *Arch. Phys. Med. Rehabil. 64*:432–433, 1983.

Levy, R. The clinical evaluation of unilateral electroconvulsive therapy. *Br. J. Psychiatry 114*:459–463, 1968.

Levy, S. D., and Levy, S. B. Electroconvulsive therapy in two former neurosurgical patients: Skull prosthesis and ventricular shunt. *Convul. Ther. 3*:46–48, 1987.

Lewis, W. H., Jr., Richardson, D. J., and Gahagan, L. H. Cardiovascular disturbances and their management in modified electrotherapy for psychiatric illness. *N. Engl. J. Med. 252*:1016–1020, 1955.

Liberson, W. T. New possibilities in electric convulsive therapy: Brief stimulus technique. *Dig. Neurol. Psychiat. 12*:368–369, 1944.

Liberson, W. T. Brief stimulus therapy. Physiological and clinical observations. *Am. J. Psychiatry 105*:28–29, 1948.

Liberson, W. T. Current evaluation of electric convulsive therapy—correlation of the parameters of electric current with physiologic and psychologic changes. *Res. Publ. Assoc. Nerv. Ment. Dis. 31*:199–231, 1953.

Liberson, W. T., Kaplan, J. A., Sherer, I. W., and Trehub, A. Correlations of EEG and psychological findings during intensive brief stimulus therapy. *Confin. Neurol. 16*:116–125, 1956.

Liberson, W. T., and Wilcox, P. Electric convulsive therapy: Comparison of "brief stimulus technique" with Friedman-Wilcox-Reiter technique. *Dig. Neurol. Psychiat.* 8:292–302, 1945.

Lingley, J. R., and Robbins, L. L. Fractures following electroshock therapy. *Radiology* 48:124–128, 1947.

Linnoila, M., Miller, T. L., Bartko, J., and Potter, W. Z. Five antidepressant treatments in depressed patients. Effects on urinary serotonin and 5-hydroxyindoleacetic acid output. *Arch. Gen. Psychiatry* 41:688–692, 1984.

Lipkin, K. M., Dyrud, J., and Meyer, G. G. The many faces of mania. *Arch. Gen. Psychiatry* 22:262–267, 1970.

Lipman, R. S., Backup, C., Bobrin, Y., Delaplane, J. M., Doeff, J., Gittleman, S., Joseph, R., and Kanefield, M. Dexamethasone suppression test as a predictor of response to electroconvulsive therapy. I. Inpatient treatment. *Convul. Ther.* 2:151–160, 1986a.

Lipman, R. S., Uffner, W., Schwalb, N., Ravetz, R., Lief, B., Levy, S., and Levenberg, D. Dexamethasone suppression test as a predictor of response to electroconvulsive therapy. II. Six-month follow-up. *Convul. Ther.* 2:161–167, 1986b.

Lippmann, S., Manshadi, M., Wehry, M., Byrd, R., Past, W., Keller, W., Schuster, J., Elam, S., Meyer, D., and O'Daniel, R. 1,250 electroconvulsive treatments without evidence of brain injury. *Br. J. Psychiatry* 147:203–204, 1985.

Liskow, B. I. Relationship between neuroleptic malignant syndrome and malignant hyperthermia [letter]. *Am. J. Psychiatry* 142:390, 1985.

London, S. W., and Glass, D. D. Prevention of electroconvulsive therapy-induced dysrhythmias with atropine and propranolol. *Anesthesiology* 62:819–822, 1985.

Lotstra, F., Linkowski, P., and Mendlewicz, J. General anesthesia after neuroleptic malignant syndrome. *Biol. Psychiatry* 18:243–247, 1983.

Lovett-Doust, J. W., and Raschka, L. B. Enduring effects of modified ECT on the cerebral circulation in man. A computerized study by cerebral impedance plethysmography. *Psychiatr. Clin.* 8:293–303, 1975.

Lowinger, P., and Huston, P. E. Electric shock in psychosis with cerebral spastic paralysis. *Dis. Nerv. Syst.* 14:2–4, 1953.

Lown, B. Sudden cardiac death: The major challenge confronting contemporary cardiology. *Am. J. Cardiol.* 43:313–328, 1979.

Lunn, R. J., Savageau, M. M., Beatty, W. W., Gerst, J. W., Staton, R. D., and Brumback, R. A. Anesthetics and electroconvulsive therapy seizure duration: Implications for therapy from a rat model. *Biol. Psychiatry* 16:1163–1175, 1981.

Lunn, V., and Trolle, E. On the initial impairment of consciousness following electric convulsive therapy. *Acta Psychiatr. Scand.* 24:33–58, 1949.

Lykouras, E., Malliaras, D., Christodoulou, G. N., Papakostas, Y., Voulgari, A., Tzonou, A., and Stefanis, C. Delusional depression: Phenomenology and response to treatment. A prospective study. *Acta Psychiatr. Scand. 73*:324–329, 1986.

Mac, D. S., and Pardo, M. P. Systemic lupus erythematosus and catatonia: A case report. *J. Clin. Psychiatry 44*:155–156, 1983.

Maletzky, B. M. Seizure duration and clinical effect in electroconvulsive therapy. *Compr. Psychiatry 19*:541–550, 1978.

Maletzky, B. M. *Multiple-Monitored Electroconvulsive Therapy.* CRC Press, Boca Raton, Florida, p. 238, 1981.

Maletzky, B. M. Conventional and multiple-monitored electroconvulsive therapy: A comparison in major depressive episodes. *J. Nerv. Ment. Dis. 174*:257–264, 1986.

Malitz, S., Sackeim, H. A., Decina, P., Kanzler, M., and Kerr, B. The efficacy of electroconvulsive therapy: Dose-response interactions with modality. *Ann. NY Acad. Sci. 462*:56–64, 1986.

Maltbie, A. A., Wingfield, M. S., Volow, M. R., Weiner, R. D., Sullivan, J. L., and Cavenar, J. O., Jr. Electroconvulsive therapy in the presence of brain tumor. Case reports and an evaluation of risk. *J. Nerv. Ment. Dis. 168*:400–405, 1980.

Mann, J. J., Brown, R. D., Mason, B. J., Halper, J. P., Kocsis, J. H., and Manebitz, A. Alteration of adrenergic receptor responsibility by electroconvulsive therapy and relationship to antidepressant outcome. In: C. Shagass (Ed.) *Biological Psychiatry 1985.* Elsevier, New York, pp. 868–870, 1986.

Mann, S. C., Caroff, S. N., Bleier, H. R., Welz, W. K. R., Kling, M. A., and Hayashida, M. Lethal catatonia. *Am. J. Psychiatry 143*:1374–1381, 1986.

Mansheim, P. ECT in the treatment of a depressed adolescent with meningomyelocele, hydrocephalus, and seizures. *J. Clin. Psychiatry 44*:385–386, 1983.

Marco, L. A., and Randels, P. M. Succinylcholine drug interactions during electroconvulsive therapy. *Biol. Psychiatry 14*:433–445, 1979.

Marjerrison, G., James, J., and Reichert, H. Unilateral and bilateral ECT: EEG findings. *Can. Psychiatr. Assoc. J. 20*:257–266, 1975.

Martin, B. A., and Kramer, P. M. Clinical significance of the interaction between lithium and a neuromuscular blocker. *Am. J. Psychiatry 139*:1326–1328, 1982.

Martin, R. D., and Flegenheimer, W. V. Psychiatric aspects of the management of the myasthenic patient. *Mt. Sinai J. Med. 38*:594–601, 1971.

Martin, W., Ford, H. F., McDonald, E. C., and Towler, M. L. Clinical evaluation of unilateral EST. *Am. J. Psychiatry 121*:1087–1090, 1965.

Mathisen, K. S., and Pettinati, H. M. Meta-analysis of effects of electrode placements. *Convul. Ther. 3*:69, 1987.

Matthew, J. R., and Constan, E. Complications following ECT over a three-year period in a state institution. *Am. J. Psychiatry 120*:1119–1120, 1964.

Maxwell, R. D. Electrical factors in electroconvulsive therapy. *Acta Psychiatr. Scand. 44*:436–448, 1968.

McAllister, T. W., and Price, T. R. Severe depressive pseudodementia with and without dementia. *Am. J. Psychiatry 139*:626–629, 1982.

McAndrew, J., Berkey, B., and Matthews, C. The effects of dominant and nondominant unilateral ECT as compared to bilateral ECT. *Am. J. Psychiatry 124*:483–490, 1967.

McCabe, M. S. ECT in the treatment of mania: A controlled study. *Am. J. Psychiatry 133*:688–691, 1976.

McCabe, M. S., and Norris, B. ECT versus chlorpromazine in mania. *Biol. Psychiatry 12*:245–254, 1977.

McDonald. I. M., Perkins, M., Marjerrison, G., and Podilsky, M. A controlled comparison of amitriptyline and electroconvulsive therapy in the treatment of depression. *Am. J. Psychiatry 122*:1427–1431, 1966.

McKenna, G., Engle, R. P., Jr., Brooks, H., and Dalen, J. Cardiac arrhythmias during electroshock therapy: Significance, prevention, and treatment. *Am. J. Psychiatry 127*:530–533, 1970.

Medical Research Council. Clinical trial of the treatment of depressive illness. *Br. Med. J. 5439*:881–886, 1965.

Medlicott, R. W. Brief stimuli electroconvulsive therapy. *NZ Med. J. 47*:29–37, 1948

Meduna, L. Autobiography. Part 1. *Convul. Ther. 1*:43–57, 1985.

Meduna, L. J. Klinische and anatomische Beitrag zur Frage der genuinen Epilepsie. *Deutsche z. Nervenkr. 129*:17–42, 1932.

Meduna, L. J. Uber experimentelle Campherepilepsie. *Arch. Psychr. Nervenkr. 102*:333–339, 1934.

Meisel, A., Roth, L. H., and Lidz, C. W. Toward a model of the legal doctrine of informed consent. *Am. J. Psychiatry 134*:285–289, 1977.

Meldrum, B. S. Neuropathological consequences of chemically and electrically induced seizures. *Ann. NY Acad. Sci. 462*:186–193, 1986.

Meldrum, B. S., and Nilsson, B. Cerebral blood flow and metabolic rate early and late in prolonged epileptic seizures induced in rats by bicuculline. *Brain 99*:523–542, 1976.

Mendels, J. Electroconvulsive therapy and depression: I. The prognostic significance of clinical factors. *Br. J. Psychiatry 111*:675–681, 1965a.

Mendels, J. Electroconvulsive therapy and depression: II. Significance of endogenous and reactive syndromes. *Br. J. Psychiatry 111*:682–686, 1965b.

Mendels, J. Electroconvulsive therapy and depression: III. A method for prognosis. *Br. J. Psychiatry 111*:687–690, 1965c.

Mendels, J. The prediction of response to electroconvulsive therapy. *Am. J. Psychiatry 124*:153–159, 1967.

Menken, M., Safer, J., Goldfarb, C., and Varga, E. Multiple ECT: Morphologic effects. *Am. J. Psychiatry 136*:453, 1979.

Merritt, H. H., and Putnam, T. J. New series of anticonvulsant drugs tested by experiments on animals. *Arch. Neurol. Psychiatry 39*:1003–1015, 1938.

Miller, A. L., Faber, R. A., Hatch, J. P., and Alexander, H. E. Factors affecting amnesia, seizure duration, and efficacy in ECT. *Am. J. Psychiatry 142*:692–696, 1985.

Miller, D. H., Clancy, J., and Cummings, E. A comparison between unidirectional current nonconvulsive electrical stimulation given with Reiter's machine, standard alternating current electroshock and pentothal in chronic schizophrenia. *Am. J. Psychiatry 109*:617–620, 1953.

Miller, E. The effect of ECT on memory and learning. *Br. J. Med. Psychol. 43*:57–62, 1970.

Miller, M. E., Gabriel, A., Herman, G., Stern, A., Shagong, U., and Klupersmith, J. Atropine sulfate premedication and cardiac arrhythmia in electroconvulsive therapy (ECT). *Convul. Ther. 3*:10–17, 1987.

Milstein, V., Small, J. G., Klapper, M. H., Small, I. F., Miller, M. J., and Kellams, J. J. Uni- versus bilateral ECT in the treatment of mania. *Convul. Ther. 3*:1–9, 1987.

Minchin, M. C., Williams, J. Bowdler, J. M., and Green, A. R. Effect of electroconvulsive shock on the uptake and release of noradrenaline and 5-hydroxytryptamine in rat brain slices. *J. Neurochem. 40*:765–768, 1983.

Mindham, R. H. S., Howland, C., and Shepherd, M. An evaluation of continuation therapy with tricyclic antidepressants in depressive illness. *Psychol. Med. 3*:5–17, 1973.

Miyasaka, M. Cortical and subcortical seizure discharge induced by bitemporal electroshock in cats. *Folia Psychiatrica et Neurol. Jpn. 13*:113–123, 1959.

Modigh, K. Electroconvulsive shock and postsynaptic catecholamine effects: Increased psychomotor stimulant action of apomorphine and clonidine in reserpine pretreated mice by repeated ECS. *J. Neural Transm. 36*:19–32, 1975.

Modigh, K. Long-term effects of electroconvulsive shock therapy on synthesis, turnover and uptake of brain monoamines. *Psychopharmacology 49*:179–185, 1976.

Modigh, K., Balldin, J., Eriksson, E., Granerus, A. K., and Walinder, J. Increased responsiveness of dopamine receptors after ECT: A review of experimental and clinical evidence. In: B. Lerer, R. D. Weiner and R. H. Belmaker (Eds.) *ECT: Basic Mechanisms.* John Libbey, London, pp. 18–27, 1984.

Moir, D. C., Crooks, J., Cornwell, W. B., O'Malley, K., Dingwall-Fordyce, I., Turnbull, M. J., and Weir, R. D. Cardiotoxicity of amitriptyline. *Lancet 2*:561–564, 1972.

Monke, J. V. Electroconvulsive therapy following surgical correction of aortic coarctation by implantation of an aortic isograft. *Am. J. Psychiatry* *109*:378–379, 1952.

Moore, M. B. Electroconvulsive therapy and the aorta. *Can. Med. Assoc. J.* *83*:1258–1259, 1960.

Moore, N. P. The maintenance treatment of chronic psychotics by electrically induced convulsions. *J. Ment. Sci.* *89*:257–269, 1943.

Moore, R. A. The electroconvulsive therapy fight in California. *J. Forensic Sci.* *22*:845–850, 1977.

Moriarty, J. D., and Siemens, J. C. Electroencephalographic study of electric shock therapy. *Arch. Neurol. Psychiatry* *57*:693–711, 1947.

Mosovich, A., and Katzenelbogen, S. Electroshock therapy, clinical and electroencephalographic studies. *J. Nerv. Ment. Dis.* *107*:517–530, 1948.

Mowbray, R. M. Historical aspects of electric convulsant therapy. *Scot. Med. J.* *4*:373–378, 1959.

Mukherjee, S. Manic states and brain dysfunction. Presented at the *American Psychiatric Association 140th Annual Meeting*, Chicago, IL, May 9–14, 1987.

Mulgaokar, G. D., Dauchot, P. J., Duffy, J. P., and Anton, A. H. Noninvasive assessment of electroconvulsive-induced changes in cardiac function. *J. Clin. Psychiatry* *46*:479–482, 1985.

Muller, D. J. Unilateral ECT. (One year's experience at a city hospital). *Dis. Nerv. Syst.* *32*:422–424, 1971.

Murray, G. B., Shea, V., and Conn, D. K. Electroconvulsive therapy for poststroke depression. *J. Clin. Psychiatry* *47*:258–260, 1986.

National Institutes of Health. Consensus conference. Electroconvulsive therapy. *J.A.M.A.* *254*:2103–2108, 1985.

Nilsen, S. M., Willis, K. W., and Pettinati, H. M. Instrument review: Initial impression of two new brief-pulse electroconvulsive therapy machines. *Convul. Ther.* *2*:43–54, 1986.

Nordin, G., Ottosson, J.-O., and Roos, B.-E. Influence of convulsive therapy on 5-hydroxyindoleacetic acid and homovanillic acid in cerebrospinal fluid in endogenous depression. *Psychopharmacologia* *20*:315–320, 1971.

Nyirö, J., and Jablonsky, A. Einige Daten zur Prognose der Epilepsie, mit besonderer Rucksicht auf die Konstitution. *Psychiatr. Neurol. Wochenschr.* *31*:547–549, 1929.

Nyström, S. On relation between clinical factors and efficacy of E.C.T. in depression. *Acta Psychiatr. Scand.* *181*:115–118, 1964.

O'Dea, J. P. K., Gould, D., Halberg, M., and Wieland, R. G. Prolactin changes during electroconvulsive therapy. *Am. J. Psychiatry* *135*:609–611, 1978.

O'Donnell, M. P. and Webb, M. G. T. Post-ECT blood pressure rise and its relationships to cognitive and affective change. *Brit. J. Psychiatry* *149*:494–497, 1986.

Osborne, R. G., Tunakan, B., and Barmore, J. Anaesthetic agent in electro-convulsive therapy: A controlled comparison. *J. Nerv. Ment. Dis.* *137*:297–300, 1963.

Ottosson, J.-O. Experimental studies of the mode of action of electroconvul-sive therapy. *Acta Psychiatr. Neurol. Scand.* *35*:1–141, 1960.

Ottosson, J.-O. Electroconvulsive therapy of endogenous depression: An anal-ysis of the influence of various factors on the efficacy of therapy. *J. Ment. Sci.* *108*:694–703, 1962.

Ottosson, J.-O. Psychological theories of ECT: A review. Psychological or physiological theories of ECT. *Int. J. Psychiatry* *5*:170–174, 1968.

Ottosson, J.-O. and Widepalm, K. Memory disturbance after ECT in low-pressure narcosis: A study of anterograde and retrograde amnesia. *Convul. Ther.* *3*:174–184, 1987.

Overall, J. E., and Rhoades, H. M. A comment on the efficacy of unilateral versus bilateral ECT. *Convul. Ther.* *2*:245–252, 1986.

Overall, J. E., and Rhoades, H. M. A reply to Mathisen and Pettinati. *Convul. Ther.* *3*:70, 1987.

Owens, D. G., Johnstone, E. C., Crow, T. J., Frith, C. D., Jagoe, J. R., and Kreel, L. Lateral ventricular size in schizophrenia: Relationship to the disease process and its clinical manifestations. *Psychol. Med.* *15*:27–41, 1985.

Pacella, B. L., Barrera, E. S., and Kalinowsky, L. Variations in the electro-encephalogram associated with electric shock therapy in patients with mental disorders. *Arch Neurol. Psychiatry* *47*:367–384, 1942.

Packman, P. M., Meyer, D. A., and Verdun, R. M. Hazards of succinylcho-line administration during electrotherapy. *Arch. Gen. Psychiatry* *35*:1137–1141, 1978.

Paivio, A. Mental imagery in associative learning and memory. *Psychol. Rev.* *76*:241–263, 1969.

Paivio, A. *Imagery and Verbal Processes*. Holt, Rinehart and Winston, New York, 1971.

Papakostas, Y., Fink, M., Lee, J., Irwin, P., and Johnson, L. Neuroendocrine measures in psychiatric patients: Course and outcome with ECT. *Psychiatry Res.* *4*:55–64, 1981.

Papakostas, Y., Stefanis, C., Sinouri, A., Trikkas, G., Papadimitriou, G., and Pittoulis, S. Increases in prolactin levels following bilateral and unilat-eral ECT. *Am. J. Psychiatry* *141*:1623–1624, 1984.

Papakostas, Y. G., Stefanis, C. S., Markianos, M., and Papadimitrious, G. N. Naloxone fails to block ECT-induced prolactin increase. *Biol. Psychiatry* *20*:1326–1327, 1985.

Paulson, G. W. Exacerbation of organic brain disease by electroconvulsive treatment. *NC Med. J.* *28*:328–331, 1967.

Penfield, W., and Jasper, H. *Epilepsy and functional anatomy of the human brain*. Little, Brown, Boston, 1954.

Penfield, W., von Kalman, S., and Cipriani, A. Cerebral blood flow during induced epileptiform seizures in animals and man. *J. Neurophysiol.* 2:257–267, 1939.

Perrin, G. M. Cardiovascular aspects of electric shock therapy. *Acta Psychiatr. Neurol Scand. 36*:1–45, 1961.

Perris, C., and d'Elia, G. A study of bipolar (manic-depressive) and unipolar recurrent depressive psychoses. IX. Therapy and prognosis. *Acta Psychiatr. Scand. 42*:153–171, 1966.

Perry, G. F. ECT for dementia and catatonia [letter]. *J. Clin. Psychiatry 44*:117, 1983.

Perry, P., and Tsuang, M. T. Treatment of unipolar depression following electroconvulsive therapy. Relapse rate comparisons between lithium and tricyclics therapies following ECT. *J. Affective Disord. 1*:123–129, 1979.

Peters, S. G., Wochos, D. N., and Peterson, G. C. Status epilepticus as a complication of concurrent electroconvulsive and theophylline therapy. *Mayo Clin. Proc. 59*:568–570, 1984.

Petito, C. K., Schaefer, J. A., and Plum, F. Ultrastructural characteristics of the brain and blood-brain barrier in experimental seizures. *Brain Res. 127*:251–267, 1977.

Pettinati, H. M., Mathisen, K. S., Rosenberg, J., and Lynch, J. F. Meta-analytical approach to reconciling discrepancies in efficacy between bilateral and unilateral electroconvulsive therapy. *Convul. Ther. 1*:7–17, 1986.

Pettinati, H. M., and Nilsen, S. Missed and brief seizures during ECT: Differential response between unilateral and bilateral electrode placement. *Biol. Psychiatry. 20*:506–514, 1985.

Pinel, J. P., and Van Oot, P. H. Generality of the kindling phenomenon: Some clinical implications. *Can. J. Neurol. Sci. 2*:467–475, 1975.

Pinel, J. P., and Van Oot, P. H. Intensification of the alcohol withdrawal syndrome following periodic electroconvulsive shocks. *Biol. Psychiatry 12*:479–486, 1977.

Pippard, J., and Ellam, L. *Electroconvulsive Treatment in Great Britain, 1980.* Gaskel, London, 1981.

Pitts, F. N. Medical physiology of ECT. In: R. Abrams and W. B. Essman (Eds.) *Electroconvulsive Therapy: Biological Foundations and Clinical Applications.* Spectrum Publications, New York, pp. 57–90, 1982.

Pitts, F. M., Jr., Desmarias, G. M., Stewart, W., and Schaberg, K. Induction of anesthesia with methohexital and thiopental in electroconvulsive therapy. *N. Engl. J. Med. 273*:353–360, 1965.

Pollard, B. J., and O'Leary, J. Guedel airway and tooth damage. *Anaesth. Intensive Care. 9*:395, 1981.

Pomeranze, J., Karliner, W., Triebel, W. A., and King, E. J. Electroshock therapy in presence of serious organic disease. Depression and aortic aneurysm. *Geriatrics 23*:122–124, 1968.

Pope, H. G., and Lipinski, J. F. Diagnosis in schizophrenia and manic-depressive illness: A reassessment of the specificity of "schizophrenic" symptoms in the light of current research. *Arch. Gen. Psychiatry* *35*:811–828, 1978.

Pope, H., Lipinski, J. F., Cohen, B. M., and Axelrod, D. T. "Schizoaffective disorder": An invalid diagnosis? A comparison of schizoaffective disorder, schizophrenia, and affective disorder. *Am. J. Psychiatry* *137*:921–927, 1980.

Position Paper on Electro-Convulsive Therapy of the Ontario Medical Association and the Ontario Psychiatric Association (excerpt), Schedule "H" of *Report of the Electroconvulsive Therapy Review Committee*, Ontario Government Bookshore, p. 87, December, 1985.

Posner, J. B., Plum, F., and Van Poznak, A. Cerebral metabolism during electrically induced seizures in man. *Arch. Neurol.* *20*:388–395, 1969.

Post, R. M., Putnam, F., Contel, N. R., and Goldman, B. Electroconvulsive seizures inhibit amygdala kindling: Implications for mechanisms of action in affective illness. *Epilepsia* *25*:234–239, 1984.

Post, R. M., Putnam, F., Uhde, T. W., and Weiss, S. R. B. Electroconvulsive therapy as an anticonvulsant: Implications for its mechanism of action in affective illness: *Ann. NY Acad. Sci.* *462*:376–388, 1986.

Powers, P., Douglass, T. S., and Waziri, R. Hyperpyrexia in catatonic states. *Dis. Nerv. Syst.* *37*:359–361, 1976.

Prakash, R., and Leavell, S. R. Status epilepticus with unilateral ECT: Case report. *J. Clin. Psychiatry* *45*:403–404, 1984.

Pratt, R. T., Warrington, E. K., and Halliday, A. M. Unilateral ECT as a test for cerebral dominance, with a strategy for treating left-handers. *Br. J. Psychiatry* *119*:79–83, 1971.

Preskorn. S. H., Irwin, G. H., Simpson, S., Friesen, D., Rinne, J., and Jerkovich, G. Medical therapies for mood disorders alter the blood–brain barrier. *Science* *213*:469–471, 1981.

Price, T. R. Unilateral electroconvulsive therapy for depression [letter]. *N. Engl. J. Med.* *304*:53, 1981.

Price, T. R. Short- and long-term cognitive effects of ECT: Part I—Effects on memory. *Psychopharmacol. Bull.* *18*:81–91, 1982.

Price, T. R. Short- and long-term cognitive effects of ECT: Part II—Effects on nonmemory associated cognitive functions. *Psychopharmacol. Bull.* *18*:91–101, 1982.

Price, T. R., and Levin, R. The effects of electroconvulsive therapy on tardive dyskinesia. *Am. J. Psychiatry* *135*:991–993, 1978.

Price, T. R., Mackenzie, T. B., Tucker, G. J., and Culver, C. The dose-response ratio in electroconvulsive therapy: A preliminary study. *Arch. Gen. Psychiatry* *35*:1131–1136, 1978.

Price, T. R.P., and Tucker, G. J. Psychiatric and behavioral manifestations of normal pressure hydrocephalus. *J. Nerv. Ment. Dis.* *164*:51–55, 1977.

Proctor, L. D., and Goodwin, J. E. Comparative electroencephalographic observations following electroshock therapy using raw 60 cycle alternating and unidirectional fluctuating current. *Am. J. Psychiatry* 99:525–530, 1943.

Prohovnik, I., Sackeim, H. A., Decina, P., and Malitz, S. Acute reductions of regional cerebral blood flow following electroconvulsive therapy: Interactions with modality and time. *Ann. NY Acad. Sci.* 462:249–262, 1986.

Prudic, J., Sackeim, H. A., Decina, P., Hopkins, N., Ross, R. F., and Malitz, S. Acute effects of ECT on cardiovascular functioning: Relations to patient and treatment variables. *Acta Psychiatr. Scand.*, 75:344–351, 1987.

Przewlocki, R., Lason, W., Stach, R., Kacz, D., Stala, L., and Przewlocki, B. In: H. Takagi (Ed.) *Advances in Endogenous and Exogenous Opioids.* Kodansja Ltd., Tokyo, pp. 238–240, 1981.

Raichel, M. E., Eichling, J. O., Grubb, R. L., and Hartman, B. K. Central noradrenergic regulation of brain microcirculation. In: M. Hanna, H. Papius, and W. Feindel (Eds.) *Dynamics of Brain Edema.* Springer-Verlag, New York, pp. 11–17, 1976.

Ray, I. Side effects from lithium. *Can. Med. Assoc. J.* 112:417–419, 1975.

Regestein, Q. R., Kahn, C. B., Siegel, A. J., Blacklow, R. S., and Genack, A. A case of catatonia occurring simultaneously with severe urinary retention. *J. Nerv. Ment. Dis.* 152:432–435, 1971.

Regestein, Q. R., Murawski, B. J., and Engle, R. P. A case of prolonged, reversible dementia associated with abuse of electroconvulsive therapy. *J. Nerv. Ment. Dis.* 161:200–203, 1975.

Regestein, Q. R. and Reich, P. Electroconvulsive therapy in patients at high risk for physical complications. *Convul. Ther.* 1:101–114, 1985.

Reichert, H., Benjamin, J., Keegan, D., and Marjerrison, G. Bilateral and non-dominant unilateral ECT. Part I—Therapeutic efficacy. *Can Psychiatr. Assoc. J.* 21:69–78, 1976.

Reichert, H., Benjamin, J., Neufeldt, A. H., and Marjerrison, G. Bilateral and non-dominant unilateral ECT. Part II—Development of prograde effects. *Can Psychiatr. Assoc. J.* 21:79–86, 1976.

Reid, A. H. Psychoses in adult mental defectives. I. Manic depressive psychosis. *Br. J. Psychiatry* 120:205–212, 1972.

Reitan, R. M. An investigation of the validity of Halstead's measures of biological intelligence. *Arch. Neurol. Psychiatry* 73:28–35, 1955.

Remick, R. A., Maurice, W. L. ECT in pregnancy [letter]. *Am. J. Psychiatry* 135:761–762, 1978.

Repke, J. T., and Berger, N. G. Electroconvulsive therapy in pregnancy. *Obstet. Gynecol.* 63:39S–41S, 1984.

Rich, C. L., Cunningham, L. A., Maher, C. C., and Woodruff, R. A. The effect of modified ECT on serum creative phosphokinase, I. With intravenous atropine. *Dis. Nerv. Syst.* 36:653–655, 1975.

Rich, C. L., Cunningham, L. A., Maher, C. C., and Woodruff, R. A. The effect of modified ECT on serum creatine phosphokinase. II. With subcutaneous atropine. *Dis. Nerv. Syst. 36*:655–656, 1975.

Rich, C. L., Spiker, D. G., Jewell, S. W., and Neil, J. F. DSM-III, RDC, and ECT: Depressive subtypes and immediate response. *J. Clin. Psychiatry 45*:14–18, 1984.

Rich, C. L., Woodruff, R. A., Jr., Cadoret, R., Craig, A., and Pitts, F. N., Jr. Electrotherapy: The effects of atropine on EKG. *Dis. Nerv. Syst. 30*:622–626, 1969.

Ries, R. K. Informed ECT for patients and families; Informed ECT for health professionals; Shock Therapy (videotape reviews). *Hosp. Comm. Psychiatry 38*:137–138, 1987.

Ries, R., and Bokan, J. Electroconvulsive therapy following pituitary surgery. *J. Nerv. Ment. Dis. 167*:767–768, 1979.

Roberts, J. M. Prognostic factors in the electroshock treatment of depressive states: I. Clinical features from history and examination. *J. Ment. Sci. 105*:693–702, 1959a.

Roberts, J. M. Prognostic factors in the electroshock treatment of depressive states: II. The application of specific tests. *J. Ment. Sci. 105*:703–713, 1959b.

Robertson, A. D., and Inglis, J. Memory deficits after electroconvulsive therapy: Cerebral asymmetry and dual-encoding. *Neuropsychologia 16*:179–187, 1978.

Robin, A., Binnie, C. D., and Copas, J. B. Electrophysiological and hormonal responses to three types of electroconvulsive therapy. *Br. J. Psychiatry 147*:707–712, 1985.

Robin, A., and De Tissera, S. A double-blind controlled comparison of the therapeutic effects of low and high energy electroconvulsive therapies. *Br. J. Psychiatry 141*:357–366, 1982.

Robin, A. A., and Harris, J. A. A controlled trial of imipramine and electroplexy. *J. Ment. Sci. 106*:217–219, 1962.

Rochford, G., and Williams, M. Development and breakdown of the use of names. *J. Neurol. Neurosurg. Psychiat. 25*:222–233, 1962.

Roith, A. I. Status epilepticus as a complication of E. C. T. *Br. J. Clin. Practice 13*:711–712, 1959.

Rollason, W. N., Sutherland, M. S., and Hall, D. J. An evaluation of the effect of methohexitone and propanidid on blood pressure, pulse rate and cardiac arrhythmia during electroconvulsive therapy. *Br. J. Anaesth. 43*:160–166, 1971.

Roth, L. H., Meisel, A., and Lidz, C. W. Tests of competency to consent to treatment. *Am. J. Psychiatry 134*:279–284, 1977.

Roth, M. Changes in the EEG under barbiturate anesthesia produced by electro-convulsive treatment and their significance for the theory of ECT action. *Electroencephalogr. Clin. Neurophysiol. 3*:261–280, 1951.

Rudorfer, M. V., Hsiao, J. K., Risby, E. D., Linnoila, M., and Potter, W. Z. Biochemical effects of ECT versus antidepressant drugs. American Psychiatric Association, *New Research Program and Abstracts*, p. 110, 1986.

Ruedrich, S. L., Chu, C. C., and Moore, S. L. ECT for major depression in a patient with acute brain trauma. *Am. J. Psychiatry 140*:928–929, 1983.

Ryan, R. J., Swanson, D. W., Faiman, C., Mayberry, W. E., and Spadoni, A. J. Effects of convulsive electroshock on serum concentrations of follicle stimulating hormone, luteinizing hormone, thyroid stimulating hormone and growth hormone in man. *J. Clin. Endocrinol. Metab. 30*:51, 1970.

Sackeim, H. A., Decina, P., Malitz, S., Hopkins, N., Yudofsky, S. C., and Prohovnik, I. Postictal excitement following bilateral and right-unilateral ECT. *Am. J. Psychiatry 140*:1367–1368, 1983.

Sackeim, H. A., Decina, P., Portnoy, S., Kanzler, M., Kerr, B., and Malitz, S. Effects of electrode placement on the efficacy of titrated low-dosage ECT *Am. J. Psychiatry, 144*:1449–1455, 1987a.

Sackeim. H. A., Decina, P., Portnoy, S., Neeley, P., and Malitz, S. Studies of dosage, seizure threshold, and seizure duration in ECT. *Biol. Psychiatry 22*:249–268, 1987b.

Sackeim, H. A., Decina, P., Prohovnik, I., and Malitz, S. Seizure threshold in electroconvulsive therapy: Effects of sex, age, electrode placement, and number of treatments. *Arch. Gen. Psychiatry 44*:355–360, 1987c.

Sackeim, H. A., Decina, P., Prohovnik, I., Malitz, S., and Resor, S. R. Anticonvulsant and antidepressant properties of electroconvulsive therapy: A proposed mechanism of action. *Biol. Psychiatry 18*:1301–1310, 1983.

Sackeim, H. A., Decina, P., Prohovnik, I., Portnoy, S., Kanzler, M., and Malitz, S. Dosage, seizure threshold, and the antidepressant efficacy of electroconvulsive therapy. *Ann. NY Acad. Sci. 462*:398–410, 1986a.

Sackeim, H. A., Portnoy, S., Neeley, P. Steif, B. L., Decina, P., and Malitz, S. Cognitive consequences of low-dosage electroconvulsive therapy. *Ann. NY Acad. Sci. 462*:326–340, 1986b.

Salzman, C. *Resident Guide to the Use of Electroconvulsive Therapy*. Massachusetts Mental Health Center Monograph, Boston, 1970.

Salzman, C. ECT and ethical psychiatry. *Am. J. Psychiatry 134*:1006–1009, 1977.

Sandford, J. L. Electric and convulsive treatments in psychiatry. *Dis. Nerv. Syst. 27*:333–338, 1966.

Savitsky, N., and Karliner, W. Electroshock therapy and multiple sclerosis. *NY J. Med. 51*:788, 1951.

Savitsky, N., and Karliner, W. Electroshock in the presence of organic disease of the nervous system. *J. Hillside Hosp. 2*:3–22, 1953.

Schultz, H., Muller, J., Roth, B., and Stein, J. Das Bioelektrische Bild

Während der Krampfbehandlung in Narkose und relaxation bei endogenen psychosen. *Arch. Psych. Nervenkrankh 211*:414–432, 1968.

Schwartz, M. Computed tomography and ECT. *Convul. Ther. 1*:70–71, 1985.

Scott, A. I. F., Whalley, L. J., Bennie, J., Bowler, G. Oestrogen-stimulated neurophysin and outcome after electroconvulsive therapy. *Lancet 2*:1411–1414, 1986.

Seager, C. P., and Bird, R. L. Imipramine with electrical treatment in depression- a controlled trial. *J. Ment. Sci. 108*:704–707, 1962.

Sebag-Montefiore, S. E. Letter: Flurothyl (Indoklon) in depression. *Br. J. Psychiatry 124*:616–617, 1974.

Senter, N. W., Winslade, W. J., Liston, E. H., and Mills, M. J. Electroconvulsive therapy: The evolution of legal regulation. *Am. J. Social Psychiatry 4*:11–15, 1984.

Serra, G., Argiolas, A., Fadda, F., Melis, M. R., and Gessa, G. L. Repeated electroconvulsive shock prevents the sedative effect of small doses of apomorphine. *Psychopharmacology 73*:194–196, 1981.

Shagass, C., and Jones, A. L. A neurophysiological test for psychiatric diagnosis: Results in 750 patients. *Am. J. Psychiatry 114*:1002–1010, 1958.

Shankel, L. W., Dimassimo, D. A., and Whittier, J. R. Changes with age in electrical reactions in mental patients. *Psychiatr. Q. 34*:284–292, 1960.

Shapira, B., Lerer, B., Gilboa, D., Drexler, H., Kugelmass, S., and Calev, A. Facilitation of electroconvulsive therapy by caffeine pretreatment. *Am. J. Psychiatry 144*:1199–1202, 1987.

Shapira, B., Zohar, J., Newman, M., Drexler, H., and Belmaker, R. H. Potentiation of seizure length and clinical response to electroconvulsive therapy by caffeine pre-treatment: A case report. *Convul. Ther. 1*:58–60, 1985.

Shapiro, M. F., and Goldberg, H. H. Electroconvulsive therapy in patients with structural diseases of the central nervous system. *Am. J. Med. Sci. 233*:186–195, 1957.

Silfverskiöld, P., Gustafson, L., Risberg, J., and Ingmar, R. Acute and late effects of electroconvulsive therapy: Clinical outcome, regional cerebral blood flow, and electroencephalogram. *Ann. NY Acad. Sci. 462*:236–248, 1986.

Siris, S. G., Glassman, A. H., and Stetner, F. ECT and psychotropic medication in the treatment of depression and schizophrenia. In: R. Abrams and W. B. Essman (Eds.) *Electroconvulsive Therapy: Biological Foundations and Clinical Applications*. Spectrum Publications, New York, pp. 91–112, 1982.

Slade, A. P., and Checkley, S. A. A neuroendocrine study of the mechanism of action of ECT. *Br. J. Psychiatry 137*:217–221, 1980.

Small, I. F. Inhalant convulsive therapy. In: M. Fink, S. Kety, J. McGaugh, and T. A. Williams (Eds.): *Psychobiology of Convulsive Therapy*. V. H. Winston and Sons, Washington, D.C., pp. 65–77, 1974.

Small, I. F., Milstein, V., and Small, J. G. Relationship between clinical and cognitive change with bilateral and unilateral ECT. *Biol. Psychiatry* *16*:793–794, 1981.

Small, I. F., Small, J. G., Milstein, V., and Moore, J. E. Neuropsychological observations with psychosis and somatic treatment. Neuropsychological examinations of psychiatric patients. *J. Nerv. Ment. Dis.* *155*:6–13, 1972.

Small, I. F., Small, J. G., Milstein, V., and Sharpley, P. Interhemispheric relationships with somatic therapy. *Dis. Nerv. Syst.* *34*:170–177, 1973.

Small, J. G. Efficacy of ECT in schizophrenia, mania and other disorders. II: Mania and other disorders. *Convul. Ther.* *1*:271–276, 1985.

Small, J. G., Kellams, J. J., Milstein, V., and Small, I. F. Complications with electroconvulsive treatment combined with lithium. *Biol. Psychiatry* *15*:103–112, 1980.

Small, J. G., Klapper, M. H., Kellams, J. J., Miller, M. J., Milstein, V., Sharpley, P. H., and Small, I. F. ECT compared with lithium in the management of manic states. *Arch. Gen. Psychiatry*, in press.

Small, J. G., Milstein, V., Klapper, M. H., Kellams, J. J., Miller, M. J., and Small, I. F. Electroconvulsive therapy in the treatment of manic episodes. *Ann. NY Acad. Sci.* *462*:37–49, 1986.

Small, J. G., Small, I. F., Milstein, V., Kellams, J. J., and Klapper, M. H. Manic symptoms: An indication for bilateral ECT. *Biol. Psychiatry* *20*:125–134, 1985.

Small, J. G., Small, I. F., Perez, H. C., and Sharpley, P. Electroencephalographic and neurophysiological studies of electrically induced seizures. *J. Nerv. Ment. Dis.* *150*:479–489, 1970.

Smith, S. The use of electroplexy (ECT) in psychiatric syndromes complicating pregnancy. *J. Ment. Sci.* *102*:796–800, 1956.

Snow, S. S., and Wells, C. E. Case studies in neuropsychiatry: Diagnosis and treatment of coexistent dementia and depression. *J. Clin. Psychiatry* *42*:439–441, 1981.

Sobel, D. E. Fetal damage due to ECT, insulin coma, chlorpromazine or reserpine. *Arch. Gen. Psychiatry* *2*:606–611, 1960.

Spiker, D. G., Dealy, R. S., Hanin, I., Weiss, J. C., and Kupfer, D. J. Treating delusional depression with amitriptyline. *J. Clin. Psychiatry* *47*:243–245, 1986.

Squire, L. R. Neuropsychological effects of ECT. In: R. Abrams and W. B. Essman (Eds.) *Electroconvulsive Therapy: Biological Foundations and Clinical Applications.* Spectrum Publications, New York, pp. 169–186, 1982.

Squire, L. R. Memory functions as affected by electroconvulsive therapy. *Ann. NY Acad. Sci.* *462*:307–314, 1986.

Squire, L. R., and Chace, P. M. Memory functions six to nine months after electroconvulsive therapy. *Arch. Gen. Psychiatry* *32*:1557–1564, 1975.

Squire, L. R., and Miller, P. L. Diminution of anterograde amnesia following electroconvulsive therapy. *Br. J. Psychiatry 125*:490–495, 1974.

Squire, L. R., Shimamura, A. P., and Graf, P. Independence of recognition memory and priming effects: A neuropsychological analysis. *J. Exp. Psychol. 11*:37–44, 1985.

Squire, L. R., and Slater, P. C. Bilateral and unilateral ECT: Effects on verbal and nonverbal memory. *Am. J. Psychiatry 135*:1316–1320, 1978.

Squire, L. R., and Slater, P. C. Electroconvulsive therapy and complaints of memory dysfunction: A prospective three-year follow-up study. *Br. J. Psychiatry 142*:1–8, 1983.

Squire, L. R., Slater, P. C., and Chace, P. M. Retrograde amnesia: Temporal gradient in very long term memory following electroconvulsive therapy. *Science 187*:77–79, 1975.

Squire, L. R., Slater, P. C., and Chace, P. M. Anterograde amnesia following electroconvulsive therapy: No evidence for state-dependent learning. *Behav. Biol. 17*:31–41, 1976.

Squire, L. R., Slater, P. C., and Miller, P. L. Retrograde amnesia and bilateral electroconvulsive therapy. Long-term follow-up. *Arch. Gen. Psychiatry 38*:89–95, 1981.

Squire, L. R., Wetzel, C. D., and Slater, P. C. Memory complaint after electroconvulsive therapy: Assessment with a new self-rating instrument. *Biol. Psychiatry 14*:791–801, 1979.

Squire, L. R., and Zouzounis, J. A. ECT and memory: Brief pulse versus sine wave. *Am. J. Psychiatry 143*:596–601, 1986.

Staton, R. D., Hass, P. J., and Brumback, R. A. Electroencephalographic recording during bitemporal and unilateral non-dominant hemisphere (Lancaster Position) electroconvulsive therapy. *J. Clin. Psychiatry 42*:264–269, 1981.

Stengel, E. Intensive ECT. *J. Ment. Sci. 97*:139–142, 1951.

Stevenson, G. H., and Geoghegan, J. J. Prophylactic electroshock. *Am. J. Psychiatry 107*:743–748, 1951.

Stieper, D. R., Williams, M., and Duncan, C. P. Changes in impersonal and personal memory following electroconvulsive therapy. *J. Clin. Psychol. 7*:361–366, 1951.

Stone, A. A. Recent mental health litigation: A critical perspective. *Am. J. Psychiatry 134*:273–279, 1977.

Strain, J. J., and Bidder, T. G. Transient cerebral complication associated with multiple monitored electroconvulsive therapy. *Dis. Nerv. Syst. 32*:95–100, 1971.

Strain, J. J., Brunschwig, L., Duffy, J. P., Agle, D. P., Rosenbaum, A. L., and Bidder, T. G. Comparison of therapeutic effects and memory change with bilateral and unilateral ECT. *Am. J. Psychiatry 125*:294–304, 1968.

Strömgren, L. S. Unilateral versus bilateral electroconvulsive therapy. Investigations into the therapeutic effect in endogenous depression. *Acta Psychiatr. Scand.* 240:8–65, 1973.

Strömgren, L. S. Therapeutic results in brief-interval unilateral ECT. *Acta Psychiatr. Scand.* 52:246–255, 1975.

Strömgren, L. S. Is bilateral ECT ever indicated? *Acta Psychiatr. Scand.* 69:484–490, 1984.

Strömgren, L. S., Christensen, A. L., and Fromholt, P. The effects of unilateral brief-interval ECT on memory. *Acta Psychiatr. Scand.* 54:336–346, 1976.

Strömgren, L. S., Dahl, J., Fjeldbörg, N., and Thomsen, A. Factors influencing seizure duration and number of seizures applied in unilateral electroconvulsive therapy. Anesthetics and benzodiazepines. *Acta Psychiatr. Scand.* 62:158–165, 1980.

Strömgren, L. S., and Juul-Jensen, P. EEG in unilateral and bilateral electroconvulsive therapy. *Acta Psychiatr. Scand.* 51:340–360, 1975.

Summers, W. K., Robins, E., and Reich, T. The natural history of acute organic mental syndrome after bilateral electroconvulsive therapy. *Biol. Psychiatry* 14:905–912, 1979.

Summerskill, J., Seeman, W., and Meals, D. W. An evaluation of post-electroshock confusion with the Reiter apparatus. *Am. J. Psychiatry* 108:835–838, 1952.

Sutherland, E. M., Oliver, J. E., and Knight. D. R. EEG., memory and confusion in dominant, non-dominant and bi-temporal E.C.T. *Br. J. Psychiatry* 115:1059–1064, 1969.

Swartz, C. M. The time course of post-ECT prolactin levels. *Convul. Ther.* 1:81–89, 1985.

Swartz, C. M. Hormone release by electroconvulsive therapy. *Lancet* 2:581, 1986.

Swartz, C., and Abrams, R. Prolactin levels after bilateral and unilateral ECT. *Br. J. Psychiatry* 144:643–645, 1984.

Swartz, C. M., and Abrams, R. An auditory representation of ECT-induced seizures. *Convul. Ther.* 2:125–128, 1986.

Swartz, C. M., and Chen, J. J. ECT-induced cortisol release: Changes with depressive state. *Convul. Ther.* 1:15–21, 1985.

Swartz, C., and Dunbar, E. Postictal prolactin elevations in rats. *Neuropsychobiology* 10:1–6, 1983.

Swartz, C. M., and Larson, G. Generalization of the effects of unilateral and bilateral ECT. *Am. J. Psychiatry* 143:1040–1041, 1986.

Swartz, C. M., and Mehta, R. Double electroconvulsive therapy for resistant depression. *Convul. Ther.* 2:55–57, 1986.

Swift, M. R., and LaDu, B. N. A rapid screening test for atypical cholinesterase. *Lancet* 1:513–574, 1966.

Szirmai, I., Boldizsar, F., and Fischer, J. Correlation between blood gases, glycolytic enzymes and EEG during electroconvulsive treatment in relaxation. *Acta Psychiatr. Scand. 51*:171-181, 1975.

Tandon, R., Grunhaus, L., Krugler, T., and Greden, J. F. Efficacy of unilateral versus bilateral electroconvulsive therapy in endogenous depression. *Convul. Ther.*, in press.

Taylor, M. A. Indications for electroconvulsive therapy. In: R. Abrams and W. B. Essman (Eds.) *Electroconvulsive Therapy: Biological Foundations and Clinical Applications.* Spectrum Publications, New York, pp. 7-40, 1982.

Taylor, M. A., and Abrams, R. Acute mania: Clinical and genetic study of responders and non-responders to treatments. *Arch. Gen. Psychiatry 32*:863-865, 1975.

Taylor, M. A., and Abrams, R. The prevalence of schizophrenia: A reassessment using modern diagnostic criteria. *Am. J. Psychiatry 135*:945-948, 1978.

Taylor, M. A., and Abrams, R. Short-term cognitive effects of unilateral and bilateral ECT. *Br. J. Psychiatry 146*:308-311, 1985.

Taylor, M. A., Gaztanaga, P., and Abrams, R. Manic-depressive illness and acute schizophrenia: A clinical, family history, and treatment-response study. *Am. J. Psychiatry 131*:678-682, 1974.

Taylor, P., and Fleminger, J. J. ECT for schizophrenia. *Lancet 1*:1380-1382, 1980.

Taylor, P. J., von Witt, R. J., and Fry, A. H. Serum creatine phosphokinase activity in psychiatric patients receiving electroconvulsive therapy. *J. Clin. Psychiatry 42*:103-105, 1981.

Taylor, R. M., and Pacella, P. O. The significance of abnormal electroencephalograms prior to electroconvulsive therapy. *J. Nerv. Ment. Dis. 107*:220-227, 1948.

Tewfik, G. I., and Wells, B. G. The use of Arfonad for the alleviation of cardio-vascular stress following electro-convulsive therapy. *J. Ment. Sci. 10*:636-644, 1957.

Thenon, J. Electrochoque monolateral. *Acta Neuropsiquiatr. Argentina 2*:292-296, 1956.

Thomas, J., and Reddy, B. The treatment of mania. A retrospective evaluation of the effects of ECT, chlorpromazine, and lithium. *J. Affective Disord. 4*:85-92, 1982.

Thompson, J. W., and Blaine, J. D. Use of ECT in the United States 1975 and 1980. *Am. J. Psychiatry 144*:557-562, 1987.

Thorpe, J. G. Learning ability during a course of 20 electroshock treatments. *J. Ment. Sci. 105*:1017-1021, 1959.

Tortella, F. C., and Long, J. B. Endogenous anticonvulsant substance in rat cerebrospinal fluid after a generalized seizure. *Science 228*:1106-1108, 1985.

Tsuang, M. T., Tidball, J. S., and Geller, D. ECT in a depressed patient with shunt in place for normal pressure hydrocephalus. *Am. J. Psychiatry 136*:1205–1206, 1979.

Turner, T. H., Ur, E., and Grossman, A. Naloxone has no effect on hormonal responses to ECT. *Psychiatry Res. 22*:207–212, 1987.

Ulett, G. A., Das, K., Hornung, F., Davis, D., and Johnson, M. Changes in the photically-driven EEG following electroconvulsive therapy. *J. Neuropsychiatry 3*:186–189, 1962.

Ulett, G. A., Smith, K., and Gleser, G. C. Evaluation of convulsive and subconvulsive shock therapies utilizing a control group. *Am. J. Psychiatry 112*:795–802, 1956.

Ungerleider, J. T. Acute myocardial infarction and electroconvulsive therapy. *Dis. Nerv. Syst. 21*:149–153, 1960.

Usubiaga, J. E., Gustafson, W., Moya, F., and Goldstein, B. The effect of intravenous lignocaine on cardiac arrhythmias during electroconvulsive therapy. *Br. J. Anaesth. 39*:867–875, 1967.

Valentine, M., Keddie, K. M., and Dunne, D. A comparison of techniques in electro-convulsive therapy. *Br. J. Psychiatry 114*:989–996, 1968.

Vetulani, J. Changes in responsiveness of central aminergic structures after chronic ECS. In: Lerer, B., Weiner, R. D., and Belmaker, R. H. (Eds.) *ECT: Basic Mechanisms.* John Libbey, London, pp. 33–45, 1984.

Vetulani, J. Relationship between receptor and behavioral changes in the course of chronic treatment with antidepressants and ECT. In: Shagass, C., Josiassen, R., Bridger, W. H., Weiss, K. J., Stoff, D., and Simpson, G. M. (Eds.) *Biological Psychiatry 1985.* Elsevier, New York, pp. 162–164, 1986.

Vetulani, J., Lebrecht, U., and Pilc, A. Enhancement of responsiveness of the central serotonergic system and serotonin-2 receptor density in rat frontal cortex by electroconvulsive treatment. *Eur. J. Pharmacol. 76*:81–85, 1981.

Vetulani, J., Szpak, J., and Pilc, A. Spaced electroconvulsive treatment: Effects of responses associated with alpha 2- and 5-HT2-receptors. *J. Pharm. Pharmacol. 35*:326–328, 1983.

Viparelli, U., Di Lorenzo, R., Capasso, G., Manieri, L., Sciorio, G., and Viparelli, G. Trattamento con e.shock di inserma psicotica gia operata di commissurotomia mitralica. *L'Ostedale Psichiatrico Fondata da M. Sciutti-diretta da G. Lavitola 2*:1–10, 1976.

Volavka, J., Feldstein, S., Abrams, R., and Fink, M. EEG and clinical change after bilateral and unilateral electroconvulsive therapy. *Electroencephalogr. Clin. Neurophysiol. 32*:631–639, 1972.

Ward, C., Stern, G. M., Pratt, R. T., and McKenna, P. Electroconvulsive therapy in parkinsonian patients with the "on-off" syndrome. *J. Neural Transm. 49*:133–135, 1980.

Weatherly, J., and Villien, L. M. Treatment of a case of psychotic depression complicated by aortic homograph replacement. *Am. J. Psychiatry 114*:1120–1121, 1958.

Weaver, L. A., Jr., and Williams, R. W. The electroconvulsive therapy stimulus. In: R. Abrams and W. B. Essman (Eds.) *Electroconvulsive Therapy: Biological Foundations and Clinical Applications.* Spectrum Publications, New York, pp. 129–156, 1982.

Weaver, L., Williams, R., and Rush, S. Current density in bilateral and unilateral ECT. *Biol. Psychiatry 11*:303–312, 1976.

Webb, M. G. T., O'Donnell, M. P., Draper, R. J., Horner, B., and Phillips, J. P. Brain-type creatine phospho-kinase serum levels before and after ECT. *Br. J. Psychiatry 144*:525–528, 1984.

Wechsler, D. A standardized memory scale for clinical use. *J. Psychol. 19*:87–95, 1945.

Weckowicz, T. E., Yonge, K. A., Cropley, A. J., and Muir, W. Objective therapy predictors in depression: A multivariate approach. *J. Clin. Psychol. 27*:4–29, 1971.

Weeks, D., Freeman, C. P., and Kendell, R. E. ECT: III: Enduring cognitive deficits? *Br. J. Psychiatry 137*:26–37, 1980.

Weil-Malherbe, H. The effect of convulsive therapy on plasma adrenaline and noradrenaline. *J. Ment. Sci. 101*:156–162, 1955.

Weinberger, D. R., Torrey, E. F., Neophytides, A. N., and Wyatt, R. J. Structural abnormalities in the cerebral cortex of chronic schizophrenic patients. *Arch. Gen. Psychiatry 36*:935–936, 1979.

Weiner, R. D. The psychiatric use of electrically induced seizures. *Am. J. Psychiatry 136*:1507–1517, 1979.

Weiner, R. D. ECT and seizure threshold: Effects of stimulus wave form and electrode placement. *Biol. Psychiatry 15*:225–241, 1980.

Weiner, R. D. The persistence of electroconvulsive therapy-induced changes in the electroencephalogram. *J. Nerv. Ment. Dis. 168*:224–228, 1980.

Weiner, R. D. ECT-induced status epilepticus and further ECT: A case report. *Am. J. Psychiatry 138*:1237–1238, 1981.

Weiner, R. D. Electroencephalographic correlates of ECT. *Psychopharmacol. Bull. 18*:78–81, 1982.

Weiner, R. D. EEG related to electroconvulsive therapy. In: J. R. Hughes, and W. P. Wilson (Eds.) *EEG and Evoked Potentials in Psychiatry and Behavioral Neurology.* Butterworths Publishing, Boston, pp. 101–127, 1983a.

Weiner, R. D. ECT in the physically ill. *J. Psychiat. Treat. Eval. 5*:457–462, 1983b.

Weiner, R. D. Does electroconvulsive therapy cause brain damage? *Behav. Brain Sci. 7*:1–53, 1984.

Weiner, R. D., Coffey, C. E., Christison, C., and Schultz, K. Factors influencing seizure endpoint determination with ECT. Paper presented at the *Society for Biological Psychiatry Annual Meeting*, Chicago, Illinois, May 9, 1987.

Weiner, R. D., Coffey, C. E., Davidson, J. R. T., Kahn, E. M., and Krishnan,

K. R. R. Regional analysis of EEG slowing with ECT. Presented at the 15th CINP Congress, San Juan, Puerto Rico, December 1986.

Weiner, R. D., Henschen, G. M., Dellasega, M., and Baker, J. S. Propranolol treatment of an ECT-related ventricular arrhythmia. *Am. J. Psychiatry 136*:1594–1595, 1979.

Weiner, R. D., Rogers, H. J., Davidson, J. R. T., and Kahn, E. M. Effects of electroconvulsive therapy upon brain electrical activity. *Ann. NY Acad. Sci. 462*:270–281, 1986.

Weiner, R. D., Rogers, H. J., Davidson, J. R. T., and Squire, L. R. Effects of stimulus parameters on cognitive side effects. *Ann. NY Acad. Sci. 462*:315–325, 1986.

Weiner, R. D., Volow, M. R., Gianturco, D. T., and Cavenar, J. O., Jr. Seizures terminable and interminable with ECT. *Am. J. Psychiatry 137*:1416–1418, 1980.

Weiner, R. D., Whanger, A. D., Erwin, C. W., and Wilson, W. P. Prolonged confusional state and EEG seizure activity following concurrent ECT and lithium use. *Am. J. Psychiatry 137*:1452–1453, 1980.

Weinstein, M. R., and Fischer, A. Electroconvulsive treatment of a patient with artificial mitral and aortic valves. *Am. J. Psychiatry 123*:882–884, 1967.

Weiss, D. M. Changes in blood pressure with electroshock therapy in a patient receiving chlorpromazine hydrochloride (Thorazine). *Am. J. Psychiatry 111*:617–619, 1955.

Welch, C. A. The relative efficacy of unilateral nondominant and bilateral stimulation. *Psychopharmacol. Bull. 18*:68–70, 1982.

Welch, C. A., Weiner, R. D., Weir, D., Kahill, J. F., et al. Efficacy of ECT in the treatment of depression: Waveform and electrode placement considerations. *Psychopharmacol. Bull. 18*:31–34, 1982.

West, E. D. Electric convulsion therapy in depression: A double-blind controlled trial. *Br. Med. J. 282*:355–357, 1981.

Whalley, L. J., Rosie, R., Dick, H., Levy, G., Watts, A. G., Sheward, W. J., Christie, J. E., and Fink, G. Immediate increases in plasma prolactin and neurophysin but not other hormones after electroconvulsive therapy. *Lancet 2*:1064–1068, 1982.

White, R. K., Shea, J. J., and Jonas, M. A. Multiple monitored electroconvulsive treatment. *Am. J. Psychiatry 125*:622–626, 1968.

Wilcox, K. W. The pattern of cognitive reorientation following loss of consciousness. *Papers of the Michigan Academy of Science, Art and Letters 41*:357, 1955.

Willerson, J. T. Acute myocardial infarction. In: J. B. Wyngaarden and L. H. Smith (Eds.) *Textbook of Medicine, 16th edition.* W. B. Saunders Company, Philadelphia, pp. 247–255, 1982.

Williams, M. Memory disorders associated with electroconvulsive therapy. In: C. W. M. Whitty and O. L. Zangwill (Eds.) *Amnesia.* Butterworths, London, pp. 139–149, 1966.

Williams, M. Errors in picture recognition after E.C.T. *Neuropsychologia* *11*:429–436, 1973.

Wilson, I. C., and Gottlieb, G. Unilateral electroconvulsive shock therapy. *Dis. Nerv. Syst. 28*:541–545, 1967.

Wilson, I. C., Vernon, J. T., Guin, T., and Sandifer, M. G. A controlled study of treatments of depression. *J. Neuropsychiatry 4*:331–337, 1963.

Wilson, W. P., Schieve, J. F., Durham, N. C., and Scheinberg, P. Effect of series of electric shock treatments on cerebral blood flow and metabolism. *Arch. Neurol. Psychiatry 68*:651–654, 1952.

Winslade, W. J., Liston, E. H., Ross, J. W., and Weber, K. D. Medical, judicial, and statutory regulation of ECT in the United States. *Am. J. Psychiatry 141*:1349–1355, 1984.

Wise, M. G., Ward, S. C., Townsend-Parchman, W., Gilstrap, L. C., 3d, and Hauth, J. C. Case report of ECT during high-risk pregnancy. *Am. J. Psychiatry 141*:99–101, 1984.

Witztum, J., Baker, M., Woodruff, R. A., Jr., and Pitts, F. N., Jr. Electrotherapy: The effects of methohexital on EKG. *Dis. Nerv. Syst. 31*:193–195, 1970.

Wolff, G. E. Results of four years active therapy for chronic mental patients and the value of an individual maintenance dose of ECT. *Am. J. Psychiatry 114*:453–456, 1957.

Wolford, J. A. Electroshock therapy and aortic aneurysm. *Am. J. Psychiatry 113*:656, 1957.

Woodruff, R. A., Pitts, F. N., Jr., and McClure, J. N., Jr. The drug modification of ECT. *Arch. Gen. Psychiatry 18*:605–611, 1968.

Wulfson, H. D., Askanazi, J., and Finck, A. D. Propranolol prior to ECT associated with asystole [letter]. *Anesthesiology 60*:255–256, 1984.

Wyant, G. M., and MacDonald, W. B. The role of atropine in electroconvulsive therapy. *Anaesth. Intensive Care 8*:445–450, 1980.

Yesavage, J. A., and Berens, E. S. Multiple monitored electroconvulsive therapy in the elderly. *J. Am. Geriatr. Soc. 28*:206–209, 1980.

Youmans, C. R., Jr., Bourianoff, G., Allensworth, D. C., Martin, W. L., and Derrick, J. R. Therapy and cardiac pacemakers. *Am. J. Surg. 118*:931–937, 1969.

Young, R. C., Alexopoulos, G. S., and Shamoian, C. A. Dissociation of motor response from mood and cognition in a parkinsonian patient treated with ECT. *Biol. Psychiatry 20*:566–569, 1985.

Yudofsky, S. C. Parkinson's disease, depression, and electroconvulsive therapy: A clinical and neurobiologic synthesis. *Compr. Psychiatry 20*:579–581, 1979.

Zamora, E. W., and Kaelbling, R. Memory and electroconvulsive therapy. *Am. J. Psychiatry 122*:546–554, 1965.

Zeidenberg, P., Smith, R., Greene, L., and Malitz, S. Psychotic depression in a patient with progressive muscular dystrophy: Treatment with multiple monitored electroconvulsive therapy. *Dis. Nerv. Syst. 37*:21–23, 1976.

Zimmerman, M., Coryell, W., and Pfohl, B. The treatment validity of DSM-III melancholic subtyping. *Psychiatry Res. 16*:37–43, 1985.

Zimmerman, M., Coryell, W., Stangl, D., and Pfohl, B. An American validation study of the Newcastle scale. III. Course during index hospitalization and six-month prospective follow-up. *Acta Psychiatr. Scand. 73*:412–415, 1986.

Zimmerman, M., Pfohl, B., Coryell, W., and Stangl, D. The prognostic validity of DSM-III Axis IV in depressed patients. *Am. J. Psychiatry 144*:102–106, 1987.

Zinkin, D., and Birtchnell, J. Unilateral electroconvulsive therapy: Its effects on memory and its therapeutic efficacy. *Br. J. Psychiatry 114*:973–988, 1968.

Zung, W. W., Rogers, J., and Krugman, A. Effect of electroconvulsive therapy in memory in depressive disorders. *Recent Adv. Biol. Psychiatry 10*:160–178, 1968.

Index